MARKET-DRIVEN MANAGEMENT

The Portable MBA Series

The Portable MBA Series provides managers, executives, professionals, and students with a "hands-on," easy-to-access overview of the ideas and information covered in a typical Masters of Business Administration program. The published and forthcoming books in the program are:

Published

The Portable MBA (0-471-61997-3, cloth; 0-471-54895-2, paper) Eliza G. C. Collins and Mary Anne Devanna

The Portable MBA Desk Reference (0-471-57681-6) Paul A. Argenti

The Portable MBA in Finance and Accounting (0-471-53226-6) John Leslie Livingstone

The Portable MBA in Management (0-471-57379-5) Allan R. Cohen

The Portable MBA in Marketing (0-471-54728-X) Alexander Hiam and Charles Schewe

New Product Development: Managing and Forecasting for Strategic Success (0-471-57226-8) Robert J. Thomas

Real-Time Strategy: Improving Team-Based Planning for a Fast-Changing World (0-471-58564-5) Lee Tom Perry, Randall G. Stott, and W. Norman Smallwood

The Portable MBA in Economics (0-471-59526-8) Philip K. Y. Young and John McCauley

The Portable MBA in Entrepreneurship (0-471-57780-4) William Bygrave

The Portable MBA in Strategy (0-471-58498-3) Liam Fahey and Robert M. Randall

The New Marketing Concept (0-471-59576-4) Frederick E. Webster

Total Quality Management: Strategies and Techniques Proven at Today's Most Successful Companies (0-471-54538-1) Arnold Weimerskirch and Stephen George

Market-Driven Management: Using the New Market Concept to Create a Customer-Oriented Company (0-471-5976-4) Frederick E. Webster

Forthcoming

The Portable MBA in Global Business Leadership (0-471-30410-7) Noel Tichy, Michael Brimm, and Hiro Takeuchi

Analyzing the Balance Sheet (0-471-59191-2) John Leslie Livingstone

Information Technology and Business Strategy (0-471-59659-0) N. Venkatraman and James E. Short

Negotiating Strategically (0-471-1321-8) Roy Lewicki and Alexander Hiam

Psychology for Leaders (0-471-59538-1) Dean Tjosvold and Mary Tjosvold

NAPIER UNIVERSITY LIBRARY

MARKET-DRIVEN MANAGEMENT

USING THE NEW MARKETING CONCEPT TO CREATE A CUSTOMER-ORIENTED COMPANY

Frederick E. Webster, Jr.
The Amos Tuck School
Dartmouth College

John Wiley & Sons, Inc.
New York • Chichester • Brisbane • Toronto • Singapore

Library of Congress Cataloging in Publication Data:

Webster, Frederick E.

Market-driven management : using the new marketing concept to create a customer-oriented company / by Frederick E. Webster, Jr.

p. cm. — (The Portable MBA series)

Includes bibliographical references.

ISBN 0-471-59576-4

1. Marketing—Management. 2. Consumer satisfaction. I. Series.

HF5415.13.W467 1994

658.8'12—dc20 93-39184

Printed in the United States of America

10 9 8 7 6 5 4 3 2 1

For Mary Alice, again

Preface

The convergence of ideas from several fields has revitalized marketing management with a new marketing concept. By many different routes, management thinking has come back to a central focus on the satisfaction of customer needs and expectations as the defining purpose of all business activity. After decades of thinking that creating *value for shareholders* was the ultimate objective, managers, consultants, and academic theorists have circled back to a *customer-value concept* of business strategy more consistent with the realities of the global marketplace and its stringent requirements for competitiveness.

For me, the most satisfying view of the world of marketing management comes from standing on the bridge between business and academe. It is essential that marketing scholars devote their energies to problems that are real and relevant for management just as it is critical that professional marketing managers stay informed about and guided by new developments in theory and research. One purpose of this book is to help strengthen the bridge by bringing together important new ideas from both business practice and scholarly research. I try to do this in a historical context of the evolution of the marketing concept over the past 40 years or so.

A major reason for the decline of the original marketing concept as a guiding philosophy of management was the lack of any strong argument or empirical support for the notion that profit was a reward for creating a satisfied customer. In the past several years, however, important new evidence has developed that builds a direct connection between creating value for customers and value for shareholders. Practical management developments have likewise forged a stronger link between customer orientation and business efficiency and effectiveness. In pursuit of customer satisfaction and lower costs, disciplines such as total quality management, reengineering, and strategic planning have come back to the fundamental notion that customers ultimately determine the success of the business. That conclusion is the common theme among many important new management ideas and concepts including relationship management, interactive marketing, management of customer loyalty, the defining of every business as a service business, distinctive competence, and strategic partnering.

In this book, I have tried to combine important new academic thinking and research with evidence of "best practice" in the field of management as reported by management consultants and other business leaders. In the past several years, it has become increasingly clear that the field of marketing is undergoing a fundamental transformation. Those changes are visible from the outside of the field looking in, but not so evident in scholarly marketing journals. Academic research and teaching still tend to focus on some obsolete notions about marketing, including an emphasis on individual transactions and sales results and a narrow focus on short-term profit maximization.

This "marketing myopia" is also characterized by the view of customers as mass markets, preoccupation with short-term price inducements and "brand switching," and the treatment of marketing as a distinct and separate management function. This is in stark contrast with the evolving business emphasis—also reflected in the strategic management literature—on customer relationships and long term profitability, direct marketing to customers as individuals, increased flexibility and product customization for individual customers and small market niches, long-term customer retention and loyalty, and marketing as customer orientation throughout the business. In the background is the fundamental reshaping of organizations that is occurring with the transition from large, bureaucratic, hierarchical structures toward flexible coalitions and networks of smaller, more entrepreneurial businesses cooperating in the shared task of creating and delivering superior value to customers. A new marketing concept is needed to guide the whole undertaking in this common purpose of satisfying customer needs.

A one-year sabbatical leave from my teaching duties at the Amos Tuck School of Business Administration at Dartmouth College provided a welcome period of reflection and refreshment and the opportunity to write this book. I want to thank Dean Edward Fox and my colleagues at the Tuck School for their support and encouragement in this effort. The best payoff has been the excitement of seeing many ideas come together into a new concept of marketing that I hope will help set the course for continued development of this vital and changeable field.

FREDERICK E. WEBSTER, JR.

Etna, New Hampshire
January 1994

Contents

1 PUTTING THE CUSTOMER FIRST—ALWAYS!

> The relationship between the man and the customer, their mutual trust, the importance of reputation, the idea of putting the customer first—always. All these things, if carried out with real conviction by the company, can make a great deal of difference in its destiny.
>
> Thomas Watson, Jr., Chairman, IBM Corporation
> The 1962 McKinsey Lectures, Graduate School of Business, Columbia University

Value is defined in the marketplace, not the factory. This simple proposition is redefining the scope and focus of business firms around the world.

It isn't a new idea. In the 1950s, American management gurus, especially Peter Drucker,[1] suggested quite simply that the purpose of a business is to create a satisfied customer. Profit is not the objective, it is the reward. Among the stakeholders in any company, the customer comes first because *all* the others are served best when the customer is satisfied.

Nothing could be easier to understand. A satisfied customer is willing to pay the firm well enough for its products and services because the customer finds value in them. Value is created for the shareholders in the form of profit when the customer pays the firm a price that is greater than the amount the firm itself paid for the goods and services that it has in its product. Thus, value is created in the marketplace by customers who perceive value in the firm's product offering.

This simple truth had barely begun to take hold across American industry in the late 1950s and early 1960s when another management concept, strategic planning, came along. At first, the marketing concept and strategic planning were integrated into a common concept of long-range planning. Over time, however, strategic planning became increasingly dominated by an apparently more sophisticated analytical framework from the field of financial management, and the customer's point of view no longer dominated.

Return on investment, the Holy Grail of strategic planning, viewed profit as the *objective* of business activity, rather than as the *reward* for creating a satisfied customer. The interests of the shareholders came first. Short-term profits, usually reported on a quarterly basis, often conflicted with the long-term interests of customers.

By the mid-1980s, the decline of American business in global competitiveness was a stark reality forcing a reassessment of the conventional wisdom of strategic planning. In industry after industry—including automobiles, consumer electronics, steel, and tires—American firms lost their dominant positions to competitors from Asia and Europe who somehow seemed better able to dial into the tastes, preferences, and buying habits of American customers. As the harsh realities slowly sank into the consciousness of American management, there was a rediscovery of the marketing concept.[2]

The marketing concept of the 1990s comes with some new twists. It is now integrated with important recent innovations from the field of strategic planning itself and with the fundamental commitment to total quality management that has become the keystone of successful survivors of the 1990s. In one sense, it is a case of old wine in new bottles: *Customer orientation* and *total quality management* are the same thing.

In another sense, however, the marketing concept of the 1990s is radically different from its predecessor because we now understand that marketing is a total organizational commitment, pervasive throughout the company's operating systems and culture, not the province of a few specialists. Even more basically, business organizations of the 1990s are taking on new forms in which the traditional functional boundaries have disappeared and the boundary between the firm and its environment is increasingly blurred.[3] Bureaucratic, divisionalized, hierarchical, functional organizations, like their cousins the dinosaurs, have evolved into more efficient organisms in the rapidly changing environment.

The purpose of this book is to describe and analyze the new marketing concept as the guiding force for successful businesses in the global marketplace of the 1990s. This chapter begins by looking at the evolution of marketing out of the sales function and contrasts the sales and marketing mandates. The following sections explore the complex relationship between the sales and marketing functions and some of the reasons for the frequent confusion of these two perspectives.

THE EVOLUTION OF MARKETING AND BUSINESS STRATEGY

Marketing in the 1950s

Let's go back to the early 1950s and look at the origins of the marketing concept more carefully. We need this historical perspective to better understand the roots of the marketing concept, the subsequent criticisms of it, and how it changed American business. This analysis will also help us to understand why the eminently sensible prescriptions of the marketing concept (which sounds so reasonable in theory) have been very difficult to implement and maintain in business practice.

We can take the year 1950 as our starting point. Consider these facts:

- The population of the United States was 150 million (compared with 250 million in 1990).
- Gross National Product (GNP) was $288 billion compared with $5,514 billion in 1990. If we adjust for inflation by using constant 1987 dollars, 1950 GNP was $1,433 billion compared with $4,885 billion in 1990. On a per capita basis, this is over $9,500 in 1950 versus $19,500 in 1990.
- Personal consumption expenditures went from $192 billion in 1950 (about $1,300 per person) to $3,743 billion (almost $15,000 per person) in 1990. Making a rough adjustment for inflation, again using 1987 dollars as the constant for comparison purposes, the average consumption expenditure per person increased from a bit less than $6,500 in 1950 to over $13,000 in 1990.
- The average consumer in 1950 enjoyed a material standard of living less than half of today's.

In 1950, the United States was still recovering from the effects of World War II, when much of the country's productive capacity was focused on the military effort; consumer products, especially durable goods such as household appliances and automobiles, were in short supply. Conditions for consumers improved rapidly in the late 1940s. Before the postwar economic recovery was complete, however, the country was brought into another major military conflict when President Truman, in June 1950, ordered American forces into South Korea after that country was invaded by troops from North Korea. The Korean War ended with a truce agreement in July 1953, putting the United States economy back into a peacetime mode. While the early 1950s did not bring the same austerity conditions that consumers had faced in the mid-1940s, they certainly prolonged the period of economic recovery from wartime conditions.

As American industry turned its attention to satisfying consumer needs, companies began to experience the benefits of the postwar "baby boom." The birth rate in the United States (per 1,000 population) went from 19.4 in 1940 to 20.4 in 1945, 24.1 in 1950, and 25.0 in 1955, peaking at 25.3 in 1957. It then declined steadily, except for a small increase in 1969, reaching a low of 14.8 in 1975. Since 1976 a slow increase has continued; the annual rate now varies between 16.2 and 16.7 births per thousand population, only two-thirds of the mid-1950s rate.

In the post-Korean War years, American industry looked optimistically at a growing market of young families with increasing incomes. Younger families needed both the durable goods required for establishing their households as well as the packaged goods and other nondurables that provide the necessities and conveniences of everyday life. Established households still had pent-up demand for durables from the war years. Services accounted for only 32% of personal consumption expenditures in 1950 compared with 54% today.

The Old Marketing Concept: Stimulating Demand for What Factories Produced

Markets became increasingly competitive as new and old firms alike sought to attract consumers. As conditions of economic scarcity waned, consumers were given a larger array of choices. New product development activity increased rapidly, fueled in no small measure by the major increases in research budgets (almost half of which had been government funded) that had accompanied the war effort. Companies began to diversify out of their core businesses—for example, oil companies into petrochemicals and rubber companies into plastics—creating new competitors in many industries. With more competing brands and the virtual end of supply scarcity, consumers could demand more precise and total response to their needs and wants. The Age of the Consumer had begun.

Changing marketplace conditions were a major stimulus in the development of the customer-oriented marketing concept. Increased competition for the consumer's patronage called for more care in understanding and responding to consumer needs and wants. Up until this time, the definition of marketing was essentially that of selling what the factory could produce. The focus of management was on products and production, not on consumers. Marketing was responsible for stimulating demand; it was different from "selling" or "sales" in that it also included advertising, sales promotion, and other forms of mass communication. Marketing management was also responsible for market research and sales planning, including forecasting and budgeting, helping manufacturing decide how much to produce. Marketing departments were found only in large companies, however. In the vast majority of firms, the little marketing activity to be found resided in the sales department.

Prior to the development of the marketing concept, the goal of marketing activity was to produce a sale, to maximize sales volume. Profitability was not a major marketing concern. The basic assumption was that sales volume was the key to profitability. The more the sales and marketing people could sell, the higher the profit the firm could expect.

Selling, product planning, pricing, and distribution were seen as separate management areas, each with a unique set of problems to be dealt with by specialists. Much of what we think of as marketing today was managed within the sales department. In addition to responsibility for the sales force, the sales department would include advertising, sales promotion, sales correspondence and service, and perhaps marketing research, if such a function existed in the company. The role of marketing was to make the sales department as effective as possible in moving the merchandise, supporting it with advertising, sales promotion, market research, and recommended pricing actions.

In most firms, product planning was not a marketing activity but fell within the purview of the research and development, engineering, and manufacturing people. The idea of an integrated marketing mix, blending product, pricing, promotion, distribution policies, and conscious strategic analysis of the interactions among them, had not yet gained acceptance.

Such was the world of the early 1950s: growing markets, increasing competition, companies focused on their current products and production capacity, marketing dominated by selling functions, and consumers with increased spending power and increased discretion in their purchasing choices.

CUSTOMER ORIENTATION AS A NEW IDEA

Perhaps the wisest viewer of this scene was Peter F. Drucker, a management consultant, lecturer, writer, and college and business school faculty member. Born in Austria in 1909, Drucker was educated in Germany in economics, politics, and the law. He worked for several years in England before coming to the United States in 1937. As a frequent advisor to banks and corporations, a reporter on economic affairs for newspapers and business journals, and a professor of politics and philosophy, he brought a unique perspective to the changing business environment in the United States. He saw things in a different way from the typical manager and management theorist.

It is fair to say that Drucker was the academic father of the marketing concept with its central tenet of customer orientation, the basic assertion that the company should put the customer first, always. In his famous book, *The Practice of Management*, published in 1954, Drucker addressed the fundamental question: What is a business? His thoughts were revolutionary:

> If we want to know what a business is we have to start with its *purpose*. . . . There is only one valid definition of business purpose: *to create a customer.*
>
> It is the customer who determines what a business is. For it is the customer, and he alone, who through being willing to pay for a good or service, converts economic resources into wealth, things into goods. What

> the business thinks it produces is not of first importance—especially not to the future of the business and to its success. What the customer thinks he is buying, what he considers "value," is decisive. . . .
>
> Because it is its purpose to create a customer, any business enterprise has two—and only these two—basic functions: marketing and innovation.[4]

Drucker believed that marketing, as opposed to selling, was an American invention, created by "the assumption of responsibility for creative, aggressive, pioneering marketing by American management." He noted that Cyrus McCormick, the inventor of the mechanical harvester, also invented market research and analysis, the concept of market share or standing, modern pricing policies, the sales/service specialist, parts and service supply to the customer, and customer credit. McCormick did all this before the middle of the 19th century, to create markets for his invention.

Drucker saw the traditional American manager's attitude of "The sales department will sell whatever the factory produces" being replaced by "It is our job to produce what the market needs." In contrast, he believed, "In Europe there is still almost no understanding that marketing is the specific business function—a major reason for the stagnation of the European economies of today."[5] Four decades later, other management authorities have made the same comparisons of Japan and the United States, but the Americans are the loser in the modern version of the story.

Drucker went on to explain:

> [Marketing] is so basic that it is not just enough to have a strong sales department and to entrust marketing to it. Marketing is not only much broader than selling, it is not a specialized activity at all. It encompasses the entire business. It is the whole business seen from the point of view of its final result, that is from the customer's point of view.[6]

As a good example, Drucker pointed to the General Electric Company's development of a new marketing approach, beginning in 1947 in some affiliated companies. By 1950, the approach had been more or less completely adopted throughout the company. The GE approach emphasized *integration of all marketing functions* and an *analytical perspective, based on market research.* In its 1952 Annual Report, GE had proclaimed the importance of putting the customer first in the process of production planning, attempting to build consumer appeal into the product from the design stage on. GE reported:

> [Its] operating managers were presented with an advanced concept of marketing formulated by the Marketing Services Division. This, in simple terms, would introduce the marketing man at the beginning rather than the end of the production cycle and would integrate marketing into each phase of the business. Thus marketing, through its studies and research, would establish for the engineer, the designer and the manufacturing man what the customer wants in a given product, what price he is willing to pay, and where and when it will be wanted. Marketing would have authority in product planning, production planning and inventory control, as well as the sales, distribution and servicing of the product. This concept, it is believed, will tighten control over business operation and will fix responsibility, while making possible greater flexibility and closer teamwork in the marketing of the Company's products.[7]

GE was in the vanguard in implementing the marketing concept. What it called the advanced concept of marketing combined customer orientation, market research, and integrated marketing. It saw the need for marketing to begin with the conceptualization of the product and its planning, not with the factory's finished product. It made a clear distinction between the new customer-oriented marketing concept and the old selling approach to marketing.

In addition to GE, a number of other large companies, such as IBM, Procter & Gamble, and General Foods (and their CEOs), were championing the marketing concept. In the consumer packaged goods area, these included Pillsbury and its president, Robert J. Keith. In a 1960 article, Keith described Pillsbury's progression from a *production* orientation to a *sales* orientation to a *marketing* orientation and, ultimately to *marketing control.* He compared this marketing revolution with the revolution caused by paradigm-shifting proposition of Copernicus that the earth revolved around the sun rather than the reverse. In this case, the company was seen to revolve around the customer rather than the customer around the company.

Keith believed that the experience at Pillsbury was one that would be followed by every company seeking steady improvement in profits. The core of the marketing orientation at Pillsbury was the development of a brand manager organization, which had evolved out of the advertising department, to integrate marketing, a system already in place at Procter & Gamble and other leading packaged goods companies. The move from marketing orientation to marketing control was basically a shift from a short-term to a long-term orientation in the business, from marketing tactics and operations to overall business policy and strategy, all focused around the consumer. Keith had a strong vision of the marketing revolution:

> Soon it will be true that every activity of the corporation—from finance to sales to production—is aimed at satisfying the needs and desires of the consumer. When that stage of development is reached, the marketing revolution will be complete.[8]

In the minds of many executives, the marketing concept was being accepted as a new management philosophy, a new concept of what it means to be a business, as Peter Drucker had proposed.

It is important to understand Drucker's early statement of what the marketing concept is, and what it is not. It is not a statement of business strategy or tactics. It does not offer a road map, checklist, or "do-it-yourself" guide. In fact, it says little about *how* to become customer oriented. Nor is it a guide to organizational structure for improved marketing. It is especially important to remember that, according to Drucker, *marketing should not be a separate business function at all.* It certainly doesn't urge, as its critics would subsequently claim, that the firm should have a strong, separate marketing department. The notion of marketing "empire building" is not part of the marketing concept.

What the marketing concept offers is a statement of management philosophy, a basic set of values and beliefs to guide the organization. Carlton McNamara, a management consultant, noted that the marketing concept is:

> . . . a philosophy of business management, based upon a company-wide acceptance of the need for customer orientation, profit orientation, and recognition of the important role of marketing in communicating the needs of the market to all major corporate departments.[9]

Today, we see the marketing concept as a statement of *organizational culture,* an agreed-on set of shared values among the employees of a company representing a commitment to put the customer first in all management and operations decision making. It calls for everyone in the organization to think about their job in terms of how it delivers value to customers. Note that Drucker specifically talked about *value* for the customer as the necessary driving force and vision for any successful company.

At the forefront in implementing of the philosophy of the marketing concept was the manager of the Marketing Services Research Service at General Electric, John B. McKitterick. McKitterick was comfortable at the interface of the worlds of business and academe, stayed current on the marketing literature, and spoke frequently at professional meetings about the marketing concept. He noted that while marketing textbooks and journals had been advocating the importance of being "market-oriented" for decades, what was new in the late 1950s was that business managers were beginning to implement these ideas. But it was the ideas, the subtle changes in meaning hidden in words, that fascinated McKitterick. He saw the focus of management shifting away from the customer as the *means* to profit and toward serving customers as the *end purpose* of business activity. Profit, he said, was becoming less the end objective of business and more a condition that must be satisfied.[10]

While the implication that customer satisfaction and profit are competing objectives is arguable, the important point in McKitterick's opinion is that management was elevating the customer's interest into the primary position in the business planning process. A key concept here was *market segmentation.* Based on the fundamental premise that no firm could do an equally effective job of delivering value to all potential customers, the marketing concept called for the firm to analyze its potential markets carefully, identifying those customers whose unsatisfied needs it could best serve.

Marketing and Innovation: A Company's Two Basic Functions

Drucker, it will be recalled, said that every firm has only two basic functions—marketing and *innovation.* Merely being "customer oriented" in the philosophical sense was not enough, nor was marketing skill, narrowly defined; constant innovation was also necessary to deliver better value to consumers in a competitive marketplace. McKitterick made the point forcefully:

> [A] company committed to the marketing concept focuses its major innovative effort on enlarging the size of the market in which it participates by introducing new generic products and services, by promoting new applications for existing products, and by seeking out new classes of customers who heretofore have not used the existing products. . . . [O]nly thinking of the customer and mere technical proficiency in marketing both turn out to be inferior hands when played against the company that couples its thought with action and actually comes to market with a successful innovation. . . . *So the principal task of the marketing function in a management concept is not so much to be skillful in making the customer do what suits the interests of the business as to be skillful in conceiving and then making the business do what suits the interests of the customer.*[11]

Implementing the Marketing Concept

The commitment to innovation and customer-oriented business decision making is only the first step in implementing the marketing concept. This commitment establishes the culture of customer orientation that is the foundation of the marketing concept.

The next step is to shift the focus away from sales volume and toward profitability. When managing for profitability, not sales volume, the firm is focusing on the value its products create for customers in the competitive marketplace. Profit does not come at the expense of the customer, as some would argue. On the contrary, it is the best possible measure of the value that has been created for customers.

Declining profitability is a signal that the company's product offering is becoming less effective, relative to substitutes and competitive product offerings, in delivering value and satisfying customer needs. It may often be the result of aggressive attempts to expand sales volume by serving a larger portion of the total market, requiring higher expenditures on promotional activities and low prices. This is where the concept of market segmentation becomes essential to our understanding. Market segmentation, targeting, and positioning constitute the third set of requirements for implementing the marketing concept.

Market Segmentation

Market segmentation recognizes that customers have distinct needs, preferences, and buying patterns. It is the process of analyzing the market creatively to define distinct groupings of customers for whom the firm has the potential to offer superior value. Market targeting involves developing products and communications aimed at specific parts of the total market to more effectively and efficiently compete. One of the drivers of the product life cycle, in which profit margins begin to erode following the early growth stage of the market, is increased competition from market nichers who selectively target parts of the total market with a superior product offering.

This brings us back to the centrality of innovation in the marketing concept. The successful firm must continuously improve its product offering to remain competitive. Inefficiency and lower profit margins inevitably creep in when the company relies on heavier promotional expenditures and aggressive pricing actions to prop up sales volume for an increasingly obsolete product aimed at multiple market segments. Superior marketing skill is a myth when applied to obsolete products in an undifferentiated or incorrectly segmented market.

The fourth requirement for implementing the marketing concept is to develop an *integrated* approach to the marketing policy variables of market segmentation, product, pricing, promotion, and distribution. The concept of integration itself is rather subtle and complex. It has three dimensions: priority, completeness, and synergy.

Prioritizing marketing decisions means putting the elements in proper sequence. First must come the market segmentation process, selecting those customers that the firm is to serve. By committing to serve a particular set of customers, the company is committing to develop a particular set of competences, resources, and skills that will define the firm. The selection of markets to be served is the single most important decision that any firm makes. It is even more important than the product offering. The product is a variable that can be tailored to the customer's needs and wants, if the customers the firm has chosen match up correctly with its unique competitive capabilities.

Second comes the product itself. Is the offering consistent with the best available technology and designed to provide the best solution for the customer in a specified use situation? The product offering must be continuously refined, improved, updated, and expanded if the firm is to be successful in meeting and exceeding customer expectations, which change over time in response to the promise of competitive product offerings. The concept of the product must go beyond the core, physical product itself, and even the "expected" product in the mind of the customer, which includes all the service features that are required to make it available to, and usable by, the consumer. It must be augmented with additional features and services that exceed the customer's expectations in important ways.[12]

Next comes pricing, which is part of the product offering and determines the economic value delivered to the customer. In fact, a given price level may be a design objective in the development of the product. The customer's use situation and competitive products may define a rather narrow range of pricing opportunities. Pricing, as part of its proper strategic role in the marketing mix, must also recognize the need for promotional expenditures and reseller profit margins.

Following market segmentation, targeting, product development and positioning, and pricing, which define the firm's product offering (and its business-level strategy, which can be thought of as the answer to the question "How do we want to compete?"), the company must establish policies relating to distribution and promotion, or marketing communications. Tradeoffs may be made between reliance on resellers in the form of wholesalers, retailers, and other forms of distributors, and the use of the company's sales force. Both the reseller organization and the direct sales force must be supported by advertising, sales promotion, publicity, telemarketing, and other forms of communication to optimize response to marketing expenditures.

Completeness and synergy are also essential factors in determining priorities. A marketing strategy must be based on careful analysis and programming of all the marketing mix elements and must consider specifically the interactions and interdependencies among them. Thus, pricing is a key dimension of product positioning. Market segmentation has specific implications for the organization of the selling effort as well as for product line development and management. Advertising message and media strategy must be consistent with the desired image called for by market targeting and product positioning. The entire effort must be coordinated at a high level of strategic management to ensure consistent and thorough marketing decisions.

Finally, organizational responsibility for marketing must be assigned. Commitment to the marketing concept and its implementation will not happen unless there is specific high level managerial responsibility for it. Here we encounter a fundamental dilemma inherent in the marketing concept. On the one hand, responsibility must be assigned. On the other hand, as Peter Drucker noted so carefully, marketing is really not a separate function at all. Rather, it is the total business seen from the point of view of its ultimate purpose, that of creating a satisfied customer. We will leave this issue unresolved for the moment but will come back to it many times in developing and analyzing the new marketing concept.

PROBLEMS IN ADOPTING THE MARKETING CONCEPT

By the mid-1960s, marketing researchers had begun to study whether American firms had actually adopted the marketing concept. They did this by looking at the extent to which management was committed to customer orientation and managing for profitability rather than sales volume. In addition, they frequently looked for the presence of a strong, central marketing department as evidence of the adoption of the marketing mandate. As noted, this is a controversial measure.

It became increasingly common, however, to equate strong marketing with a large marketing department. Hise, for example, in a 1965 study, defined a firm's adoption of the marketing concept as including:

1. Customer orientation.
2. Profit orientation of marketing operations.
3. "An organizational structure in which all marketing activities are performed by the marketing department, and where the chief marketing executive is accorded a place on the company's organization chart equal to that given the top financial and manufacturing executives."[13]

He found that the companies surveyed were doing market research and surveys and giving marketing partial responsibility for product development but in general were not managing for profitability. Large firms were more likely to use market research. In most of the firms surveyed, the top marketing executive reported to the president of the firm. Hise's overall conclusion was that most large and medium-size manufacturing firms had adopted the marketing concept, especially in terms of customer orientation and organization structure, with large firms showing a somewhat stronger tendency.

In 1972, McNamara published the results of another survey of American manufacturing firms practices with respect to adopting the marketing concept. He used primarily organizational criteria in making his judgments, including:

- The organizational level of the top marketing executive.
- The presence or absence of people with marketing backgrounds in top management positions.
- Whether marketing was centralized at the corporate or product/division level.
- The scope of the marketing research function.

He did not consider direct measures of customer- or profit-orientation, but for these constructs he used such organizational surrogate measures as the presence of marketing executives on nonmarketing committees and the presence of formal training and communications programs.

His primary conclusions were that large firms and consumer goods companies were more likely to have adopted the marketing concept than were smaller companies and those marketing to industrial customers. In large companies, with centralized marketing at the corporate level, the role involved coordinating and consulting functions rather than direct operations. Smaller companies and industrial firms indicated a limited amount of integration of marketing functions, but with more of an operational focus.[14]

By the mid-1970s, it had become clear that most companies did not easily or readily accept the rather simple strictures of the marketing concept. Instead of true customer orientation, managing for profitability, and integrated marketing at the business unit level, what was often found was continued product and manufacturing orientation, continued emphasis on sales volume rather than long-term profitability based on customer satisfaction, and weak integration among marketing functions and of marketing with other functions such as R&D and manufacturing. In most companies, sales still dominated. The job of marketing was to sell what the factory could produce.

The original marketing concept saw it as pervading all aspects of the business, putting the customer in the center of all operational and strategic decision making. The objective was to do the best possible job of satisfying customer needs. At both GE and Pillsbury, for example, it was explicitly proclaimed that as the marketing function came to fruition, all operations management, from product design to production planning to manufacturing to inventory control and distribution, would ultimately be coordinated, integrated, and directed by marketing. Keith's fourth phase in the development of the marketing—marketing control—stated this vision.

Instead of a blurring of the boundaries between the traditional management functions (sales, finance, manufacturing, engineering, etc.) called for by the move to total customer orientation, the functional boundaries grew higher and stronger. In large consumer goods companies, marketing had typically become the dominant managerial function and now provided a large portion of the top management of the company. In smaller companies, and in firms serving industrial markets, marketing, if it existed at all, was relatively weak. There was still manufacturing and engineering dominance, and there was a sales volume and selling orientation. Marketing was typically a staff function, perhaps within the sales department or else as part of the administrative structure reporting to the president or chief operating officer.

Champions of the marketing concept were troubled by what they saw in the mid-1970s. Marketing had not lived up to its promise of revolutionizing American business. Many companies in several key industries were facing non-American competitors who were taking significant market share and apparently were much more in touch with the American consumer. Automobiles, consumer electronics, office machines, and photographic equipment and film were just a few of the industries under siege.

Why was the marketing concept, so simple an idea to understand, so hard to implement? There are three areas to consider:

1. The validity and soundness of the marketing concept per se.
2. Errors and shortcomings in its implementation.
3. Inherent conflicts with other management functions.

Flaws in the Marketing Concept

This chapter has stressed, as did Drucker, that the marketing concept is a management philosophy, a way of thinking about the business and its fundamental purpose: to create a satisfied customer. From a societal point of view, customer orientation is the strongest source of legitimation for business as an institution, especially for a business grown too large to be controlled by its owners and their wishes for business purpose. In its simple form, where its intent is most clear, the marketing concept does not contain significant *strategic* content. It says virtually nothing about *how* the firm should satisfy customer needs. Indeed, it says nothing about *which* customer needs a firm should focus on. Because of these unanswered questions, the nebulous quality of the marketing concept makes it difficult for marketing managers and other advocates of customer orientation to defend themselves against the other management functions.

Difficulty in Analyzing Customer Needs

A key part of customer orientation and integrated marketing is the use of market research to analyze customer needs and wants and to provide feedback of the results to other parts of the business. The implication is that marketing has the ability to discover, to understand, and to communicate to others the essence of customer needs. The even more basic implication is that customers know their needs. Suppose they don't. Where does that leave the marketing concept and customer orientation?

There are a number of situations where customers do not and even cannot know their own needs and wants. Consumers could not know they wanted television or electronic fuel injection or compact discs or fluoride toothpaste before they existed. A possible retort here is, "Of course, but they had defined needs for information and entertainment, dependable engine performance, improved musical listening, and better dental health." From a practical standpoint, how useful is that level of analysis? What good does it do a firm in the radio manufacturing business to have its marketing research learn that people want better information and more entertainment?

The real challenge for the firm is *to create new markets,* not just to serve existing ones. The legendary success stories—Ford, IBM, Xerox, Federal Express, Apple, and the like—did just that. These managers did not start with a clean piece of paper when they asked customers what they wanted. They had a vision of a capability to produce a unique product or service that would revolutionize the way customers solved a problem. They could lead their customers into the future, especially if they listened to customers as the company developed and refined the features of its product offering. They were committed to leading and educating their customers in the use of their products. They had a vision.

Not all real business opportunities are as revolutionary. Consider those instances in which customers can come closer to expressing their unsatisfied needs; for example, "I would like to have a toothpaste that will make my children want to brush their teeth three times a day and that will prevent cavities." There is still the question whether the company has the capability to develop the called-for solution or whether the solution is even remotely technically feasible.

In his classic statement of the marketing concept, "Marketing Myopia," Ted Levitt built a convincing argument that the business should define itself not by its products but by the basic customer needs it was committed to satisfying.[15] His examples of firms in the industrial graveyard because of failure to do so included railroads and buggy whip companies. The argument was that the railroads should have defined themselves as being in the transportation business and that buggy whip manufacturers should have been able to develop new lines of business to serve the automobile owner. Putting aside the fact that government regulation prevented the transformation, there seems little point in telling a railroad that it should go into the trucking business to compete with the truckers or into the airline passenger business to keep the customers who used to travel by rail. The buggy whip people could probably have used their leathercrafting skills better in making belts or hats than in trying to develop new products for the automobile market. Fundamental questions about the capability of the firm—its resources and skills, and even more basically its values and mission—must be answered before a company can match up a business strategy with a set of market needs.

Understanding What the Firm Can Do Well

The market alone cannot tell the firm what to do. It requires a creative process to look at the market, understand potential customer needs and wants, consider the basic capabilities of the firm, conceive potential product offerings based on those present and potential capabilities, design and develop such products, and actually make and deliver them with the full bundle of supporting services to a clearly defined target market. It is just as important to understand the firms capabilities as it is to understand customer needs. The marketing concept does not deny this fact; it just doesn't say anything about it.

A literal interpretation of the marketing concept would suggest that the firm should take information from the marketplace as the sole basis for deciding what to do. Somehow, this implies that the market itself provides not only information about customer needs but also the criteria that tell the firm what to do. Carried to this extreme, the marketing concept begins to make less and less sense. To that extent, therefore, the marketing concept is an incomplete management philosophy.

One insightful commentator, Andrew Kaldor, a management consultant, addressed this issue in the early 1970s with his concept of *imbricative marketing*, a phrase that, not surprisingly, never caught on. "Imbrication" is an overlapping of edges, and the concept of imbricative marketing involved four steps:

1. Identification of the organization's skills.
2. Identification of the objectives of the organization.
3. The identification of the leading part of the system in which the firm operates, which can be thought of as its position in the value chain.
4. The identification of market needs compatible to the organization's needs.[16]

More recent authors have made much of the concept of the firms "distinctive competence," but Kaldor was using the concept in 1971:

> By concentrating on the firm's competencies, the concept of imbrication attempts to outline the areas in which the firm may actualize its potential. It is a framework for strategy selection because it includes the firm and its environment, recognizes the repercussive nature of policy making, and concentrates on those areas in which the firm can maximally utilize its resources. Thus, the framework defines those areas of choice confronting the firm through the conjunction of the freedom the environment allows the firm and the capabilities within the firm. The integrity of the firm is preserved by interpreting and translating information about the environment from the perspective of the firm and not from the perspective of the environment.[17]

No firm can be all things to all potential customers.

If the marketing concept was to be a useful management tool, not just a statement of corporate culture and business purpose, it would need to be expanded to include a more strategic focus on matching up market needs and the firm's capabilities.

Errors in Implementing the Marketing Concept

Beyond the conceptual problems with the marketing concept, which it is fair to assume a lot of managers had not thought about deeply, there were a number of problems at the implementation level:

- The failure to make customer orientation the true priority.
- Underinvestment in marketing.
- Weak performance by the marketing organization.
- The creation of a marketing bureaucracy.

The Difficulty of Making Customer Orientation the Priority

First, for many companies, the adoption of the marketing concept was mostly at the conceptual level. It is easy for top management to say the firm is committed to a customer orientation. That has the familiar ring of "motherhood and apple pie." It is harder to make the resource commitments to marketing information systems, strategy development, processes for identifying and developing professional marketing management talent, and organizational structures necessary to keep the total organization focused on the customer. It may be even harder to develop and maintain a true culture of customer orientation: a set of values and beliefs that put the customer's interests first, ahead of those of the other constituencies and stakeholders served by the organization.

Not all chief executive officers are truly committed to putting the customer first, even if they say they are. Some CEOs put the shareholders first; all too often, shareholders' interests dominate, in terms of the priority of return on investment and quarterly earnings per share. Especially in publicly owned corporations where large institutional investors (notably pension funds) often control huge blocks of stock, top management would seem to have little choice but to make short-term profit the number one objective.

The argument that, over the long run, all constituencies including the shareholders are served best by putting the customer first is a bit nebulous, especially for financial analysts whose job is to focus on return on investment. The marketing concept's assertion that profit is the reward for creating a satisfied customer and that the firm that does the best job for the customer will be the most profitable lacks sound empirical support and may appear to its critics to be little more than wishful thinking.

If top management does not truly put the customer first, they have put something else first—usually earnings per share. The rest of the organization can figure this out in a hurry and will behave accordingly, especially if they are evaluated and rewarded in terms of short-term measures of profitability and financial performance.

Underinvestment in Marketing

The marketing concept requires specific resource commitments, most of which do not pay off in the short term. There is an obvious requirement for information from the marketplace about customer needs, wants, preferences, usage patterns, and buying habits, and about competitive product offerings. This information must be collected and professionally analyzed. Models must be developed for examining relationships among market characteristics, marketing actions, and customer response to marketing efforts. Professional marketing requires the development of truly professional marketing personnel and marketing information systems.

These are long-term investments with long-term payoffs and long-term strategic consequences for the firm. Budgeting for these investments puts the marketing function in direct conflict with other management functions for scarce financial resources. Such requests may conflict directly with the short-term profit orientation of the firm.

The marketing department may be trapped in a "self-fulfilling prophecy" cycle: Lack of investment in information and analysis, resulting in failure to develop the professional marketing personnel and analytical systems necessary to identify and track the strategic and financial consequences of marketing actions, makes it difficult to justify rigorously the request for funds to develop and maintain such systems. As financial management gained ascendancy in the 1970s, the representatives of the marketing function in many companies looked less professional than other management colleagues, who had often been trained more completely and more rigorously in the management and analytical disciplines. To quote one executive:

> Marketing tends to be peripatetic. They do less homework than the other business functions such as finance, manufacturing, and engineering. They tend to fly by the seat of the pants and their approach is much less documented. They are less even, more in-and-out than the other functions. I have great affinity for the marketing people. I like to talk to them. But when they go away I wonder if they were really listening.[18]

Weak Performance by the Marketing Function

All too often, marketing promised more than it could deliver. This is true both on the academic side, where marketing scholars were struggling to develop a rigorous analytical base for the marketing discipline, and on the business side, where marketing departments were often staffed with people poorly prepared for their responsibility.

From the academic perspective, management science, using the tools of rigorous mathematical and statistical analysis, had not lived up to its promise in marketing.[19] Although there had been a lot of overpromising in the 1960s and 1970s, that is not the principal point here. Rather, there is a fundamental difficulty inherent in the nature of marketing problems for the manager who wishes to justify marketing expenditures by establishing cause-and-effect relationships between marketing actions and sales and profit results. In a competitive marketplace, where consumers are exposed to thousands of selling messages from dozens of competing suppliers, where customers have limited ability to process information and a number of other constraints on their decision making, where every sale is the result of many complex interactions between marketing variables and buyer characteristics, it is virtually impossible to find strong causal relationships.

The financial manager can run a computer model to predict return on investment given assumptions about risks and interest rates. The manufacturing manager can rather precisely determine the amount of production output that will result from specified inputs of raw materials, machine time, workforce hours, energy, and so on. The marketing manager must often answer "It all depends . . ." when asked to predict the results of a given investment. At best, the manager may be able to specify what "it depends" on. More commonly, he or she may not be able to provide even that general level of analysis.

In the best companies, marketing management talent was being recruited from leading universities and exposed to rigorous in-house training and management development programs. Such excellence was characteristic of the large consumer packaged goods companies such as Procter & Gamble, General Mills, and Gillette, and some of the more prominent industrial firms such as General Electric and IBM. In many other companies, however, as their managers will readily admit, marketing was still seen as an adjunct to the sales department. Field sales managers were brought into headquarters to head up a poorly conceived marketing operation. The long-term, strategic, research-based requirements of the marketing concept were superseded by the short-term, tactical, intuitive emphasis and skills of the sales manager, who continued to be under pressure to produce maximum sales volume in the short term.

In a 1980 study of top management views of the marketing function, many of the respondents commented on the separation of sales and marketing. The president of one of the American "Big 3" automobile companies commented:

> The auto companies are in the Dark Ages. They confuse sales and marketing. The "sales and marketing guys" are all sales guys. They don't sell cars to the public, they sell them to the dealers. The auto companies do not see that they have any incentive to become customer and marketing oriented.[20]

The chief executive officer of a major paper products company, with more than 30 years experience in a variety of both consumer and industrial businesses, commented from this broad perspective:

> The marketing concept is only 25 or 30 years old and to get it understood and accepted is the biggest challenge any organization faces. Marketing tends to degenerate into a sales orientation and into an exclusive concern for marketing communications. . . . In industrial companies like this one, the experience ladder is usually built on direct sales or a related function, and this can create a very narrow viewpoint. They bring the values of a salesman into the marketing function, partly because they feel they have been successful and have been promoted into marketing. In an industrial organization, there is an almost inevitable

> pressure from individual customers that creates a short-term orientation, a concern for specific orders, specific customer problems, specific requests. It is a continuing uphill battle to get marketing people to see their job in broad strategic terms. It is difficult for anybody to think broadly, reflectively about what they do. But sales people will never be able to develop a marketing plan. There are many, many more sales people in the typical organization than marketing people, and this also helps to explain why the sales viewpoint tends to drive out the marketing viewpoint.[21]

Marketing Bureaucracy

Over time, the marketing department became a distinct organizational entity in many companies, in part because of the inherent conflict between the sales and marketing viewpoints. Assigning marketing responsibility to sales organizations in general did not work very well. Marketing was identified with marketing research and product development, whereas sales was associated with promotion, distribution, and pricing. Integrated marketing required something more.

Despite the urging of Drucker and others that marketing was really not a separate business function, it was necessary to find organizational mechanisms for implementing the marketing concept. There must be responsibility for market information, market analysis, and integrated marketing—coordination of the parts of the marketing mix and of marketing with other functions, especially manufacturing and distribution.

In the consumer packaged goods firms, organizational responsibility typically resided in a brand management function. Here, marketing was a line management function with profit-and-loss responsibility implemented through a rigorous annual budgeting process. Some firms in other industries such as paper, chemicals, office machinery, and computers also found it possible to organize around product managers or market managers who had clear P&L responsibilities.

In many other cases, however, marketing remained a staff function, reporting through a sales vice president or marketing vice president to a chief executive officer such as the president. Within the marketing function, there were managers of advertising and sales promotion, market research, and sometimes product development, distribution, packaging, public relations, and publicity. Pricing responsibility was often diffused across marketing, sales, and financial management. Sales was frequently a separate function, with its own vice president, who reported directly to the CEO.

Organizational separation of marketing and sales obviously created a number of issues of responsibility and coordination. Some firms attempted to manage the inherent conflict with a kind of matrix organization in which salespeople also had a "dotted line" responsibility to a product manager or market manager. Seldom did these arrangements work well. Again, the sales viewpoint tended to dominate. The product or market manager was a general without troops. Market development activities, for example, would receive inadequate attention from a sales force focused on making the sales revenue numbers for the current period. Marketing planning remained an advisory or consulting function with unclear responsibility for results, and it was often viewed as an impediment to quick response in the increasingly competitive marketplace.

If marketing was a separate staff function, it was not a profit center but a cost center. It had a budget and a staff, assigned costs, and no assigned revenue. When the cost-cutting, downsizing, and delayering mandates of the 1980s came along, marketing departments were in an exposed position. Marketing staffs were reduced significantly and in some cases eliminated altogether. The rationalization was sometimes that of the old marketing concept—marketing should not be a separate staff function; rather it is the responsibility of the businesses, the operating units, to become customer focused and market driven. That didn't mean better marketing would result at the operating unit level, however. The basic problems of the marketing concept and its implementation remained, regardless of the level in the organization to which they were assigned.

Having marketing as a separate function also had another negative consequence: It let the rest of the organization "off the hook" in terms of customer satisfaction. Other functional managers could follow the mandates of their own disciplines, not the customer's requirements. (If the marketing department is going to worry about the customer, the other departments can go about their own business.)

When marketing became a function, it was no longer a focus. Someplace along the line, market*ing* orientation was substituted for market or customer orientation. Perhaps it was Pillsbury's Keith with his concepts of marketing orientation and marketing control who unwittingly first made the substitution. It should come as no surprise that managers of other functions were not ready to buy into the notion of a firm controlled by its marketing department.

Conflict between Marketing and Other Management Functions

Marketing, as a separate management function, has an inherent conflict with the other management functions. Under the marketing concept, that management function is charged with responsibility for telling the rest of the organization what to do. It is marketing's job to research customer needs and wants and to direct the firm's product development, manufacturing, and distribution activities, and indeed all other support functions from credit to human resources to purchasing to financial management, toward the delivering of maximum value for customers. Marketing is charged with being *expert on the customer,* for keeping the rest of the organization both informed about and focused on the customer. Marketing is an advocate for the customer's point of view.

There are two problems with this:

1. Managers in other functions have other constituencies that must be served and satisfied.
2. Marketing managers are not alone in thinking that they know best what is in the customer's best interest.

Any organization is a complex coalition of interests. According to the stakeholder theory of the firm, each of the company's functional specialists is responsible for securing the favor and serving the needs of a group of persons and organizations who provide resource inputs to the firm or who constrain its activities:

- Financial managers are accountable to the firm's shareholders and others who provide funds.
- Purchasing managers must manage relationships with suppliers of raw materials, components, services, and other inputs to the operations of the business.
- Engineers and scientists represent the *scientific community* and are caretakers for a body of professional knowledge.

- Human resource managers and line managers share responsibility for the *employees* who contract with the firm.
- Manufacturing management is accountable to multiple constituencies including the *employees,* the *owners* of the productive assets, *vendors,* and *customers.*

It is the job of top management to coordinate and manage the tradeoffs between these potentially conflicting interests.

The marketing concept asserts that customers should be first among equals, so to speak, the constituency that must be served first because customers have veto power over all the other decisions made within the organization. If the customer doesn't buy, the other inputs and constraints are irrelevant because the firm will be out of business. This should give legitimacy to the mission of the marketing function to make the rest of the business customer oriented.

Managers in other functions may honestly believe that they are putting the customer's interests first when they look at things from their own internal company perspectives. The research scientist, the engineer who specializes in product development and design, the manufacturing manager, the purchasing manager, and all the rest are not willing to concede that their own viewpoint about what serves the customer best is in error. A manufacturing manager for a chemical company once said to me, for example: "I'll tell you what is best for the customer—it is what runs best through my plant!"

R&D people are certainly entitled to the view that they know better than the customers themselves what is in their best interest because they, the scientists, have a better view of what is possible. They know the technology, the customer doesn't. Some may think they even know better than customers themselves what is best for the customer. This can be a problem especially in firms dominated by the disciplines of physical or biological sciences and engineering.

Can the Marketing Concept Improve Organizational Performance?

A final, and perhaps most basic problem with the marketing concept is that there was virtually no convincing evidence that a commitment to the strictures of the marketing concept would actually improve profitability or other measures of organizational performance. The argument that profit was a reward for creating a satisfied customer seemed to be based on faith rather than hard data. It would be a hard argument to prove, because the relevant profits were *long-term* profits. Furthermore, concepts like *customer orientation* and *integrated marketing* would prove very difficult to make operational, observable, and measurable.

In the absence of empirical support for the argument, and given the marketing concept's call for a long-term, strategic view of a firm that put the customer's needs first, it was no surprise that the emphasis on strategic planning and sophisticated financial management that evolved in the 1970s would revolve around short term measures of profitability such as cash flow, return-on-investment, and earnings per share. The current interests of the shareholders and sales volume as the key to short-term earnings would continue to dominate firm management, at the expense of the interests of customers and long-term profitability. Global competitors found an interesting opportunity in the United States, the largest domestic market in the world, where management attention was not sharply focused on the changing needs and preferences of an increasingly sophisticated consumer.

SUMMARY

Thus, the marketing concept ran into rough times as it matured. While no one argued with the basic wisdom of customer orientation, managing for profitability, and integrated marketing, implementing this concept proved to be difficult work. First, there was the problem of the rather weak strategic links of customer orientation back to the resources, skills, and other competences of the firm. It was often unclear whether the customers could say what they needed or wanted or whether it was reasonable to assume that customers could direct the development of potential technological and other capabilities.

Second, there were difficulties of implementation including the tension between the demand for short-term earnings based on current sales volume and the need for a long-term, strategic focus on future earnings requirements. Short-term needs tended to drive out attention to long-term goals; sales dominated marketing. Firms that underinvested in marketing tended to weaken their marketing activities, undercutting the ability of the marketing function to gain credibility with the other management functions and contribute to organizational effectiveness. Marketing didn't always live up to its promises.

A separate marketing department and the development of a marketing bureaucracy added to the problem. If marketing and sales were separate functions, the inherent conflict was usually won by the sales department. If the company had not made a commitment to a strong marketing department, as opposed to simple lip service to the concept of being customer oriented, it was easy for the other management functions to refuse to be guided by the information provided by a marketing department. Information is the key, and to be useful, it must be credible. If marketing has low credibility, the other functional managers can in good faith hold onto their belief that they know best what is in the customer's best interests.

A new marketing concept would have to address these questions, but in the context of the new organizational forms that have emerged in the global marketplace in the 1990s—*network organizations* consisting of smaller, more entrepreneurial business units, some as traditional divisions of larger corporations, others as joint ventures, strategic alliances to develop new technologies, strategic partnerships with vendors, and a variety of long-term relationships with resellers, customers, and suppliers of services of all kinds. The traditional functional, bureaucratic, hierarchical, divisionalized corporate structure, defined by the pyramid of its organizational chart and its shiny corporate offices, is obsolete. As these new organizational forms evolve, the marketing concept must be reinvented for the 1990s.

That is the purpose of this book.

2 STRATEGIC PLANNING AND MARKETING

> The strategic aim of a business [is] to earn a return on capital, and if in any particular case the return in the long run is not satisfactory, then the deficiency should be corrected or the activity abandoned for a more favorable one.
>
> Alfred P. Sloan, Jr.
> Quoted in Ansoff, *Corporate Strategy* (1965), p. 1

The marketing concept, articulated as a management philosophy in the 1950s, melded into a broader concept of strategic planning in the 1960s and the marketing concept was soon overshadowed.

A financial management orientation dominated the strategic planning process in the late 1960s and into the 1970s. Firms were seen as investment portfolios of businesses, defined as product/market combinations, with the objective of maximizing return on investment. Members of top management focused their attention on allocating financial resources among the businesses in the portfolio to maximize the shareholders' total return.

It wasn't until the mid-1980s that business leaders began to revisit the fundamental notions of customer orientation and integrated marketing that had been popular 25 years earlier. By the end of the decade, many managers were trying to repair the damage inflicted on their competitive positions by short-term financial objectives and to recreate their companies as customer-focused, market-driven businesses.

This chapter examines the evolution of the marketing concept into strategic planning and back again.

EMERGENCE OF LONG-RANGE STRATEGIC PLANNING

As the ideas of the marketing concept were gaining popularity in the 1950s, managers were also developing the practice of *long-range planning*. This was an attempt to get beyond annual sales forecasting, budgeting, and production planning and adopt a longer time horizon that would permit more careful development and commitment of financial and human resources. Long-range planning was distinct from product planning, which was part of the product development process.

Also in the late 1950s, an interest developed—especially on the academic side—in rigorous, quantitative approaches to management decision making. The field of management science and decision analysis was based on mathematics, statistics, economics, and psychology. The curricula of leading business schools very quickly began to teach these more rigorous approaches to decision making and to apply them in the functional fields of marketing, production/operations, and finance.

In his famous study, *Strategy and Structure,* published in 1962, the business historian Alfred Chandler had concluded that the evolution of the country's largest and most successful corporations had followed a consistent pattern. These successful firms had been able to identify changes in the external environment that created new opportunities and required some fundamental changes in management operations. The firms had been able to adopt new strategies required by the changing environment and to implement them through new organizational forms. It was this willingness to adapt form and structure to the changing environment that distinguished the successful firms. Chandler's observations led to the simply following simply stated conclusion: *Structure follows strategy.*[1]

The result of the evolutionary process that Chandler had identified in these successful companies was the now familiar organizational concept of centralized policy making and decentralized control, through a profit center form of organization. Large, bureaucratic, divisionalized companies must balance the need for consistency, coordination, and control on the one hand with the need to push decision-making responsibility and authority down and out into the operating units on the other.

One of the management issues inherent in such arrangements is how to achieve the proper balance between attention to current operating problems and long-term strategic challenges, between short-term and long-term decisions, despite the inevitable tendency of operating management to focus on short-term problems and results. Formal, long-range planning was a method for keeping the entire enterprise moving in a coordinated fashion toward the achievement of long-term objectives. The practice of long-range *strategic* planning, which focused on the long-run strategic objectives of the firm, emerged in the 1960s as a new discipline, a new management practice to address these needs.

Three Types of Decisions: Operating, Strategic, and Administrative

An early voice bringing these ideas together in a coherent framework was that of H. Igor Ansoff, then a professor at Carnegie Institute of Technology, noted for its rigorous approach to the study of industrial management. Ansoff's approach to the concept of strategy is particularly interesting because it highlights the confusing and often conflicting relationship between strategic planning and the marketing concept. In his book *Corporate Strategy,* Ansoff spelled out the differences among three types of decisions: operating, strategic, and administrative.[2]

Operating Decisions

Operating decisions allocated the firm's productive resources to various activities, determining the levels of the various physical, financial, and human inputs into the firm's operations. Ansoff gave the following examples of operating decisions:

- Pricing.
- Marketing strategy (his words).
- Setting production schedules and inventory levels.
- Relative expenditures for R&D, marketing, and operations.

In an early example of how confusing the use of the word strategy can be, marketing *strategy* was said to be an operating decision, not a *strategic* decision.[3] Operating decisions were said to have a primarily *internal* focus, while strategic decisions had an *external* focus. From the beginning of the field of corporate strategy, there has been confusion and uncertainty about the relationship with marketing as a concept, as a discipline, and as a business function.

Strategic Decisions

These were defined by Ansoff as those that establish what business the firm is in. They do so by selecting among alternatives for the product-market mix, the products to be offered, and the markets to which they will be sold. Apparently, Ansoff did not consider the choice of products or markets to be marketing decisions. As previously noted, marketing was defined as a set of operating decisions. This becomes significant as we consider what will happen to the acceptance and implementation of the marketing concept. Ansoff was also specific as to the objective of strategic decision making: to select a product-market mix that maximizes the firm's return on investment potential.[4] The emphasis on financial criteria was inherent in a more rigorous, economics-based approach to management decision making that focused on the optimum allocation of the firm's scarce resources among investment alternatives.

Administrative Decisions

These decisions establish the shape and structure of the firm. The objective of administrative decisions was to structure the firm's resources to maximize the firm's profit performance potential. Administrative decisions included those relating to:

- The development and acquisition of productive resources such as raw materials and personnel.
- The organization of the firm, including authority and reporting relationships.
- The flow of work and information.
- The location of facilities.
- The design and management of channels of distribution.

How the Marketing Concept Fits into Strategic Planning

Thinking back to the marketing concept and relating it to Ansoff's schema, if product-market selection is a strategic decision and distribution is an administrative decision, then the balance of what he would call *marketing* is pricing and promotion (personal selling, advertising, sales promotion, etc.) decisions, which he saw as *operating decisions*. Marketing was one of the functional competences that the firm needed to maintain. In Ansoff's words:

> *Marketing* is taken as a broad activity concerned with creating product acceptance, advertising, sales promotion, selling, distributing the product (including transportation and warehousing), contract administration, sales analysis, and, very importantly, servicing the product.[5]

As a practical matter, it would seem more appropriate to consider sales force management issues as being administrative in nature, but that is a small point. Ansoff's concept of corporate strategy and three types of decisions implicitly broke marketing into administrative and operating decision components and explicitly separated marketing from strategic decision making. It was a reversion to the days before the marketing concept, when marketing was equated with selling. Ansoff added distribution and service to the marketing function but specifically excluded concern for customer focus and innovation. These were now the province of "strategy" although the marketing concept had intended to provide a long-term, strategic focus for the business.

Long-Term Challenges versus Short-Term Focus

Ansoff observed that management, under the pressures of day-to-day business life, tended to approach decisions sequentially, and that attention to short-term operating problems tended to drive out attention to long-term strategic issues. If a problem was identified—for example, sales volume below forecasted levels—management tended to treat it first as an *operating* decision and might adjust the level of resources by increasing advertising or decreasing the rate of production. If the problem persisted, it would next be defined as an *administrative* decision—resulting in some change in the structure of the firm or its resources, for example reassigning sales representatives or managers or perhaps reorganizing the production department.

Only if the problem continued to persist would it be defined as a *strategic* problem that questioned the company's commitments to products and markets. In familiar words, the focus would shift from asking, "Are we doing things right?" to "Are we doing the right things?" Strategic decisions were those that required a realignment of the firm's resource commitments with a changing market environment.

The problems of General Motors and IBM in the mid-1990s, as they attempt to downsize, realign, and refocus their organization into smaller, more flexible business units, show the process that Ansoff described at work. Only after a series of operating and administrative decisions failed to stop the erosion in sales and earnings did top management at GM and IBM face up to the need for fundamental strategic shifts and total reorganization. Both strategic and structural change came too slowly. GM, cited as an example of a successful firm in Chandler's studies three decades ago, could now be used as an example of what happens when firm does *not* respond to a changing environment with a changed strategy and organization. It could equally well be cited as an example of a firm that had lost touch with its customers as well as its ability to provide innovative solutions for customer problems.

Creating a Strategic Planning Function

A clear concept of corporate strategy and strategic planning required ongoing surveillance of the changing environment so that important developments could be seen as they occurred rather than being detected after-the-fact through their problematic impact on operations. This called for a separate, centralized strategic planning operation that could assume responsibility for this critically important function of environmental assessment, objective analysis of the strengths and weaknesses of the firm, and a carefully managed process of matching up the firm's capabilities with changing market opportunities.

Using this approach, the company could overcome the basic management tendency to focus on short-term operating and administrative decisions and to lose sight of the need for strategic response to a changing environment. Management could make an up-front judgment about whether a given problem was primarily operating, administrative, or strategic in nature rather than proceeding sequentially on a trial-and-error basis to the identification of the vital strategic issues. Strategic planning moves the firm from a pattern of lagged responses to a changing environment to one of anticipatory or self-triggered responses.

Strategic planning also addressed an important limitation of the marketing concept identified in Chapter 1. The marketing concept called for customer orientation and directed the firm to concentrate on satisfying customer needs. It did not say how the firm could determine *which sets of customer needs* to focus on. Product development was to be guided by market research on customer needs, wants, and preferences. However, the marketing concept offered firms no guidance in deciding in which areas to concentrate efforts at innovation in response to changing customer needs. The marketing concept said nothing about which markets to serve or which technologies to develop and exploit in creating products for those markets.

Implicit within the marketing concept, but not clearly or completely developed, was the concept of market segmentation—dividing the total market into smaller, more homogeneous segments within which buyers had similar needs and patterns of response to product characteristics and communications. After those segments have been identified and analyzed, the strategic problem is to choose among them and to tailor the firm's offerings for each. Should the company try to serve all segments or select one or a few? This is the market targeting and product positioning problem. Ansoff incorporated these fundamental notions and made them explicit in his concept of strategy—the selection of markets to be served and products to be offered there. How should a firm decide which markets to serve and which products to offer in those markets? He saw these as strategic decisions, not marketing decisions.

The Financial Emphasis of Strategic Planning

Corporate strategy as a distinct field had a predominant financial emphasis from the very beginning. Ansoff followed traditional economic wisdom in assuming that the long-run objective of any business was profit maximization, an assumption in the microeconomic paradigm that puts the interests of the owners ahead of all other participants in the business system. He also recognized, however, that it was virtually impossible to predict accurately the stream of profits from a given business—defined by the commitment of resources to a product/ market.

After considering issues involved in forecasting and measuring profitability, Ansoff stated that, in his theory of corporate strategy, ". . . the primary economic objective is to optimize the long-term rate of return on the equity employed in the firm."[6] The problem of corporate strategy was to allocate scarce financial resources across the portfolio of businesses (product-market combinations) in ways that maximized return on investment.

Ansoff rejected classical capital investment theory as the basis for his theory of corporate strategy because it provided a mechanism only for evaluating and ranking alternative investment projects. It did not address the prior problems of defining strategic challenges and opportunities and searching for investment alternatives. Instead, he based his theory, in part, on a new approach to traditional portfolio selection theory proposed by Clarkson.[7] Clarkson's enhancement of Markowitz's[8] original model allowed the incorporation of flexible decision rules and multiple objectives, depending on the situation and preference of the investor, including attitudes toward risk. The new approach appealed to Ansoff because it incorporated important qualitative considerations while retaining rigorous analysis.

The virtual impossibility of accurately predicting long-term profitability remained. How could a firm pursue a goal of maximizing long-term return on equity if long-term profit could not be forecasted? Ansoff proposed to "abandon efforts to measure long-term profitability directly and to measure, instead, characteristics of the firm that contribute to it."[9] The variables that he chose as surrogates for long-term profitability set the stage for the rapid demise of the customer-focused marketing concept. We will return shortly to a specific discussion of these surrogate measures.

KEY ELEMENTS OF STRATEGIC PLANNING

The fundamental purpose of strategic planning was to ensure the survival, growth, and profitability of the firm over the long run in a changing and potentially hostile competitive environment. Any firm faced two basic challenges: (1) maintaining its competitive strength and (2) continuously improving its internal efficiency. These challenges can be thought of as simply the revenue and cost elements of the profit equation.

To maintain its competitive strength, the firm needed to grow at a rate at least equal to the rate of market growth. Failure to do so would result in loss of market share. Thus, *market share* becomes a key strategic variable in the most basic sense. In addition, the firm must grow revenues and profit margins in ways that minimize seasonal and cyclical fluctuations. Such fluctuations can lead to inefficient use of assets from under- and overcapacity utilization, causing reduced return on investment and diminished competitive strength. Stability—of sales, growth rates, and earnings—thus becomes an important strategic objective. The twin strategic objectives of growth and stability dominate the strategic planning process.

Turning to the efficiency/cost elements of the profit model, the factors to be considered include the firm's skills in research and development (R&D), management, and the labor force, the age of physical assets including plant, equipment, and inventory, the rate of turnover of its financial assets and inventories, the ratio of sales to inventories, and the rate of return being earned on sales. These relationships are summarized in Figure 2–1.

Surrogate Variables for Profitability

It has been often said that what gets measured gets emphasized. When management incorporated surrogate variables for profitability identified by Ansoff and others into formal strategic planning systems, it focused attention on specific, short-term operating measures. In pursuit of long-run maximum returns on equity, guided by the twin objectives of competitive strength and internal efficiency, Ansoff's framework identified a number of operating measures to guide management as described in the following sections. Subsequent authors quickly adopted and expanded these ideas.

Sales Growth

The objective of continuous sales growth at or above the rate of market growth, to maintain market share, is a prelude to achieving increased market share. The position of the firm relative to its competitors is

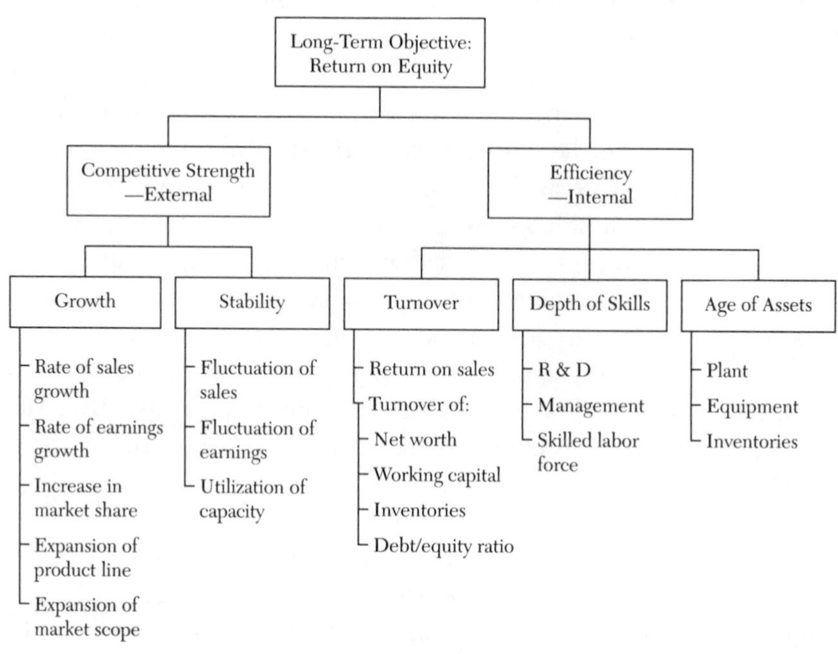

FIGURE 2–1. The hierarchy of strategic objectives: surrogates for long-term profit/ROI Maximization. *Source:* Adapted from H. Igor Ansoff, *Corporate Strategy* (New York: McGraw-Hill, 1965), p. 53. Used with permission.

a fundamentally important determinant of the firm's competitive strength. Market dominance is a source of market power, permitting more control over pricing and a larger expenditure for sales- and market-expanding activities such as R&D and marketing/selling.

Market Share

Increasing market share is essential to improve efficiency of the firm relative to competitors. Market share becomes important because of the *experience curve,* the phenomenon of a constant percentage reduction in cost per unit each time the cumulative volume produced by the firm doubles. This is a first cousin to the older concept of the learning curve. Logically, the argument is that the largest firm, in terms of total units produced over its lifetime, should be the most efficient, lowest cost producer.

Earnings Growth

Profits must increase to permit reinvestment in skills, resources, and assets. If the firm is to grow at or preferably above the rate of market growth, it needs to continually reinvest in human and physical resources, in the development of new sources of raw materials and components, and in R&D. The funds to support this investment must come from operating earnings as well as from new capital investment.

Growth in Earnings per Share

Improved performance attracts new capital. The firm with the best earnings per share should be able to attract more new investment at lower cost than firms with weaker earnings performance.

Innovation

Addition of new products and product lines is vital. Because of the dynamics of the competitive marketplace and product life cycles, with declining profit margins over time, new products are the lifeblood of the business, the engine for growth.

Customer Growth

New customers expand the customer base and reduce the dependence on a few large customers. Major dependence on one or a few large customers is a sign of strategic weaknesses and relatively low competitive strength. These large customers can demand increasingly lower prices by means of threats to take their business elsewhere. The loss of a major piece of business can also contribute to substantial instability in sales and earnings.

Stability

Excessive seasonal or cyclical fluctuation in sales and earnings, can cause the loss of competitive position through inefficient use of resources. Orderly investment decisions, the logic of the experience curve, and the need for continuous improvement in skills, resources, and the product mix call for stability in sales and earnings. Otherwise, the firm could find itself in situations of over- and undercapacity, leading to higher relative costs and weakened competitive position.

These core concepts came to dominate the strategic planning field. Many of the ideas were developed and promoted by managers and consultants, not only by academic thinkers and writers. Some of the nation's most respected and most successful businesses, including General Electric and Norton Company, sometimes in collaboration with major consulting firms such as McKinsey & Company and the Boston Consulting Group, began to popularize and promote these ideas. *Market share* became the Holy Grail, followed closely by the importance of steady *revenue and earnings growth* from growing markets, a focus on becoming the *low-cost producer* by exploiting the *experience curve,* and *stability* in earnings growth enhanced by *diversification* into unrelated businesses to spread risk and balance seasonal and cyclical trends that might characterize certain industries.

Defining the Business: To Satisfy Customer Needs or to Develop Technical Competence?

While this book cannot offer a complete review of Ansoff's model of corporate strategy, one other important feature is directly relevant in its connection to the marketing concept. The basic calculus of the strategic planning approach being developed by Ansoff and others was to match up the strengths and weaknesses of the firm with the evolving set of competitive threats and market opportunities. Ansoff was particularly concerned with the problem noted earlier: The marketing concept did not specify how the firm should choose among the multiple market opportunities potentially available to it. He rejected the mandates of the earliest advocates of the marketing concept, especially Drucker[10] and Levitt,[11] to define the business in terms of the customer needs that the business was committed to satisfying. He argued against customer orientation in its pure form and advocated, instead, a view that focused internally on the firm's technological capabilities—the things it could do best. On the other hand, traditional definitions of the business, which focused on a particular industry, were also too narrow.

Ansoff believed that definition of the business in terms of customer need satisfaction (for example, defining a railroad as being in the business of satisfying customer's needs for transportation) was imprecise and impractical. First, such definitions were too broad. It was highly unlikely that a railroad would have the skills and resources necessary to be an effective competitor in the airline or trucking or pipeline or barge business. Second, such definitions did not provide what Ansoff called "a common thread," a relationship between the firm's present and future markets that would enable managers and outsiders, especially investors, to see where the firm was headed and to give it guidance. A useful definition of the business would focus on the range of missions, customers, and products that the firm wished to pursue.

Focusing on a particular set of customers also was rejected as the common thread. Each customer has many needs and wants and a given firm can serve only one or a few of these. The customer also "belongs" to many other businesses, including many of the firm's competitors. Thus, Ansoff argues that the customer cannot provide strategic focus for a business.

Defining the Business with a Product *and* Market View

Instead, Ansoff believed that the fundamental concept of *product/market scope* was the most practical definition of a common thread for a business unit. To be useful and provide the necessary guidance for management, the concept of product/market scope should concentrate on a particular set of submarkets and technologies with similar characteristics.[12] This led to the definition of four growth strategies:

1. Market penetration—gaining a larger share of an existing market.
2. Product development—pursuing new product opportunities for existing markets.
3. Market development—expanding present markets and finding new markets for existing products.
4. Diversification—the more risky strategy of simultaneously pursuing new products for new markets.

Ansoff referred to these strategies as "growth vectors."

By focusing on the firm's strengths and weaknesses and the need to develop specific competences as a source of competitive advantage,

Ansoff had addressed a serious shortcoming in the marketing concept. At the same time, however, he had softened the commitment to a customer orientation, to putting the customer first. Was this necessary? Was it wise? Does a firm really have to choose between focusing on its customers or its core technologies?

By the late 1960s, the business community initiated the development of several concepts of strategic planning and corporate strategy. They had many common themes:

- These concepts of strategy all adopted a portfolio approach and incorporated many of the ideas in Ansoff's seminal work.
- They all recognized the strategic importance of growth and internal efficiency.
- They all were concerned with matching up the firm's strengths and weaknesses with market opportunities and threats.
- They all emphasized the strategic importance of market share.
- And they all incorporated the criterion of maximum return on equity and attempted to address the problem of allocating scarce financial resources across a portfolio of competing investment opportunities.

Ansoff's work was a seminal influence in many respects. The concept of product/market scope as the common thread in a business became a central element in the several different approaches to corporate strategy developed by leading business firms and management consultants. Highly visible among these was Bruce Henderson, founder of the Boston Consulting Group, called "BCG." Henderson had been an executive at Westinghouse and worked briefly with the Arthur D. Little consulting firm before founding his own company to exploit the new interest in corporate strategy.[13] The approach promoted by Henderson and BCG was built around three central concepts:

1. The strategic business unit.
2. The experience curve.
3. The growth/share matrix.

Each of these concepts is discussed in the following sections.

Strategic Business Units

The strategic business unit, or SBU, was an operationalization of the concept of product/market scope and was the central unit of analysis in the strategic planning process. The term was proposed by McKinsey & Company in a study they did at General Electric in 1969, borrowing freely from the language of an internal study concluded at GE in 1957.[14] The general definition of a strategic business unit was that it could be recognized as a distinct business unit selling a product or a product line to a definable market and not competing directly with another SBU within the corporation. (If businesses were serving the same market and therefore competing they were part of the same SBU.)

In addition, the SBU was defined by a set of activities built around a common thread such as technical competence, access to critical raw materials, a dominant position in a marketing channel, or a particular management skill such as sales promotion. In practice, the definition of SBUs became highly flexible and creative. At one point, General Electric had over 60 distinct SBUs ranging widely in size and defined in many different ways, prompting one manager to comment: "I'll tell you how an SBU is defined—however the Chairman wants it defined!"

The SBU was a freestanding entity with its own chief executive and/or operating officer. In the annual strategic planning and budgeting process, the SBU management team had to prepare a strategic plan that served, most importantly, as a request for funding. Corporate management reviewed the plans of the SBUs, evaluated performance against previously stated objectives and plans, considered the attractiveness of the markets in which the SBU was competing, assessed the competitive strength of the SBU in its chosen markets, and judged the management's proposed strategy for competing in those markets. Based on these evaluations, financial assets were allocated among the SBUs. Some businesses received new funding, whereas others were expected to provide the cash (from earnings) to fund the businesses with greater future potential.

Defining the "served market" was critical in defining a strategic business unit because this identified the competitors with which the business must compare itself in assessing its strengths and weaknesses. Markets were defined as sets of competitors rather than as sets of customers.

The Experience Curve

The focus on internal efficiency as the key to competitive strength led directly to a concern for achieving the lowest possible costs among firms vying for the same customers. The Boston Consulting Group, as part of its strategic planning practice, developed the concept of the experience curve, an update of the old idea of the learning curve. In the manufacturing of aircraft in the 1930s, it was observed that the cost of producing an airplane tended to diminish consistently over time as production workers became more familiar with the task and improved their skills. This process was called "the learning curve," and it could be used to forecast costs. The experience curve refined the learning curve by noting that the cost per unit would decline by a predictable amount each time the total cumulative production doubled. The BCG formulation also extended the learning notion to all costs, not just those narrowly defined by manufacturing activities.

The relationship between cost and volume was described by a logarithmic function in which cost declines in an amount described by the gradually decreasing slope of the curve, the cost elasticity. For example, with a 15% curve, unit cost would decline by 15% with each doubling of volume. BCG research found this predictable consistency in cost reduction in many distinct product/market groups—including long distance telephone calls in the United States, integrated circuits, life insurance policies, bottle caps in Germany, refrigerators in Britain, polystyrene molding resins in the United States, and Japanese motorcycles.[15] Experience curve effects were attributable to learning, technological innovation, and economies of scale. Many solid econometric studies have confirmed the existence of the experience curve, often by studying the decline of *prices,* as a surrogate for costs, over time.

To have a favorable cost position, a business (SBU) needed to achieve a dominant position in its served market, which would assure its being furthest down the experience curve and thus the low-cost producer. The name of the game was *dominant market share.* One strategy for exploiting the potential of the experience curve was to use price to gain a dominant market position, thus moving down the experience curve faster than competitors as well as discouraging competitive market entry.

A number of critical assumptions are operating here, each of which is subject to debate:

1. It is assumed that all competitors face the same experience curve; otherwise, the comparison is invalid. This in turn requires the assumption that all competitors are using approximately the same production technology.
2. It is also assumed that market share is highly correlated with cumulative production. There is no consideration of the possibility that a late entrant into the market could adopt a newer, more efficient product form or production technology, and achieve both a dominant market share and a low-cost position without having the largest cumulative production volume.
3. Another assumption is that all cost components decline at the same rate. Whereas the analysis is performed on total costs, the implicit assumption is that costs of manufacturing, selling, distribution, and so on are all declining in similar fashion. In fact, the relative changes in individual cost elements may vary widely and behave differently over time.

In addition, there are all the issues associated with administrative rules for allocation of costs among products and activities. The data for performing experience curve cost analysis are provided by normal company cost accounting methods with all their arbitrary rules of thumb. These become especially serious issues when many of the relevant costs are joint costs, shared by multiple products and activities.

The Growth/Share Matrix

In the strategic planning process, as top management appraised the plans and performance of the multiple SBUs and determined where to allocate financial resources, the major problem was how to apportion scarce resources, especially cash, among the competing investment opportunities. The strongest business opportunities, with the greatest potential for maximizing return on investment, were those with the strongest growth prospects and those in which the firm could achieve a dominant competitive position. The central idea was that certain basic economic rules in the marketplace could be analyzed and that these factors determined the success or failure of a business. It was necessary to understand these structural characteristics of markets as barriers to competitive entry and as contributors to competitive strength. The growth/share matrix provided a mechanism for making the necessary comparisons in the context of different competitive market structures.

While the BCG product portfolio became the best known and most widely used of the growth/share models, several others were developed including the company position/industry attractiveness matrix developed by McKinsey & Company for General Electric, the Arthur D. Little product life cycle/market position matrix, and the Shell Chemical International product portfolio.[16] In each model, the two most important dimensions in the matrix were the company's *market share/competitive position* and the *market's rate of growth,* the latter being a proxy variable for stage in the product life cycle.

In the BCG model, the two dimensions are industry growth rate and market share. Industry growth is said to be high if it is more than 10%, low if less. Market share is defined as *market share relative to the market share of the largest competitor,* on a logarithmic scale. Thus, a firm's position is measured by dividing its market share by the largest competitor's share. The result is a number that is more than one if the SBU is the dominant competitor, less than one if it is not dominant. Why is *dominance* the critical concept? Because of the logic of the experience curve. If the SBU is not a dominant player, it has an inferior cost position and is an inefficient competitor with weak prospects for success in this market.

These definitions result in the two-by-two matrix shown in Figure 2–2. Various names have been used to describe the businesses that end up in each of the four boxes. In our terminology, the *stars* are the businesses with high growth and dominant market position. They require substantial investment for growth and are users of cash. Despite their cash requirements, they are the most sought-after SBUs, the most attractive. They are the subject of a *Growth* strategy.

The businesses with good growth characteristics but whose firm has an inferior position have been called *question marks, problem children,* or *wildcats.* They also need cash to finance their growth but their prospects are uncertain because the company has a relatively weak

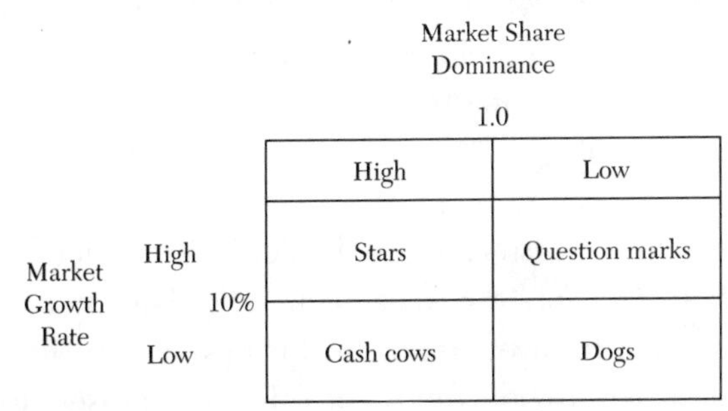

FIGURE 2–2. The Boston Consulting Group growth/share matrix.

competitive position. These businesses have a poorly defined strategic role. They must be fixed, strengthened, and repositioned, or else removed from the portfolio. They are candidates for either a *Fix* or *Divest* strategy.

The SBUs characterized by a strong competitive position in a slow growth market are the *cash cows* for the corporation. Because they do not require major new investments, due to slow growth, and because the firm's dominant position confers a degree of market control and is also likely to mean a favorable cost position, these businesses can be sources of cash for reinvestment in other SBUs. They are often selected for a *Harvest* strategy.

The weakest performers in the portfolio are those businesses where the firm has a weak position in a slow growth market. These are the *dogs.* Given the prospects of slow growth, a weak competitive position, and the likelihood of zero-to-negative returns on investment, these SBUs are identified for a *Divest* or *Withdrawal* strategy, freeing up funds for investment in businesses with better prospects.

As this brief review suggests, the product portfolio was concerned primarily with sources and uses of cash and the allocation of financial resources among competing investment projects, not with how to manage those businesses. Nothing in the growth/share matrix suggests the specific business strategies appropriate for a given SBU. Saying that a business is a star or a question mark or a cash cow does not say what the firm must do to compete effectively in that business. (The Arthur D. Little and Shell Chemical International models did go the next step and suggest broad categories of appropriate generic strategies for each box in the matrix but could not prescribe specific business strategies.) The growth/share matrix could help decide strategic issues at the *corporate* strategy level—"What businesses do we want to be in?" It could not specify a *business* strategy—"How should we attempt to compete in the business we have chosen to be in?"

Also, the focus on cash flow led, by definition, to a relatively short-term orientation. Corporate management's fundamental question was whether to continue to invest funds in this business in the next year or whether to use it to provide funds for other businesses. Financial urgency usually called for a relatively short-term orientation in assessing business prospects.

Market share was in many respects the most important strategic indicator of competitive strength. More than one CEO announced that his company was not going to stay in any business where it could not be in the number one or number two competitive position. In the hundreds of firms that developed a strategic planning competence, usually in the form of a manager of strategic planning with a supporting staff, the focus on market share was paramount.

This led to some interesting managerial behavior as SBU managers tried to define their served market so that they *were* in the number one or number two position. Defining the boundaries of any market is never an easy task, and the temptation to tautological argument is great. It is easy for a manager to try to dismiss a major competitor by observing that it has a different product strategy and a different market niche and therefore should not be considered as being in the same business. Thus, there was a time when the American automobile manufacturers dismissed the European and Japanese marques that were beginning to appear in the United States because these cars were smaller and supposedly less safe and poorly made, and not competing for the same customers. These "inferior" competitors ended up with over one-third of the U.S. domestic market.

Notice how long it has been since this discussion last mentioned *customers.* Nowhere in the strategic planning approach and in product portfolio analysis was there any consideration of customers. Markets were defined as collections of competitors. Competitive strength was measured in terms not of satisfying customer needs but of achieving a dominant position based on lowest total cost. Basic concepts of customer value were simply not part of the strategic planning conversation.

In many respects, the strategic planning approach, with its emphasis on return on investment, cash flow, market dominance, low cost, and markets defined as sets of competitors was in direct conflict with the marketing concept and its focus on customer orientation, innovation, and long-term profit as a reward for creating a satisfied customer.

PIMS: THE PROFIT IMPACT OF MARKET STRATEGY

In the beginning of the formal strategic planning discipline, arguments about the central importance of market share were based largely on the logic of economic analysis. There was little empirical support for the notion that higher market share would lead to higher return on investment. That was to change with the advent of the PIMS project at General Electric Company.

The PIMS (*P*rofit *I*mpact of *M*arket *S*trategy) project grew directly out of the corporate strategic planning department at GE. After the McKinsey & Company consulting project had been completed in 1969, the company reorganized itself around 43 SBUs, a sharp reduction from 190 separate business plans that the CEO had had to review under the old organization. These 43 SBUs, each of which might contain several businesses, covered 23 of the 26 two-digit SIC (Standard Industrial Classification) codes used by the Bureau of the Census. GE was a highly diversified company competing in virtually every industry imaginable.[17] GE management recognized that this breadth of experience offered a natural laboratory for examining the fundamental determinants of competitive strength and business performance. To follow up on this possibility, the PIMS program of research was launched in 1972. Later, the PIMS project would leave GE and be set up as the independent Strategic Planning Institute, eventually attaining a database of more than 450 companies and 3,000 business units.[18]

The Importance of Market Share to Profitability

The basic methodology of the PIMS project was regression analysis, a form of correlation analysis in which n variables are arranged in an $n \times n$ matrix and the correlation of every pair of variables is determined. Equations are then built to combine variables in terms of the strength of their association with the *dependent* variable, that variable the analyst is interested in explaining and predicting. In the PIMS analysis, the dependent variable was profitability, measured as return on investment. There were 36 other, "independent" or explanatory variables in the database that could be examined for their influence on the profitability of a business. Among all the variables examined, it was *market share* that had the strongest association with return on investment.[19] This finding was entirely consistent with the theory and conjecture of the strategic planning school and gave new life to the belief in the strategic importance of market share.

To put these results into perspective, it is helpful to understand a bit more about the PIMS database, especially because the critics of the PIMS findings often focused their attention on the quality of the data. Among the variables in the PIMS database, in addition to market share, were such things as advertising expenditures, product quality, stage in product life cycle, type of business (service, durable goods, etc.), frequency of product changes, rate of technological change, type and number of customers, average size of purchase, and several items taken from a profit and loss statement or balance sheet (sales, percentage of revenue spent on purchases, R&D expenditures, fixed assets, profits, etc.). The data were provided by the managers of the business as answers to a series of questions. Product quality and price were assessed *relative to competition*.

The finding of the importance of market share was subsequently duplicated, dissected, and expanded by other PIMS researchers. The result was surprisingly robust. Many studies confirmed the strong relationship of profitability (ROI) and market share. Critics were quick to point out, however, that correlation does not imply causality. It would be a mistake to use the PIMS regression results to argue that market share *causes* profitability although that was the argument of the early strategic planning theorists. A person could just as well argue, using the PIMS findings, that *profits cause market share*—perhaps by giving the business the resources that it needs to invest more heavily in promotion and R&D. Still others could argue that *both* profits and market share might be caused by some third variable such as product quality or loyal customers.

In fact, the early PIMS findings about the correlation between market share and profitability, when analyzed further, showed that the major factor explaining the relationship was the ratio of purchases to sales. The firm with the largest market share seemed better able to achieve economies of scale in its purchasing expenditures. While there was no particular theory to explain this result, it was a strong statistical finding. Several later studies found the same result—that the large-share firms have the lowest ratios of cost of purchases to sales.[20]

Reducing Price to Improve Market Share

A possible interpretation of the findings of the strong association between market share and return on investment is to conclude that the firm that increases its market share will increase its profitability. This is a problematic conclusion because the statistical finding is based on a "cross-sectional" analysis that makes comparisons among many businesses, whereas the proposed conclusion makes an assertion about changes in a single business over time. Nonetheless, it can be argued that if a firm increases its market share, it is moving down the experience curve faster than its competitors and that a dominant market share will provide the low-cost position and resulting competitive strength.

How can a firm improve its share of market? One way, of course, is to lower prices. Especially if the firm is selling a relatively undifferentiated product, customers might readily shift their purchase preference to the firm with the lowest prices. This interpretation of the market share findings could lead to the following strategic argument:

Volume Strategy:

Low Price ——► High Share ——► High Volume ——► Low Cost ——► Profit

---

Called a "high-volume/low-cost strategy," this combination of high volume and low cost could supposedly lead to higher return on investment. This strategy was frequently advocated by BCG and others who were impressed by the strength of experience curve effects.[21] The problem is that the combination of low price and resulting low margins makes it difficult to earn above-average returns on the large investment necessary to support the high-volume strategy, especially if high-cost debt is used to finance the volume/growth strategy.

Such a strategy can also lead to disaster if the company puts its price cutting ahead of its cost cutting, anticipating (sometimes based more on hope than analysis) that greater volume will produce the necessary cost improvements. Many companies have been trapped by this unwarranted assumption. There is nothing magical about the experience curve. Cost improvements do not come automatically with volume. Rather, they result from careful, programmatic attempts to reduce specific costs. Cost reduction must be managed.

The business landscape is littered with the remains of companies that tried to use price to gain share to achieve low cost and, finally, above-average return on investment. They are found in many industries from airlines, to automobiles, to consumer electronics, to computers, and even retailing. Even Japanese industries have not been immune from the negative consequences of the low-price, high-share, high-volume strategies for which they have been well known and, in some cases, emulated. In the past few years, the Japanese automobile industry has faced declining world demand for its products, excess plant capacity, and increased cost of capital, putting some of the weaker players into a loss position and bringing the likelihood of industry consolidation.

Improving Quality to Increase Market Share

Further analysis of the PIMS database, which was adding many new companies and businesses into the 1980s, suggested that the relationship between market share and profitability was more complicated. Market share did not influence profitability directly.

Some studies found many examples of small-share firms enjoying superior rates of return. Others found that both market share and return on investment tended to be jointly determined by other factors including product quality, marketing expenditures, management skill, luck, and unanticipated changes in the environment, such as entry or exit of a major competitor, a change in government regulations, or the introduction of a new technology. Others found the suspected reverse causal link between profitability and market share—profits leading to higher share. In general, it was often found that the magnitude of the relationship between market share and return on investment was very small. And always lurking in the background was the basic question of how a market was to be defined to calculate market share.[22]

It became obvious that low margins, which would be characteristic of low-price competitors, were typically not associated with above-average return on investment, even for firms with dominant market share. Rather, it was a combination of *high price* and low cost that yielded superior profitability. Do high price and low cost represent a contradiction? Isn't higher quality associated with a higher price because of higher cost? Yes and no. High price *is* associated with high quality, because customers are usually willing to pay more for a better, more differentiated product. It is *not* necessarily true that high quality leads to high cost. In fact, the reverse may be true. In many situations, "quality costs less."

The common way to think about the relationship between quality and profitability is what has been called a "margin strategy," as contrasted with the "high-volume/low-cost strategy" or market dominance strategy:

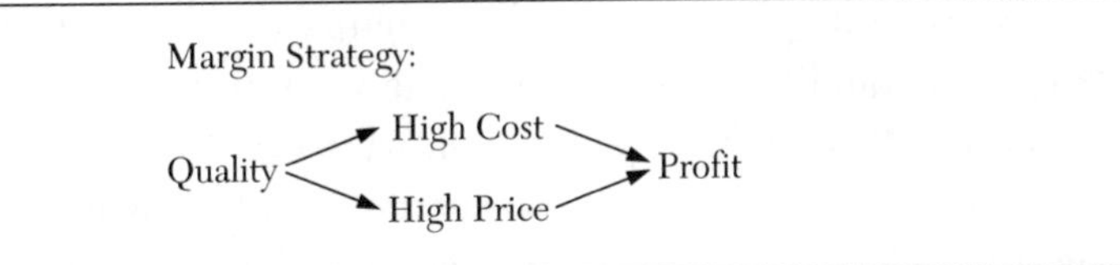

With a margin strategy, the company is typically pursuing one or more well-defined market niches, a set of customers with needs and wants that are served by the unique features and superior quality of a differentiated product. The margin strategy is usually also a market-niching strategy.

A well-known author in the strategic management area, Michael Porter, offered some evidence in support of the notion that either a volume strategy or a margin strategy could produce superior results. He proposed that firms should choose which of the two strategic options they were pursuing and not try to find some combination or compromise of the two. Firms that were "stuck in the middle," with neither a superior quality/market niching strategy nor a dominant, low-cost market position, had the lowest return on investment.[23]

The assertion that low cost and high quality are mutually exclusive is debatable. Another way to think about the relationship between market share and profitability is to see both market share and low cost as driven by superior quality. If customers really value the superior quality supposedly being built into the product or service, the demand for it will be higher and it will command a relatively higher price. In this instance, what we can call simply the "quality strategy" (superior quality) leads to both high volume and high margin, and volume, in turn, produces a favorable cost position:

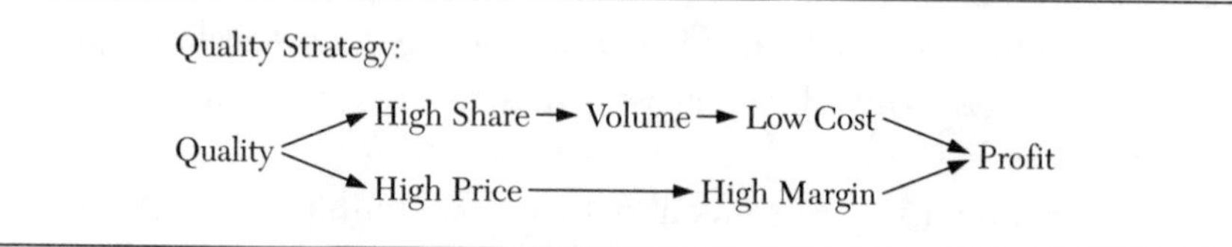

Further analysis of the PIMS data led the officers of the Strategic Planning Institute to move away from their focus on market share and toward an emphasis on product quality (actually, "perceived relative product quality," because the data were based on managers' perception of their product quality relative to that of competitors). One PIMS study, using a more sophisticated analytical technique called "causal modeling," showed there was no evidence to support the argument that high quality was incompatible with low cost relative to competitors. It was found that the higher prices associated with higher product quality did not deter market penetration. Thus, quality had a positive effect on return on investment, not directly but indirectly, through its influence on market share, which yielded both higher volume and lower cost.[24]

The PIMS researchers then attempted to disassociate the market share arguments from those based on experience curve effects, as advocated by Bruce Henderson and BCG, and to associate market share with quality.[25] Reinterpretation of the PIMS data reinforced the conclusions of the "quality strategy" model. Today, the first of the "PIMS Principles" is stated as:

> In the long run, the most important single factor affecting a business unit's performance is the quality of its products and services, relative to those of competitors.[26]

The firms with the most favorable performance were those that had been able to dominate a market niche, not the whole market, with superior quality offering both the advantages of high-price/high-margin and the low costs associated with higher volume. The basic wisdom of a strategy of product differentiation, market segmentation, and positioning was confirmed, and the low-price-driven experience curve strategy was discredited.[27]

Delivering Value to Customers to Increase Market Share

One of the most interesting examinations of the relationship between market share and profitability was conducted by Cathy Anterasian of McKinsey & Company and Lynn W. Phillips of the Stanford University Graduate School of Business, in a study published by the Marketing Science Institute.[28] They revisited the question of the direction of causality between share and profit and the role of product quality, using both PIMS and Federal Trade Commission (FTC) "Line of Business" data. What makes their study especially interesting is the model that they used to analyze the data, which they called "the value delivery theory of competitive advantage." Conceptually, it puts the customer's definition of value back into the center of strategic focus.

The central proposition of the value delivery theory is that sustainable competitive advantage has its roots in the ability of the firm to deliver superior value to customers at a profitable cost, not in the "structural barriers" to competition at the core of the experience-curve-based arguments. A business may capitalize on a particular set of skills in selecting, producing, delivering, or communicating superior value to a target market. That skill set could be unique to the firm or one in which it is merely superior to its competitors. These skills may reside in individuals, in technological capabilities, or in business systems designed and managed by the organization. Market share is the result of superior value delivery, as is profitability. Profit and market share are caused by the same forces.

This strategic formulation brings us back to a point of view consistent with the original marketing concept: Profit is a reward for creating a satisfied customer. Market share is also not a strategic objective; it is a result. In their analysis of the PIMS and FTC data, Anterasian and

Phillips could find no instance in which market share had a significant, positive, and temporarily prior influence on return on investment. In fact, they found stronger evidence of reverse causality—higher profit can lead to higher market share.

Significant environmental discontinuities or "shocks" were factored into the value delivery model in terms of their effect on the customer's definition of value and the resulting change in the skills and resources that the firm needed to deliver superior value to customers at a profit. Profitable firms had the management skills necessary to redefine strategy and reconfigure the resources and skills of the organization to fit the new market requirements. The more profitable firms were more likely to have the skills and resources, and the financial strength, necessary to respond to the changing environment. For these well-managed firms, discontinuities and shocks created an opportunity to improve their market position. This finding certainly sounds like conclusions Chandler reached three decades earlier. Successful firms monitor and respond to a changing environment with new strategies and organization structures.

In the strategic planning discipline, and in the related field of marketing strategy or "strategic marketing," product quality and value delivery have replaced market share and low cost as the key strategic variables. The ascendance of such brands as Honda, Komatsu, and Kawasaki helped to focus management attention on the central importance of product quality in determining market share. Superior business strategy based on product quality resulted in market shares. Simplistic thinking about the value of market share as a strategic objective in itself had been an expensive mistake for many firms.

COMPETITOR-CENTERED VERSUS CUSTOMER-CENTERED PLANNING

The most important contribution of strategic planning may also have been its critical shortcoming. Strategic planning focused the firm on its competitors and its strengths and weaknesses relative to them. It introduced the basic notions of market structure and competitive forces from economic theory into management thinking. Market share was the summary measure of competitive strength. Product quality was assessed relative to competitors. Dominant market share was important in attaining a favorable cost position relative to competitors. Strategic planning, especially with the incorporation of the experience curve, focused the attention of industry on cost as a strategic variable. This was a critical development as American firms faced global competitors, many of whom had favorable cost positions based on lower labor costs, government support, and lower cost of capital.

But the customer fell out of the equation in this market view. Markets were defined as a set of competitors, an "industry," not a set of customers with needs and wants that must be satisfied. Product quality was defined in terms of managers' perceptions of their product quality relative to that of competitors, not in terms of the ability of the product to satisfy customer needs better than the products of competitors.

The new strategy of value delivery reintroduced the customer into the concept of business strategy. The firm is assessed relative to its competitors in terms of its ability to deliver superior value, as perceived by the customer.

The other major contribution of the strategic planning era was to recognize that the firm's distinctive competence had to be taken into account, along with customer needs and wants, in defining the strategy of the firm and its selection of product/market combinations where it wished to compete. The original marketing concept had left some important questions unanswered. Strategic planning put the company and its competence into the concept of business strategy whereas the marketing concept had focused only on the customer's needs and wants.

A more complete approach to planning business strategy combines both customer-centered and competitor-centered analysis and matches the company's distinctive competence with a set of market needs and wants that is less than completely served by competitors. It focuses on the customer in developing a definition of value and then assesses the skills and resources of the firm in terms of its ability to deliver superior value compared with competitors. Effective business strategy must be based on a balanced combination of competitor-centered and customer-centered analysis. The goal is a strategy that permits the firm to deliver superior value to a well-defined set of customers in the competitive marketplace, capitalizing on its unique sources of competitive advantage. Every strategy problem must be approached in terms of "The Three C's": Customers, Company, and Competitors.

A NEW BALANCE: CUSTOMERS, COMPANY, AND COMPETITORS

The key strategic concept here is the *value proposition,* a statement of how the firm proposes to deliver superior value to customers. The value proposition is important both internally and externally. Internally, it focuses everyone's attention on customer requirements. Externally, it is the means by which the firm can position itself in the minds of customers. The value proposition should be the firm's single most important organizing principle.

Day and Wensley have offered a new model for balancing the analysis of customers, the company, and its competitors in a strategic planning framework.[29] Their model is summarized in Figure 2–3. In the center of their model is *superior customer value,* seen as the major determinant of the firm's strength relative to competition. The other source of advantage is *lower relative cost.* Both of these are assessed relative to competitors, but it is the *customer's perception of value relative to competitors' product offerings* that is important.

These positional advantages are based on the firm's distinctive competence—its superior skills and resources. But, there is nothing automatic about superior skills and resources leading to positional

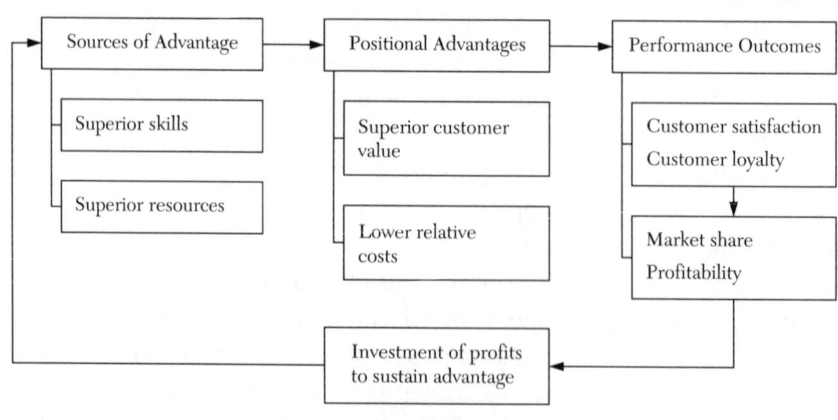

FIGURE 2–3. A value-based view of business strategy. *Source:* George S. Day and Robin Wensley, "Assessing Advantage: A Framework for Diagnosing Competitive Superiority," *Journal of Marketing,* 52, 2 (April 1988), pp. 1–20, at p. 3. Reproduced with permission of the American Marketing Association.

advantages. Whether the firm's distinctive competences can be turned to positional advantages depends on the quality of the analytical and strategy formulation skills of management. Chief among these is the ability to understand customers and their needs. In formulating strategy, management must understand how customers define value, based on their needs, wants, and product use systems, and how they evaluate the firm's offering relative to those of competitors. Management must also understand their competitors' business strategies, critical skills and resources, and value propositions. How do they propose to satisfy customer needs? On what basis are they trying to deliver superior value? What are their strengths and weaknesses? Thus, customer-centered and competitor-centered analysis blend in creating a concept of value delivery for a target market, based on the company's unique skills and resources as a source of sustainable competitive advantage.

Just as turning the company's potential sources of advantage into real positional advantages in the marketplace requires superior skills in strategic analysis and planning, so does achieving positive performance results depend on managing the firm's positional advantages and implementing the strategy successfully. The quality of the tactics, programs, and systems developed and employed by the business to implement its strategy are just as important as the quality of the strategy itself. Strategy formulation and implementation are inseparable determinants of business performance.

The old approach to strategic planning emphasized strategy formulation and had little to do with actual implementation. Portfolio models looked at strategy from the corporate perspective—What businesses should the firm be in? The answer to the business strategy question—How should we compete in those businesses?—was phrased simplistically in terms of low-cost/high-volume or high-quality/market-niche strategic options. How to do that, how to implement the business strategy with functional-level strategies for marketing, operations, R&D, and so on was not addressed.

Strategic planning was dominated by professional planners on the corporate staff as advisors to top management. The people who were actually charged with responsibility for operating the businesses profitably were involved to the extent that they provided the required information and business plans. In many cases, the corporate strategic planning process became so time consuming that operating management lost track of the details of running their businesses. They had to focus all their attention on achieving the bottom-line financial results called for by their strategic plan and the role of their SBU in the business portfolio. Thus, long-range strategic planning had the undesirable, even self-defeating, result of focusing corporate management on long-term objectives (primarily financial) while focusing operating management attention on very short-term (usually quarterly) goals.

In the new value-delivery view of strategy, business performance is measured primarily by customer satisfaction and loyalty. These *lead to* market share and profitability. This causal sequence is essential to understanding the new viewpoint embodied in the value delivery view of strategy. Remember that Ansoff's principal measures of business success—sales growth, market share, earnings growth—accepted the futility of predicting long-term profitability. None of those measures reflected on customer preference or satisfaction. In the new view, market share and profits are the rewards for creating a satisfied customer. Back to the marketing concept!

Assuming that the long-term objectives of the firm are survival and growth, the firm must reinvest profits in the maintenance and enhancement of the critical resources and skills that define its distinctive competence and are the source of its unique, sustainable competitive advantage. While the owners' interests are vital, they are not paramount. In the old view of strategy, the shareholders' interests were put first. The objective was to maximize return on equity. In the new view of strategy, the customer is first among equals because the customer must want the company's products and be willing to pay a reasonable price for them if any of the other constituencies of the firm—owners, employees, managers, suppliers—are to achieve their objectives over the long run.

It is the unique responsibility of top management to balance the claims of all these constituencies and to optimize the firm's total performance. More and more, top management has recognized the wisdom and necessity of putting the customer first.[30]

SUMMARY

This chapter completes our historical overview of the evolution of the marketing concept from its origins through its eclipse by strategic planning and into a new value-driven concept of strategy. The failure of the original marketing concept to address the fundamental issue of matching customer needs with the things the firm could do best left unanswered the critical question of how the firm could find sustainable competitive advantage. Strategic planning addressed that issue but redefined markets as collections of competitors and obliterated customer-orientation.

The integration of long-range planning, capital budgeting, and the marketing concept into a new discipline of strategic planning shifted management attention in many American companies away from customers and toward competitors and the interests of shareholders. Thinking of firms as portfolios of investments emphasized short-term profitability (ROI) at the expense of long-term relationships with satisfied customers. Newly emerging competitors in many global industries from automobiles to financial services were able to take advantage of the opportunities this created for providing superior value to customers.

The value-driven concept of strategy has emerged out of a reconsideration of the relationship between market share and profitability. The conclusion that market share *caused profitability* proved to be overly simplistic. Rather, *quality* as perceived by the customer has been identified as the critical strategic force leading to both lower costs and higher sales (and, thus, higher market share), which combine to yield superior profitability. Strategy must be based on analysis of the company, the competition, and the customer, identifying those opportunities for the firm to deliver superior value to customers based on its distinctive competences. The firm's *value proposition* becomes the primary organizing force for the business.

3 QUALITY EQUALS CUSTOMER SATISFACTION

A manufacturer is not through with his customer when a sale is completed. He has only then started with his customer.

Henry Ford
My Life and Work (1922), p. 41

While strategy researchers and consultants were discovering that quality was the critical strategic variable, the total quality management (TQM) movement was gaining a strong foothold in American industry. Japanese firms had for decades been learning and following the precepts of the American fathers of the quality movement, W. Edwards Deming and Joseph Juran (born in Romania but raised in the United States), with almost religious zeal. Japanese industry had created the Deming Prize to honor Mr. Deming and to encourage total quality management that would spur Japanese firms to world-class competitiveness. Only in the 1980s did American firms begin to pay serious attention to the dictates of a commitment to total quality.

TQM and the value delivery concept of strategy have much in common. The total quality movement has been a major force for the revitalization of the marketing concept. More and more, businesspeople and academics realized that TQM and customer orientation were really the same thing. While some companies and their management had continued to be advocates for a customer-centered view of the business throughout the 1970s and into the 1980s, many more had not. It was only when quality was defined, under the pressures of global competition, as the major issue facing American industry that the shift back to putting the customer first began to occur in earnest. Even then, the path was not a direct one.

HOW NOT TO DEFINE QUALITY

Not all views of quality put the customer first. Some are internally focused and use product-oriented, technical definitions of quality—meeting specifications for product dimensions or performance, defects or rejections per thousand pieces produced, visual standards for fit and finish, and so on. When quality is defined by statistics about the product or the manufacturing process, there is a good chance that the customer has still been left out of the equation.

Other definitions of quality focus on the people of the organization, processes for managing those people, their obligations to one another, and team building in the pursuit of organizational excellence. It is common in companies with this focus to talk about "the internal customer," the people in the organization whose work is most directly affected by what the person does, who use the output of that person's function.

One well-known company promotes 10 "Quality Principles" including "Build a spirit of working together toward common goals," "Promote a climate of open communication and feedback," "Encourage and recognize innovation and teamwork," and "Provide honest, fair and equitable treatment of all and develop an atmosphere of trust and mutual respect." Those are lofty principles for organizational functioning, but they do not have a direct bearing on quality. The customer is only mentioned in 2 of the 10 principles: "Encourage every person to strive continually for understanding of and mutual agreement on all requirements of customers and suppliers," and "Require that products will not be shipped nor services performed if they do not meet customer requirements." (Why does this last principle need to be stated at all?)

The most aggressive and successful quality programs recognize that definitions of quality in terms of product characteristics and organizational behavior miss the point. Quality, like the marketing concept, means putting the customer first, always. There is only one customer, the one who pays the bills. Talk of the "internal customer" is dangerous and misleading because it puts another organizational actor first rather than the real customer. This can create all kinds of interesting internal politics and intraorganizational conflict requiring energy that could be better used to solve real customer problems in the marketplace.

QUALITY IS DEFINED BY THE CUSTOMER

The true definition of quality is *meeting and exceeding customer expectations.* This definition may leave a technical expert with an uneasy feeling because it appears to be very subjective. How can you make a definition of quality operational if it relies on something as soft and mushy as customer expectations? How can you define quality in terms of people's feelings? These are good questions, but there are also good answers. It *is* possible to measure customer expectations and to measure performance against those standards.

The bigger problem is that customers keep changing and increasing their expectations. "What have you done for me lately?" is the standard response when a company gives its customers what they want, especially in the industrial market. When a company succeeds in meeting customer expectations, two things are likely to happen. First, the customer says "Thank you" and, realizing that this company has the capability for superior performance, will now expect it as a matter of course. Second, competitors improve *their* performance (or promise the customer that they will) and try harder to gain a share of the customer's business. Thus, three forces drive customer expectations upward:

1. The customer's dynamic needs and wants.
2. The company's promise and delivery of superior performance.
3. Competitors' promises that they can do even better.

The "Three C's" of strategy—Customers, Company, and Competitors—become the "Three C's" of quality. The customer's expectations change, his or her definitions of value change, and the definition of quality keeps evolving. For business-to-business marketers, there is added pressure because the *customer's* customers continue to increase *their* expectations and demands for superior performance.

Thus, quality and continuous innovation go hand in hand as dual requirements of the new marketing concept. Customer expectations, technological developments, and competitive pressures intersect and combine to equate continual improvement with success. Any firm that attempts to make customers satisfied with what they currently have, that is not committed to continuous improvement in products and processes, and that is unable to offer new and better solutions to customer problems is doomed to failure in the global marketplace.

Merely promising and promoting "new, improved, better" products and services won't do the job. The firm's value proposition must be based on skills and resources that deliver value as perceived by the customer. The old definition of marketing—one limited to the functions of selling, advertising, promotion, distribution, and customer service—is worse than inadequate: It is self-defeating and certain to lead to competitive disaster and business failure. The quality revolution is real, the changes it has brought are permanent, and a customer-centered view of the business is essential. There is no other choice.

QUALITY IS DELIVERING SUPERIOR CUSTOMER VALUE

Quality should be defined from the customer's perspective because, as noted in Chapter 1, value is defined in the marketplace. In the factory, we add costs. Value is not created in the factory, it is created in the market when the customer pays us more for the product or service we have produced than the sum total of the costs we incurred to create and deliver the product/service bundle. The difference between what the customer is willing to pay and the costs we have incurred is value. Profit is a measure of the value we have created. It is the reward for creating a satisfied customer, for solving a customer problem.

The Concept of the Value Chain

The value chain describes all the activities that must be performed from the time raw materials are taken from mines, forests, farms, oceans, lakes, rivers, and air (for many gases); combined with human labor;

turned into goods and services; delivered to the marketplace; often resold several times to create additional utilities of form, time, and place; and ultimately consumed.

"Consumption" often, even usually, does not mean that the product or service disappears. Most acts of consumption result in the production of waste in the form of refuse, gases, or spent products that must be reclaimed, recycled, or destroyed. Some products, such as information services, may even become more valuable with use. The value chain doesn't end until these postconsumption effects have also been taken into account. Value for one person may be cost for another, especially in the frequent case of public consequences from private consumption such as air pollution from automobile use and water pollution from construction activities.

In companies with a mature commitment to total quality management, the quality process extends back into vendors' processes and forward to those of the customer. The company operates in a fairly narrow range of the value chain and depends heavily on vendors for inputs that must meet all the quality standards defined by customers. Integrating forward into the customer's processes may also be essential to assure delivery of the full range of benefits promised, especially if the company has capabilities that the customer does not have. For example, manufacturers of industrial coatings may take responsibility for the paint spraying operations in the plants of their appliance and automobile manufacturer customers. Through dealer organizations, automobile manufacturers try to maintain control over the maintenance and parts used by customers, to ensure satisfactory performance over the life of the car. Chemical companies work with their customers on training personnel, applications engineering, process improvement, recovery of used materials, and other value-enhancing services.

In addition to the flow of products from manufacturers to customers, there is also a flow of information that, in many instances, is more important to customer satisfaction than the product itself. There is also a continuous flow of information from the customer back to the manufacturer, providing feedback on customer satisfaction, identifying the need for additional assistance, and suggesting the need for new products and services. In the best buyer-seller relationships, both parties are totally committed to continuous improvement in their interdependent processes for creating and delivering superior value.

Marketing to Define, Develop, and Deliver Value

One definition of marketing is built around the concept of the value chain. *Marketing* is the process of *defining, developing, and delivering value:*

- *Defining* value consists of identifying, measuring, and analyzing customer needs and translating that information into requirements for creating satisfied customers.
- *Developing* value incorporates the activities of product development (completing the product offering with services) and pricing consistent with customer needs, competitive conditions, and the value inherent in the product bundle.
- *Delivering* value includes not only the obvious functions of distribution—transportation, storage, risk taking, sorting and providing an assortment of goods—but also the process of communicating the product offering through personal selling, advertising, sales promotion, publicity, and display, to the intended target market. Customer service functions such as applications engineering, installation, warranties, and after-sale service can be thought of as an integral part of delivering value.

The concept of the value chain incorporates focus both on the customer, inherent in the marketing concept, and on the company's capabilities, resources, and skills, inherent in the strategy concept. Customer needs, perceptions, and use systems define value. The company's capabilities determine its ability to deliver value. The company's chosen strategic position in the value chain, and its value proposition to the customer, represent management's best judgment as to the way to achieve unique, sustainable competitive advantage within the constraints of the resources and skills it has or can reasonably expect to develop.

The new marketing concept calls for defining the business "from the outside in": finding customer needs that are incompletely satisfied, customer problems that are not solved; being "expert" on that class of customer problems—knowing the customers and their needs and problems better than they know themselves; creating solutions to those problems through innovation; and communicating and delivering those solutions to a carefully defined set of prospective customers whose needs the business is committed to serving.

The new marketing concept involves more than simply understanding and serving customer needs. The new marketing concept recognizes that customers are interested in the company's total capabilities. They want to be educated about the class of problems and solutions that the company claims to be expert about. They expect the marketer to provide leadership in the future, especially where technical capabilities are concerned. A purchase of a personal computer, for example, is based partly on the expectation that there will be a continuous flow of product enhancements, new applications software, and other innovations.

These fundamental notions concerning the value proposition are the subject of Chapter 4, which discusses designing and communicating that proposition. This chapter concentrates on the challenges of total quality management, its relationship to customer satisfaction, and its integral role in the new marketing concept.

Achieving Quality and Customer Expectations: Developing an Augmented Product

Quality is defined by how well the product meets customer expectations, which involves much more than the physical product or the simple service that is being purchased. The customer has expectations for the entire product offering and defines quality to encompass the shopping, buying, after-sale, use, and disposal processes. A concept of the augmented product developed by Theodore Levitt helps in understanding customer expectations and their central role in defining quality.[1]

First, there is the *Generic Product.* In the case of physical products, it is "the thing you can drop on your foot," such as the portable computer on which this is being written. For a service product, it is the basic service feature, such as $100,000 worth of term life insurance. Generic products, even for products as sophisticated as personal computers and term life insurance, and certainly for basic commodities such as chemicals and air travel, tend to be undifferentiated and to be bought and sold largely in terms of price. Definitions of quality that focus on physical characteristics, specifications, and defects per thousand deal only with the generic product and fall short of the mark of thinking about quality from the customer's perspective. Every company hopes to offer more. Every customer expects more.

What the customer is buying is the *Expected Product.* The expected product includes the generic product plus all the features and services that the customer simply expects as part of the product offering. The expected product of this portable computer included a bright legible screen, easy-to-use software for word processing and spreadsheets, rechargeable batteries, and the availability of a local dealer for product support and assistance when needed. The term-insurance customer expects efficient billing procedures, easy-to-understand terms, a friendly helpful agent, and guaranteed prompt payment in the event of a claim. The industrial customer buying emulsifiers expects overnight delivery in either bags, drums, or trailer loads, technical assistance on product applications when requested, and efficient order-entry and billing procedures.

Competitive prices are still an important part of the expected product, and it is assumed that the generic product meets all technical specifications. The service bundle is also simply assumed to be part of the product offering; it is expected to be there without having to ask for it or to negotiate terms and conditions for its delivery. The generic product is what Levitt calls "the table stakes"; it is necessary but not sufficient to create a satisfied customer. Delivering the expected product is both necessary *and* sufficient. However, merely doing a sufficient job of meeting customer expectations may not be adequate for long-term survival in the competitive global marketplace. It is better if the company can *exceed* customer expectations.

The *Augmented Product* includes features and services that were not expected, creating the possibility of not merely meeting but actually exceeding customer expectations, *delighting the customer,* as it is often said. The screen on this computer is much brighter and easier to read, even in strong light, than I had expected. Response to commands and the scrolling feature are even faster than on my office computer. The battery recharges much faster than I had expected. I am not merely satisfied; I am delighted.

In other examples, the term-insurance customer was delighted to learn that the policy included a conversion option that adds a savings and capital appreciation feature. And the emulsifier customer, a manufacturer of soaps and detergents, was delighted to find that the distributor who agreed to serve his requirements has excellent field sales personnel as well as technical support staff available by telephone. He can order for multiple plant sites from multiple distributor stocking points using the distributor's electronic data processing and telecommunications capabilities to ensure overnight delivery anyplace in the United States and Canada. The distributor also offers a total care program that takes responsibility as required for reclamation and disposal of process byproducts and stands ready to help with any spills, accidents, or other problems. While the chemical product itself is manufactured by a large national company with an excellent reputation, the critical features of the augmented product are provided by the distributor-partner.

Can the manufacturer or distributor who offers a superior augmented product declare victory? Hardly. It doesn't take long for the augmented product to become the expected product. The customer may go to other potential suppliers to see if they can meet or exceed the service bundle now being purchased, but at a better price. The initial successful seller has educated and informed the customer, who now exercises more discretion and power. The customer, whose expectations have increased, becomes more demanding. The competitive battle rages. So, even the augmented product may not be enough to ensure competitive survival over the long run.

The successful firm is always thinking about the *Potential Product,* opportunities to innovate and serve customers better. Success requires staying ahead of customers' perceived needs and competitors' product offerings. The company cannot merely meet defined customer needs. It must look at its own capabilities and work with customers to apply them in new areas, not just doing what the customer says, but forming a partnership that looks to the future.

The trick is to be able to do so at a profit: to find value enhancing features, activities, and services that will improve the efficiency with which the customer is served and/or for which the customer is willing to pay more. It is the customer's definition of value that determines profitability. Product enhancements and improvements may not worth their cost to the customer. Appliances with spoken instructions provided by voice-chip technology did not receive favorable market response, for example.

Service bundling, the strategy of adding services to the product offering at a fixed price, can be an attractive way to offer superior value to customers. It can be unprofitable, however, if the customer is unwilling to pay for it. On the other hand, service *un*bundling may be disastrous if some competitors offer the full bundle at no additional charge or if service specialists offer specific pieces of the service bundle at lower costs and prices.

The dynamics of the expected, augmented, and potential product are the driving force on the need for continuous innovation in the competitive marketplace. Levitt's intriguing concept is extremely useful to managers thinking about total quality management, customer satisfaction, and the need to define value from the customer's perspective in a competitive marketplace where the definition of value keeps changing.

QUALITY AS A WAY OF DOING BUSINESS

Early definitions of quality, which focused on the product itself, defined it negatively, in terms of things that could go wrong. The emphasis was on measures such as defects or parts rejected per 1,000 produced. It defined quality as protecting customers from annoyances rather than delighting them with superior performance. The traditional quality measures were "defensive" measures to eliminate defects and preempt product failure.[2]

The most successful quality programs define quality not in terms of products, but in terms of a total way of doing business, a total commitment to the customer. These manufacturers think of themselves as partners for their customers. In industrial markets, this incorporates the order-entry, purchasing, credit, and billing procedures; help with applications; careful introduction of new technology and new products and services as they become available; educational programs for customer personnel; and more. The partnership is based on a thorough understanding of the customer's processes and how they interact with the seller's processes, and careful management of their integration. The effort is focused on making the business partners more competitive in their markets and goes well beyond simply offering "good products."

These concepts of partnership and relationship management are also being implemented more and more by consumer marketers. It may be something as simple as the manufacturer listing a telephone number on each package that customers can call for product information. Or it may be the automobile manufacturer who regularly calls customers after they have visited a dealership for service or who offers an extended warranty program at modest additional charge. It is seen in the frequent traveler programs offered by airlines and hotel chains. Hotels and campground chains give special rates, discounts, and services to customers who join their travel "clubs." Credit card companies provide not only the convenience of the card but quarterly summaries of expenses, services such as airline reservations, special entertainment and dining packages, and traveler's checks and check-cashing privileges. They go beyond the expected product and the individual transactions and look at multiple aspects of their relationships with customers over an extended period.

For these sophisticated companies, quality becomes a competitive business strategy, the central theme of their business strategies in the competitive marketplace. Xerox, for example, has defined quality simply as "a way of doing business, one that is focused wholly on the customer."[3] Other large companies whose quality programs are emulated include L.L. Bean, Federal Express, Fidelity Investments, Motorola, IBM, Corning, Disney, and Ford.

How *Not* to Manage Quality

The quality movement has produced many positive results, but it also has had some negative consequences. These negative aspects of the quality movement result from the tendency of companies, paradoxically most likely to be those with the strongest departments or managers of quality, to focus their quality management internally, rather than on the customer. Unfortunately, for some companies, going after the brass ring of a quality prize caused the rider to fall off the quality carousel. By focusing efforts myopically on their internal processes, they lost sight of the customer.

Competing for quality prizes, such as the Baldrige Award (created by the U.S. Congress in 1987 and administered by the National Institute of Standards and Technology) or the Deming Prize, is a challenging and complicated endeavor. A bad example of what can go wrong is provided by Florida Power and Light, which for several years was held up as a paragon of TQM. The company made an all-out effort to become the first non-Japanese winner of the Deming Prize and succeeded in doing so in 1989. The quality department, at its height, employed 85 people; there were 1,900 quality teams involving three-fourths of the employees.

Efforts were focused on the measurements called for under a very sophisticated statistical quality-review system. Unfortunately, improvements in service delivery seen by customers were insignificant. A new head of quality was appointed who described his job as trying to "clear up the mess." The quality department was reduced to six employees.[4]

Every Business Is a Service Business

When we combine the definition of quality as meeting or exceeding customer expectations, the concept of the augmented product, and the value delivery concept of business strategy, we come up with an interesting result: It is possible and desirable to define any business as primarily a service business. Customers don't buy products, they buy a set of benefits and solutions to problems. Furthermore, the majority of economic activity in developed nations is in the production and marketing of services rather than physical products. Even more interesting is the fact that most of the companies we tend to think of as "industrial giants" with a predominance of their revenues from manufacturing activities, such as General Electric and IBM, actually derive the majority of their revenues from the sale of services.

For most businesses, the reconceptualization of themselves as a service business is an enormous challenge. Traditional ways of thinking about the business usually center on products; for example, GE in power generation equipment, motors, and lamps; and IBM in large mainframe computers, as well as smaller machines, personal computers, and a total line of peripheral equipment. The fact is that GE's largest and most dynamic businesses are in the services sector: GE Capital Corporation, NBC in television and radio, nuclear plant servicing and operations, and so on. IBM derives over half its revenues from sales of software, consulting services, networking, and other service businesses.

Thinking about the business in terms of the expected product and the services provided to the customer develops a customer orientation, a way of looking at the business from the customer's perspective. It is better to think in terms of what the customer is buying as opposed to what the company is making and selling. Evidence that different customers expect and derive different benefits from the same product can identify distinct market segments with different strategic requirements. Such insights are not possible if the business is defined in terms of its products.

Defining the business as a service business helps to create a value proposition rich enough to capture all the important dimensions of the expected and augmented product, as perceived by customers, and to define the key success factors for the business. It leads to a definition of quality as a total way of doing business rather than to a narrow focus on product dimensions and features. It can help to ensure that the company won't go to market with an incomplete product.

THE SERVQUAL MODEL

While the conversation about TQM began in traditional manufacturing settings, innovative adaptation of ideas about quality management to the field of services has produced some interesting insights into the concept of quality itself. One of these is the importance of defining quality in terms of meeting and exceeding customer expectations, critical in services marketing because it is much harder to develop precise specifications for product characteristics.

The SERVQUAL model, shown in Figure 3–1, provides a useful conceptual framework. The SERVQUAL model has been developed, tested, and refined in a program of research supported in part by the Marketing Science Institute and with the cooperation of many service businesses in a wide range of industries.[5] Two central features of the SERVQUAL model are the definition of quality in terms of the comparison of expected and perceived benefits and the identification of "gaps" in the service delivery process. These gaps identify the following important ways in which the business can fail to perform in the mind of the customer:

- Misunderstanding customer expectations.
- Developing inadequate specifications for product/service performance.
- Developing products/services that do not meet the performance specifications.
- Not communicating product/service benefits accurately and realistically to potential customers.
- Creating expectations that cannot be met, by overpromising in marketing communications.

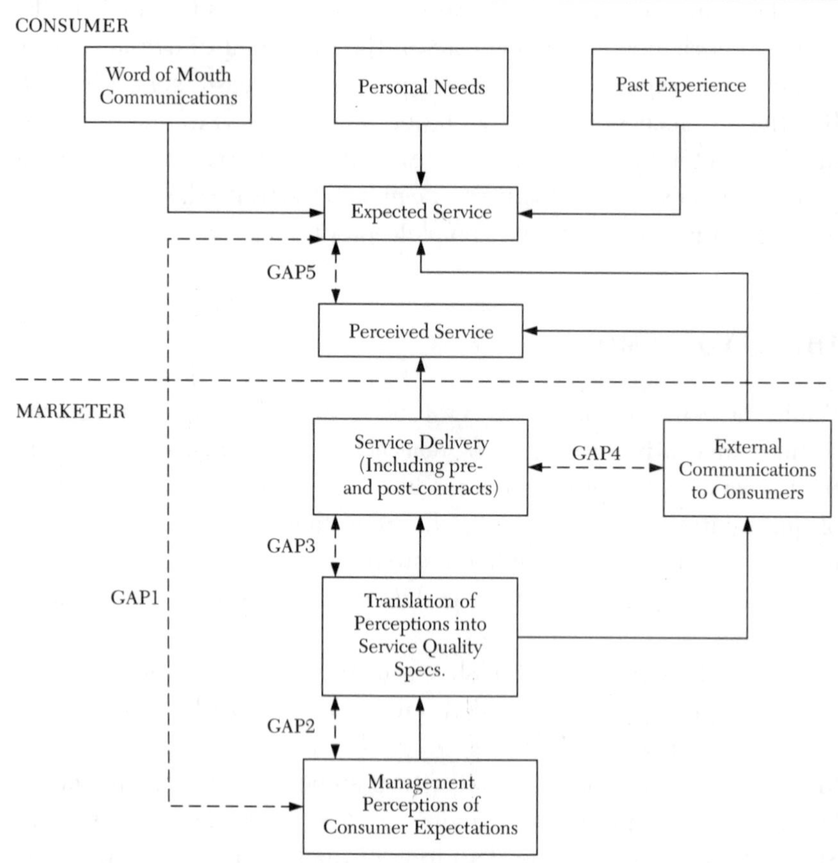

FIGURE 3–1. The SERVQUAL Model. *Source:* A. Parasuraman, Valarie A. Zeithaml, and Leonard L. Berry, "A Conceptual Model of Service Quality and Its Implications for Future Research," *Journal of Marketing*, Fall 1985, pp. 41–50. Copyright 1985 by the American Marketing Association; reproduced with permission.

ANALYZING CUSTOMER NEEDS AND WANTS

Often, the most important gap in the delivery of service or product quality results from a failure to understand the customer's needs and wants and the product-use system in which the company's offering will be used. The company must have procedures for gathering and analyzing the necessary information about customer needs, wants, buying habits, and usage patterns, and for communicating that information to those in the organization who can use it to design, develop, produce, and deliver superior customer value. Being customer-oriented is more than a mindset; it is, more specifically, having current, correct, and complete information, carefully analyzed about customers, their value perceptions, and their assessments of competitors' product offerings.

Providing such information is the major reason for a separate marketing function in the company, a group of people who are responsible for being experts on the customer and communicating that information throughout the organization. The value of the marketing function is determined by the extent to which these other organizational actors value and use this information. As noted in Chapter 1, however, that is part of the problem of implementing the marketing concept.

These other organizational actors, including the R&D people, the product designers, the applications engineers, the sales force, the customer service personnel, and the rest, may sincerely believe that they know better than the marketing people what it is the customer needs and wants. And, in fact, they might. Each of them, however, is likely to view the customer with a functional bias and an incomplete understanding of the customer's total requirements.

Establishing Cross-Functional Teams to Focus Attention on the Customer

Cross-functional teams are an important tool for implementing a total quality management program. The overarching objective is to coordinate the traditional management functions including engineering, production, credit, transportation, and customer service, and to break down the functional walls that have often prevented the delivery of the intended level of performance in the marketplace. Cross-functional teams are a mechanism for focusing everyone's attention on the customer. They must be guided by information about customer needs, wants, expectations, and purchasing and consumption behavior.

"Quality circles" are another device for focusing organizational actors and their actions on the customer. These small groups are typically set up within a given department or function and meet regularly to identify and discuss problems requiring action. Such groups must be given the tools and training to be effective, including guidelines for identifying what is important and what is not, problem-solving techniques for identifying solutions, and organizational resources and support necessary to implement their recommendations. An essential part of the quality circle concept is teaching the participants how to measure the significant aspects of their operations. Such measurements should be based on an understanding of customer expectations and how customers define value. Quality circles without specific, ongoing measurements are not likely to be effective.

The challenge is to coordinate the design, development, delivery of value to customers among all the players in the system, who are guided by the same vision of the customer. The first part of the challenge is to develop a common perception, or base of information and understanding about the customer. The second part of the challenge is to develop team-building mechanisms that can cross, if not eliminate, traditional functional boundaries.

Customer analysis addresses the first part of the challenge, gathering and analyzing information about customers. Traditional survey research methods, studying a large representative sample of customers to find central tendencies in their attitudes, preferences, and behavior, are generally inadequate for developing the broader understanding of customer definitions of quality and value. The "average customer" is of little use in a concept of value delivery that looks at all aspects of the business and its relationships with customers over an extended period.

Developing Customer Visit Programs to Open Lines of Communication

Some industrial companies, such as Hewlett-Packard, have developed customer visit programs to learn more about the problems facing customers, the way in which the company's products get used, their influence on customers' operations, and opportunities and requirements for future product development and improvements. Customer visit programs are an important device for achieving cross-functional coordination and creating an organizational culture of customer orientation. Feedback from customer visits can also become part of the system for measuring customer satisfaction although this is not the primary purpose.[6]

Dr. Katherine Tobin, the leader of the customer visit program at Hewlett-Packard, has cited the following benefits for the company:

- Updated knowledge of customer environments and needs.
- Updated knowledge of competitors' products.
- Information to improve product strategy.
- Information for HP engineers about market conditions.
- Reinforced customer perceptions that HP is concerned about their needs.
- Enhanced cooperation between the R&D labs and the marketing organization.
- Better mutual understanding between the factory and the field sales and service organization.[7]

Using Quality Function Deployment to Help Meet Customer Needs

Quality Function Deployment (QFD) is a sophisticated tool for addressing the gap between understanding customer needs and turning this understanding into specifications for product design or service. It involves people from multiple business functions in the product development and planning effort and facilitates interfunctional cooperation. It is a planning method for translating customer needs and expectations into requirements not just for products but for total company performance. QFD can make the marketing concept operational and can match up customer requirements and company capabilities.

The concept of "the house of quality" is a central feature of QFD. It was developed in 1972 at the Kobe shipyard of Mitsubishi and further refined by Toyota and its suppliers.[8] The central purpose of QFD is to design, manufacture, and market products that customers will want to purchase, based on an understanding of customers' needs and wants. The house of quality provides the conceptual map for this task, recognizing that customer wants are complex, multi-dimensional, and at times fundamentally in conflict with one another.

The house of quality approach involves first listing the attributes that customers want. These can be identified in a number of ways; for example, by watching customers examine or use the product. These attributes are broken down into several sub-levels of detail and bunched together into groupings that capture overall customer concerns, using actual customer language wherever possible, to guide design decisions.

Consumer research is also used in assigning importance weights to various bundles of attributes, in order to assess the necessary tradeoffs because of technical constraints. These result in the assignment of percentages (totaling 100%) to attribute groupings.

Customer ratings are also used to evaluate competitive product offerings on each attribute grouping, creating a map of consumer preferences. Designers then define opportunities for improving products, based on the company's skills and capabilities, in ways that will be important to customers' perceptions of value and provide a source of competitive advantage. The house of quality provides a visual tool in the form of a matrix of customer perceptions of product attributes on one dimension and engineering characteristics on the other. Specific target objectives for design work emerge from matching what is possible in terms of engineering capabilities and the customer's desires. The technique can potentially be applied to any process within the company that is part of the process of defining, developing, and delivering superior value to customers.

Quality function deployment and the house of quality are useful for visualizing the relationship between customer requirements and engineering capabilities. They can be modified and creatively expanded to meet the needs of any design team. They do not offer a panacea for developing successful products, but they offer a flexible approach to achieving an operational commitment to customer orientation.

ANALYZING COMPETITORS THROUGH BENCHMARKING

The new marketing concept balances customer and competitor analysis. It recognizes that customer perceptions of value result from the interaction of their evaluations of the alternative product offerings available from competing firms. *Benchmarking* is a widely used technique for analyzing competitors' product offerings, identifying the best products and processes, and adapting them to the company's own products and activities.

Benchmarking has been defined as stealing somebody else's best ideas and improving them. The practice began in the United States at Xerox in 1979, when the company began to address its loss of market share and its unfavorable cost/price position relative to competitors, especially Japanese brands. Initially focused on product problems, benchmarking was extended throughout the company into all functions, including marketing. Today, when other American firms want to benchmark their benchmarking activities, they look to Xerox, which now offers training and consulting in the technique.

Benchmarking can be done on different divisions and functions within a company, on competitors, or on any company from which something can be learned that will help the business improve its products and processes. For example, the following companies have been widely recognized as world-class leaders in these designated areas:

- *Marketing.* Procter & Gamble.
- *Customer Satisfaction.* L.L. Bean, Federal Express, GE Plastics, Xerox.
- *Distribution and Logistics.* L.L. Bean, Wal-Mart.
- *Billing and Collection.* American Express, MCI, Fidelity Investments.
- *Product Development.* Beckman Instruments, Calcomp, Cincinnati Milacron, DEC (Digital Equipment Corporation), 3M, Xerox, Hewlett-Packard.
- *Benchmarking.* Xerox, AT&T, Ford, Texas Instruments, IBM, DEC.
- *Supplier Management.* Ford, Bose, Motorola, Xerox, 3M, Levi Strauss.[9]

The highly successful Ford Taurus/Mercury Sable automobiles were developed using benchmarking. Fifty competitive midsize automobiles from Germany, Sweden, Japan, and the United States were analyzed in detail to discover best-in-the-world designs for everything from brake pads to transmissions to door handles. The dismantling of competitors' products, sometimes called "reverse engineering," is only one aspect of benchmarking and competitor analysis. Other forms of analysis include visiting factory sites, interviewing customers, and reviewing publicly available information contained in product brochures, news releases, corporate annual reports, trade show exhibits, and other sources.

Knowing competitors' product offerings and distinctive competence can create a better understanding of how customers define value, where the company can improve its own performance in products and processes, and where it is best to avoid head-to-head competition. Benchmarking is simultaneously focused on improving performance and lowering costs, in products and in all the processes and activities needed to achieve value for customers.

While benchmarking can be performed on all the company's products and processes, not all of them are equally important in the competitive marketplace. A focus on essential internal processes, such as order processing, production planning and scheduling, inventory control, and billing, will influence the level of customer satisfaction, but benchmarking may not be dealing with the most important issues strategically if the focus is internal only. These issues may define the requirements and necessary costs of being in the business, "the table stakes," to use Levitt's phrase again, but they are not likely to identify the sources of unique, sustainable competitive advantage. World-class dining facilities don't count, even if management loves them!

ANALYZING YOUR COMPANY'S INTERNAL RESOURCES

The key to successful competition is to select market niches where the company's skills and resources will deliver the highest value to customers compared with its competitors. The company must understand its distinctive competences, the things that it does best. When it identifies weaknesses relative to competitors, management must decide which areas to strengthen and where there is an ongoing competitive weakness that suggests avoiding direct battles with other companies.

Defining Your Company's Distinctive Competences

When management appraises the strengths and weaknesses of the business to assess its competitive position, it needs to concentrate on those areas of capability that really matter. Among the strengths that the typical company might identify are "loyal employees, stable management, full product line, and community support." Similarly, a list of weaknesses might include "limited access to capital at reasonable rates, unresolved liability for site contamination, aging production facility, and lack of management depth and provision for managerial succession." While these are important areas and issues, with weaknesses that should be addressed by the commitment of additional resources, they do not define key success factors in the competitive marketplace.

The central calculus of strategy is to match the firm's capabilities with customer needs. Chapter 1 pointed out that the old marketing concept only addressed one side of the equation—customer needs—and was silent on the question of identifying the firm's capabilities. The concept of imbricative marketing was an early attempt to blend company capabilities and market needs. Chapter 2 showed how long-range strategic planning, with the concepts of product/market mission and strategic business units, lost sight of the customer by defining markets as collections of competitors. Capability was narrowly defined in the portfolio approach to strategic planning as the ability to achieve the position of lowest-cost producer and the ability to dominate a market, to achieve the largest market share.

A distinctive competence is something that the firm does better than any of its competitors *and* that is valued by its customers. There is a tremendously important definitional point here—the firm cannot define its distinctive competence except in the context of its chosen market. Customer selection is the critical strategic choice that any firm makes. At the same time, the selection of market targets must be based on the assessment of distinctive competences. The firm must choose those market niches where its skills and resources can deliver superior value to customers.

The Criteria for Distinctive Competence

To be a meaningful and real strategic variable, the distinctive competence must meet three criteria:

1. It must be important to potential customers in terms of their perception of value.
2. It must be knowledge based, which often means that it is technology based.

3. It should apply across multiple products and offer potential access to multiple market segments.

A truly distinctive competence defines an area where the company is uniquely capable among all companies in the world. Because the competence is knowledge based, it is not easily copied. It resides in key individuals and in tightly designed and controlled proprietary systems. It may be protected by patents or copyrights. Some key distinctive competences are based on information technology, including airline reservations systems (American, Delta, and TWA), small package delivery systems (United Parcel Service, Federal Express), and elevator maintenance and repair service (Otis).

Distinctive competence is at the core of a spectrum of products or potential products. It may become a global industry standard as a component of the products of many firms. The distinctive competence is the knowledge, not the products themselves.[10] Among some of the best-known examples of distinctive competences are Hewlett-Packard's laser-printing technology, Intel's computer-chip-making technology, and Corning's capabilities in ceramics. These companies' products have achieved dominant positions in the world market, often through strategic alliances with partners whose own distinctive competences create the possibility for new products through bringing together convergent technologies.

Although most distinctive competences are knowledge based in a general sense, not all are technology based. Marketing skills in such areas as sales promotion and media advertising are knowledge based, often supported by sophisticated information systems. Marketing skills are core competences for Procter & Gamble, Pepsico, and General Mills. Access to, and dominant position in, a channel of distribution may be a distinctive competence for the company, as in the case of Norton Company (now a part of Saint Gobain) in abrasives/industrial distribution and Monsanto in performance chemicals/chemical distribution. A dominant channel position may preclude weaker competitors from gaining a viable place in the market.

Physical assets may also be a source of distinctive competence, especially if they are based on a unique locational advantage, such as access to a scarce raw material. In most cases, however, physical resources do not offer a unique, sustainable competitive advantage because they are susceptible to duplication, often with improvements, by competitors. Unique production skills, however, meet the tests of distinctive competence because they are likely to be embedded in skilled production workers or in technology-based systems and proprietary knowledge.

The definition, development, and nurturing of distinctive competences is a key step in a program of total quality management and the implementation of the new marketing concept. It defines the competitive arena in which the company is going to strive to deliver superior value to customers, the things it promises to do better than any other business in the world.

Distinctive competences define areas where the firm must invest heavily if it is to maintain its competitive advantage. Given the inevitable progression of customer expectations, competitive imitation, and technology, the company must continue to develop the relevant knowledge, skills, and capabilities by reinvesting profits or obtaining new capital as necessary. Distinctive competence is intertwined with the need for continuous innovation, a key element of the new marketing concept.

MEASURING COMPANY PERFORMANCE BY OBTAINING CUSTOMER FEEDBACK

The final and perhaps most important step in a total quality management program is developing a program for measuring customer satisfaction and providing feedback to all members of the organization. Customer feedback measures the last and most important gap in the service delivery process—the difference between what customers expected and what they perceive was actually delivered by the company. Customer satisfaction measures must find their way into systems for evaluating and rewarding individual performance. In this way, quality becomes the most important strategic driver for the entire company. If the company is to succeed in always putting the interests of the customer first, customer satisfaction must be linked to the methods by which people are evaluated and rewarded.

Defining What to Measure

A maxim for public speakers advises, "Tell 'em what you're going to tell 'em; tell 'em; tell 'em what you told 'em." That is also good advice for measuring the successes and failures of a total quality management program. The process must begin with the customer and we might paraphrase the steps as, "Ask 'em what they expect; give it to 'em; ask 'em if they got what they expected."

The first step in the process is to determine customer expectations. How do customers define value? What do they expect? The essential point is that the customer defines quality, so the customer must also define standards for evaluating company performance. Internal measures (for example, number of units per thousand produced requiring rework, percentage of orders shipped complete, or percentage of orders shipped within 24 hours of receipt) may be important in delivering value and meeting expectations but may not reflect true customer satisfaction or lack thereof. Internal measures should be based on those parts of the process that result in true differences in customer satisfaction, such as discrepancies between promised and actual delivery dates.

Listening to customers and watching how they use products may reveal some surprises about the basis for measuring performance. For example, having prompt repair service for home appliances may not do much to improve customer satisfaction if the customer's primary expectation is that the product will work satisfactorily from the very beginning. Time spent waiting for a reservations clerk to answer a telephone may be more important in defining quality than the courtesy with which the phone is finally answered. Mediocre airline food may meet customer expectations, while a dirty seat cushion may not.

One expert divides customer feedback into five principles, or phases:

1. *Know why* you are measuring and how the results will be used to improve performance.
2. *Let customers* define what to measure.
3. *Monitor continuously* company performance versus competitors' performance.

4. *Track the internal processes* that are tied to the results customers value as well as the end results themselves.
5. *Communicate the results* throughout the organization, to everyone involved in the value delivery process.[11]

The company must learn to evaluate itself, and its management, based on specific measures of customer satisfaction. The feedback from customers must be meaningful to people within the organization in terms of how they evaluate their own performance.

Since the process must start with the customer, the following approaches can be useful: focus groups, customer visits, surveys, laboratory simulations, and field observation. The first step is to define the customers' evaluation criteria. The second step is to arrange these criteria in proper priority and to put weights on the multiple criteria, basing those weights on customer research. The third step is to design measurements that capture the performance of the company on each of these important dimensions. The final step is to develop summary measures and to compile the results in reports for management and employees on an ongoing basis.

For industrial products and services, or for complex consumer products such as automobiles and major appliances, the measurement challenge may be complicated by the fact that many people are involved in the purchase and use of the product. Each may use somewhat different criteria. For example, purchasing managers may focus on price and order processing, manufacturing managers on on-time delivery and reject rates, engineers on product performance characteristics, and customer service personnel on spare parts availability. Measurement systems must incorporate the criteria emphasized by each of the important people in the system.

Several excellent commercial research firms are available to help companies develop measurements required. Traditional market research firms such as Yankelovich Partners, the Forum Corporation, Elrick & Lavidge, and Walker Research are able to design customer surveys that will identify and prioritize important evaluation criteria. They can design instruments that will track customer satisfaction over time and analyze and summarize the results in reports to management on a regular basis. Management consulting firms such as MAC/Gemini and McKinsey and Company have practices devoted to using such information in TQM programs and in management evaluation and reward systems. No company, regardless of size, can afford to do business today without current, complete, and correct information about customer satisfaction, integrated into a TQM program, as part of its commitment to putting the customer first, always.

Influencing Customers' Word-of-Mouth Messages

One of the most powerful forces in marketing is word-of-mouth, one customer speaking to another. Word-of-mouth is a significant source of customer expectations for the performance of products and services, as noted in the model of service quality shown in Figure 3–1. It can be used for the company or against it. Word-of-mouth is powerful because of its believability. When customers talk about products or companies, they are doing so based on personal experience or what they have learned from another consumer/user, or perhaps what they have read or seen in the media. In any event, because the customer appears to have no commercial interest, no intent to sell the listener anything, word-of-mouth appears to be objective and credible.

Word-of-mouth is motivated behavior, for both the listener and the source. The listener is motivated to learn more about the product or service, as a potential buyer and user. Listeners may actually seek out the opinions of others as part of their buying decision. It is common, for example, for people to try to find someone who has already seen a movie, and to solicit the person's opinion, before actually going to see the movie (or renting the video) themselves. Industrial buyers routinely contact buyers in other companies to get information about the performance of vendors and their products.

The motivation of the source of word-of-mouth messages is more complex. People may talk about advertising and other forms of marketing communication, but they are much more likely to talk about their actual experience with a product. Whether they have had a positive or negative experience, users of products and services may be motivated to talk about them to test and confirm their own experience. It is a way of reducing postpurchase doubt, or "cognitive dissonance," as well as gaining positive affirmation for a decision. It is well known that new car buyers like to "show off" their purchases, by talking about them and showing them to friends. This activity generates positive feedback in the form of compliments and questions that permit buyers to demonstrate their knowledge, expertise, and buying skill as well as to review the positive aspects of their decision, thus reinforcing, in their own minds, the wisdom of that decision.

For marketers, perhaps the most interesting fact is that unhappy customers are more likely to talk about their purchase experience than are those who are satisfied. The motivation of the communicator in this instance may be to seek advice, to seek affirmation for the negative opinion, to help a friend or colleague avoid a similar problem, or to inflict damage on the reputation and the sales of the seller. Or the negative information may simply come out of a conversation initiated by the receiver who is looking for advice, as is often the case, for example, with potential purchasers of automobiles, major appliances, or home entertainment products. The would-be buyer of a car, for example, is likely to look for owners of the make of automobile being considered and ask their opinion. When they report a negative experience, this helps the person know what questions to ask the dealer or why it may be best to eliminate that brand from the consideration set. If the owners are really unhappy with some feature or angry about some unresolved problem, this is a chance to "get it off their chest" and to seek affirmation for their decision to buy in the first place by demonstrating that they were misled, misinformed, or deceived rather than that they simply made a bad decision. Their opinions will be highly believable because they are based on actual experience and are communicated within the bonds of acquaintance or friendship with no need to misrepresent the true situation.

Companies can take specific steps to increase the amount of positive word-of-mouth generated by their customers, and to intercept and manage the negative word-of-mouth or, more importantly, root out the causes of dissatisfaction. An important step in generating positive word-of-mouth is to follow up with the customer, to be sure they know how to use and enjoy the product to the maximum extent, and to help them through any difficulties in the early stages of usage and ownership. Providing customers with information that they can share with others can be very helpful, especially when their opinions are sought out by other potential customers.

The Value of Customer Complaints

Contrary to the widely held opinion of most businesspeople, customer complaints are a valuable business asset. Whereas the conventional wisdom is to minimize complaints and to avoid them at all costs, a moment's reflection suggests that they can have great value. Four facts support this observation:

1. Unhappy customers are likely to complain to someone, and it might as well be the company. This minimizes the negative impact on other potential customers and it gives the company the opportunity to correct the problem.
2. Customers keep changing (increasing) their expectations, and the complaint is an opportunity to understand how customer expectations may be changing.
3. It is the best opportunity to learn when there really is something wrong that might not come to management's attention in normal channels for weeks or months. (A burned-out lightbulb in a hotel room is a good example.)
4. The cost of satisfying an unhappy customer is usually much less than the cost of acquiring a new customer.[12]

Customers who are less than completely satisfied are a fact of business life that cannot and should not be avoided. It does no good to pretend they are not there. It is not part of the psychological makeup of every customer to be completely satisfied. Customer expectations keep changing in the competitive marketplace, making historical levels of satisfaction obsolete. A customer complaint can be a window on the changing world even when the product has performed properly. If there is a problem with the product itself, then it is doubly important to identify and correct it. Companies must learn to listen to the customer, not only through the traditional means of market research, but through the vitality of a customer complaint tracking system.

Customer complaint tracking is more than the usual survey of customer satisfaction. It requires following up with at least a sample, if not the total population of recent customers. It requires asking them to identify specific problems they may have perceived that did not come out in the routine questioning about levels of satisfaction. The standard "How satisfied were you?" or "How would you rank our service?" kinds of questions will not necessarily reveal useful customer complaints. Customers must be asked why they assign those rankings and must have specific opportunities to tell the company about real and perceived problems. Since such questions are open-ended, without preassigned response categories, they must be analyzed one at a time using seasoned judgment. Focus groups with actual customers, while quite expensive, can be an effective interview method for studying customer complaints. Many companies put a toll-free telephone number on their packages or product information brochures so that customers know where to call with questions and complaints.

Feedback in the form of customer complaints is the opportunity to hear the voice of the changing customer, to gain information to be shared with all employees who are involved in delivering value to customers, and to identify those opportunities to innovate, solve problems, and continue to develop the firm's distinctive competence in directions important to the customer.

SUMMARY

Total quality management is synonymous with a commitment to customer satisfaction. Quality is defined by customer expectations. Defining, developing, and delivering value to customers is a process of understanding, influencing, and responding to those customer expectations. This is a dynamic process because customer expectations keep changing as the result of the interaction of competitive product offerings and increased customer sophistication.

A commitment to customer satisfaction and total quality is also a commitment to continuous innovation on behalf of the customer. In Chapter 4, we consider the development of the firm's value proposition. This process begins by defining the target market that the firm has decided to serve, given the unique combination of skills and resources that define its distinctive competences. Chapter 5 examines the management of customer relationships as an extension of total quality management in the implementation of the new marketing concept.

4 MARKET TARGETING AND THE VALUE PROPOSITION

> The essence of positioning is sacrifice. You must be willing to give up something in order to establish that unique position.
>
> Al Ries and Jack Trout
> *Positioning: The Battle for Your Mind* (1986)

The most important strategic choice any company makes is choosing the customers it wishes to do business with. It is a choice that defines the business. It must be a *conscious* choice, based on the desires and values of the owners and managers of the business as well as an assessment of the company's strengths and weaknesses, resources and capabilities, compared with those of competitors. It should be based on a management vision of the potential of the company for creating and serving markets, for exploiting its unique strengths, and for achieving substantial profitability.

Customers define the business by the demands they place on it, by asking the firm to do certain things effectively and efficiently. The decision to provide solutions to customer problems, to work with specific customers, to accept their demands, is a commitment of resources. The choice of markets and customers shapes the business even more than the choice of products to be offered. Over time, the product offering is adjusted to changing customer needs. In a stable business, the product is a variable; the served market and the customer are the constants.

Changing the definition of the served market changes the definition of the business. Customers shape the business, which is why customer choice is the critical strategic decision. If management has not defined a strategic vision of what it wants to be, and who is the desired customer, it has no control over the forces shaping its business. A business that tries to be all things to all customers is not a business at all, because it has failed to define its product/market scope. It should be obvious that no business can satisfy the demands of all potential customers. But it is not.

THE SIREN SONG OF SALES VOLUME

In contrast to the marketing concept stands the sales concept. Under the marketing concept, profit is the reward for creating a satisfied customer. Under the sales concept, profit is tied to sales volume. The apparent logic of a sales-volume orientation by management is rooted in marginal profit contribution. Given high fixed costs, the logic goes, every additional sales dollar helps to make a contribution to fixed costs and brings the company closer to a position of profitability. Once fixed costs have been covered, the total contribution above variable costs per unit sold "falls to the bottom line" as operating profit.

The lure of the next sales dollar is very great. Think of an industry with high fixed costs, usually associated with large investments in plant and equipment, and you have probably identified an industry where the sales concept is more prevalent than the marketing concept: Pulp and paper, lumber, agricultural chemicals, and textile fibers are good examples.

BIGGER IS OFTEN NOT BETTER: THE REPUBLIC AIRLINES CASE

Republic Airlines, which resulted from the merger of North Central Airlines with Southern Airways in 1979 and incorporated Hughes Airwest in 1980, provides a classic example of a company almost destroyed by a sales-volume orientation.[1] In 1983, Republic was the nation's sixth largest passenger carrier, serving most of America's metropolitan areas and many intermediate-size cities. Republic's routes reached from

Seattle/Tacoma to Miami, from San Diego to Boston and Montreal (but not to Hawaii or Alaska). It carried 17.8 million passengers a total of 9.7 billion passenger miles in 1983, an average of 545 miles per passenger. And it lost about $111 million in the process.

The airline business, like most transportation businesses, is characterized by high fixed costs. Looking at the total airline company, there are the high fixed costs of airplanes, baggage handling and other ground equipment, airport leases, signage, local sales and operating staffs, and administration. For an individual flight, even most of the operating expenses such as fuel (25% of revenues for Republic) and labor (37% of revenues) are fixed costs that will be incurred for each scheduled flight regardless of the number of passengers. True variable costs for food (2%), inflight service, ground service, and so on are virtually negligible.

A major element of fixed costs for Republic Airlines was the debt burden incurred as a result of the mergers (equal to 6% of total revenues). Their fixed costs per flight were also significantly above industry norms because their aircraft, including the worlds largest fleet of DC-9s, were old and inefficient, their experienced labor force earned above-average wages, and their route structure was dominated by relatively short flight segments.

These conditions created a perfect setting for the trap of a volume orientation. Management focused on filling the seats and increasing the number of cities served. More cities served meant more passengers being funneled through Republic's four hubs in Minneapolis-St. Paul, Detroit, Memphis, and Phoenix onto outgoing flights. In none of these hubs did Republic enjoy a dominant market position in either number of flights or passenger preference. Frequent fliers who used Republic often did so because they had to, given their originating cities and destinations, not because they wanted to. Republic's in-flight personnel were regarded as friendly and helpful but the airplanes were described as old, dirty, and poorly decorated. Informed passengers knew that Republic was struggling for survival in the unfriendly skies created by deregulation of the industry and were worried about its survival.

An estimated 130 airlines were certified to carry passengers in 1984, many of them in weak financial condition. In addition to the familiar transcontinental carriers (American, United, and TWA) and the large regional airlines that had tended to fly north-south routes extending into the Caribbean and Latin America (Braniff, Eastern, and Delta) or east-west routes extending to international destinations in Europe and Asia (Northwest Orient and Continental), there were the start-up, low-cost, low-service airlines (People Express, Southwest, Midway, and others), as well as the commuters. Large regional carriers such as USAir, Piedmont, and Western were also a major competitive factor. Republic's extensive route structure of more than 150 cities meant that it competed with all of them.

How to compete? Republic had no jumbo jets, few international destinations (Montreal in Canada, Mazatlán and Puerto Vallarta in Mexico, and Grand Cayman in the West Indies), and a reputation for unreliable schedules. The answer seemed obvious: price and promotion. Initially, Republic had tried to hold out against the low-fare competitors and saw its load factor (percentage of seats filled on the average flight) fall to just above 50%, which was below the breakeven level. Republic then decided to respond with aggressive pricing. It was committed to a "big airline" strategy, competing in the national market against the transcontinental carriers, the large regionals, and the new low-cost airlines as well. So Republic lowered its fares to attract passengers and continued to expand the route structure.

Advertising carried the headline "What's Bigger Than 140 Cities And Flies?" and featured the tag line "Nobody Serves Our Republic Like Republic." Promotions aimed at infrequent pleasure travelers included a "Kids Fly Free" promotion with Chex cereals and a two-for-one "Pair Fare." Such promotions produced virtually no incremental revenue on the non-fare-paying passengers but were assumed to attract fliers who would not have otherwise flown. These revenues, it was assumed, were purely incremental revenue that would not have been earned without the promotion. In the meantime, it was obvious that some business travelers were taking advantage of the new low fares. Republic succeeded in increasing its load factor to well over 55 percent. It also increased its losses.

For the average flight distance of 545 miles, the average passenger paid only $77.99. While Republic's costs were an estimated 15.9 cents per revenue passenger mile, its revenues were about 14.3 cents. Thus, they were losing an estimated 1.6 cents per revenue passenger mile flown. That is bad enough for a small airline. For a big airline, which is what Republic aspired to be, flying 9.7 billion passenger miles, that is a disaster. Republic's cargo revenues of about $125 million per year during this period, all of which are truly incremental in an aircraft committed to passenger travel, helped to mitigate the financial disaster, reducing the loss on operations to about $31 million as did the sale of tax benefits and a small amount of interest and nonoperating income. Interest expense of $98 million brought the total loss to $111 million in 1983. It was a classic case of the old saw "We lose money on every unit we sell but we hope to make it up on volume." It would be funnier if it wasn't so true. The engine of sales volume multiplies the consequences of inefficiency very rapidly!

Fortunately, new management was able to get on top of the situation and reverse Republic's fortunes, with the help of a new advertising agency, Dancer Fitzgerald Sample. After negotiating a new labor agreement that reduced labor costs by about 15 percent, the new chief executive officer, Stephen Wolf (who would subsequently work a similar turnaround at Flying Tiger, the freight airline, and then move on to United Airlines), retrenched by cutting back the number of cities served to less than 100 and concentrating aircraft on stronger schedules out of the major hubs.

Republic offered a number of new services aimed at the business traveler, especially the younger traveler who did not currently have a strong preference for another airline, in those markets where Republic had the advantage of service frequency and an established market position. Often, these markets—cities like Omaha, Rochester (New York), and Madison—had not attracted competition from the major national carriers. Instead of presenting itself as a big airline, Republic was repositioned as a regional carrier, national in scope, with service through efficient, less congested hubs. Services for the business traveler included a more attractive frequent flyer program, airport lounges, a $15 upgrade to first-class cabin, and a tie-in with Pan American Airlines that offered generous international travel awards for frequent-flier mileage.

The value proposition for the business traveler was captured in the revamped marketing communications program, which featured "Perks" for the frequent flier. Republic's new advertising carried the tag line "We Make You Feel Like Flying," which emphasized the airline's commitment to providing services for the business traveler. Republic was focused on the frequent business traveler and on those cities where it could achieve some competitive superiority through schedules and service. Instead of chasing after the pleasure traveler who was interested primarily in price and who could choose when, where, and how to travel based on finding the lowest fares, Republic tailored its product offering and communications for the business traveler, who had to travel to a certain place at a certain time and often had little or no discretion except, perhaps, in the choice of airline.

Republic returned to profitability in 1984. In 1985, it merged with Northwest Airlines which was headquartered, like Republic, in Minneapolis-St. Paul. The purchase price was about $884 million and the buyer acquired debt of over $600 million. From a balance sheet where shareholder's equity had declined to something around $1 million or less in 1983, the merger placed a value on Republic of almost $1.5 billion, which may have been excessive but which shows the value of a successful repositioning based on market segmentation and targeting. By focusing on the young business traveler in underserved secondary and regional markets, Republic defined a profitable market niche where its smaller aircraft, frequent flight schedules, and friendly cabin personnel, along with the many new services for business travelers, were able to deliver superior value.

SEGMENTING THE MARKET AND TARGETING CUSTOMERS

Choosing customers begins with market segmentation. This is both an analytical and a creative process, requiring the collection and analysis of data about the potential market and the imaginative interpretation of those data by the marketing manager. The essence of market segmentation is to break a large market into smaller pieces, consisting of customers who are similar to one another in ways important to the marketer such as their needs, preferences, buying habits, usage patterns, or media exposure. Customers within a given market segment should be similar in their response to the company's product offerings and/or communications. This similarity in response is the key to market segmentation, and response should be related to one or more customer characteristics that can be observed and measured.

Customers *within* a given market segment should be as *similar* to one another as possible on these important characteristics; customers in different market segments should be as *different* from one another as possible. (Statistically, this means minimizing within-group variance and maximizing among-group variance.) The customer characteristics chosen as the basis for market segmentation can be demographic (age, income, occupation, family status, type or place of residence) or psychographic (self-concept, life-style, risk aversion, buying decision process). Psychographic segments are often hard to develop, however, because it is difficult observe and measure such characteristics, unless they can be related to more observable attributes such as age or place of residence.

Benefit segmentation is based on the fact that different customers are looking for different sets of benefits from the same product, although this also requires matching up some observable and measurable characteristics of the customer with these benefit sets. For example, benefit segments for toothpaste might be based on the relative importance the consumer places on cavity prevention, taste, or whitening. These preferences are likely to be related to the presence of children in the household and the age and marital status of the consumer. Income, education, and occupation may also be usefully correlated with these benefit preferences, making benefit segmentation feasible and operational. Often, however, benefit segments are hard to define in operational terms.

Once the company has identified distinct segments, it has the choice of trying to serve one, some, or all of those segments. In concentrated marketing, the company sells to one or a few segments, leaving the other segments to competition. In differentiated marketing, the company develops distinct products and communications for each segment and tries to serve a larger number of segments, perhaps even the total market. Undifferentiated marketing, selling the same thing the same way everywhere, returns the company to a sales-volume orientation.

Republic Airlines moved from undifferentiated marketing back toward concentrated marketing. By focusing in their regional markets on frequent business travelers aged 25 to 44 who did not have a strong preference for another airline, Republic was matching up its limited resources with a relatively underserved portion of the total market.

The essence of market segmentation and targeting is in the willingness to *not* serve certain customers. It requires the ability to "just say No," to walk away from business that might be available. The ability to turn down business is not part of the genetic makeup of many businesspeople, especially salespeople. The new management at Republic was willing to let competitors have those potential customers who wanted very low fares, who were traveling strictly for pleasure and on a flexible schedule, who wanted to fly on wide-body aircraft to attractive foreign destinations. Republic made a conscious choice not to compete aggressively in the major markets such as New York, Atlanta, Dallas, Los Angeles, Miami, and Chicago and not to try to switch the preferences of those business travelers who participated in the frequent-flyer programs of American, United, Delta, Northwest, and the rest. Some of those markets were dominated by a single, large competitor, whereas others were fiercely competitive with many carriers, including the low-cost operators. Republic didn't have the skills and resources to compete in those markets and could not meet customer expectations.

Market Segmentation and Product Differentiation

Market segmentation and product differentiation are related but distinct concepts. Sometimes they are used interchangeably, which is incorrect and has led to some confusion.

Over the years, the term "product differentiation" has been used to mean three very different things. In the first instance, it means simply offering products with features different from those of more standardized competitive offerings. This is at the base of Levitt's concept of the augmented product, examined in Chapter 3. Thus, manufacturers of commodity chemicals *differentiate* their products by offering services as part of the purchase price, including special packaging, transportation options, applications assistance, and more. Banks differentiate their services on the basis of their convenient locations and helpful personnel.

The second meaning of product differentiation is related more closely to market segmentation. In this usage, product differentiation refers to the practice of offering somewhat different products for different market segments. Thus, Coca-Cola comes in two standard flavors, new "Coke II" and "Coke Classic," as well as Diet Coke and Caffeine-free Coke. Coca-Cola also markets Tab, another sugar-free cola, plus many noncola products including the Sprite and Fanta brands. Likewise, Mercedes-Benz offers a large range of models from the lowest-priced 190 series Baby Benz sedans up through somewhat larger and more expensive 300 and 400 series models, to the very expensive luxury sedans in the 500 and 600 series, along with the SL roadsters. Each of these products has distinctive features and is aimed at a specific market segment.

The third meaning of product differentiation is the use of communication tools, especially advertising, to make claims infusing a product or service with value that is not obviously part of the service or physical product itself. For example, Budweiser beer is promoted as "Beechwood Aged," Ford promises that "Quality is Job 1," Connecticut is "The State That Thinks Like a Business," Avis "Tries Harder" and Fidelity Investments offers "Common Sense. Uncommon Results." We often talk about using advertising to create a "brand image" that differentiates the product from competitors in the mind of the customer.

The Power of Brand Images

It can be argued that, from a competitive standpoint, brand image is the most powerful form of product differentiation because it is virtually impossible for a competitor to duplicate it. Once United Airlines put major advertising dollars behind the campaign, it had a preemptive claim on "The Friendly Skies." An established brand image cannot be copied except to the benefit of the original owner. Pepsi-Cola and BMW can compete with Coca-Cola and Mercedes-Benz by offering a parallel range of products based on physical product characteristics but they cannot hope to compete based on the same brand images. Rather, they must make huge promotional investments to create distinct brand images for their own products and pursue their own market segmentation strategies. Thus, Pepsi advertising creates a more youthful brand image and BMW is presented as a sporty sedan.

The values inherent in a strong brand image, now commonly referred to a "brand equity," are often based on the communication strategy surrounding the brand rather than the physical characteristics built into the product. IBM may be the best example of a brand image based almost entirely on communication, in this instance not only from the company's advertising but also the professionalism of its sales force and all supporting communications about the company and its products and services. IBM managers would be the first to tell you that their excellent products were often no better than those of their best competitors but what really made the difference in the mind of the customer was the image of IBM as the world leader in computing and its supportive relationship with every customer. Sadly, IBM was unable to maintain that distinction in the viciously competitive markets of the 1990s.

Some authors have confused market segmentation and product differentiation or have mistakenly presented them as competing marketing strategies.[2] Market segmentation is the strategy of conceptually and statistically identifying different market segments with different characteristics—needs, wants, preferences, buying habits, usage patterns, communication exposure, or whatever. Product differentiation is the strategy and tactics of offering products with distinctive characteristics—based either on product design and engineering variables or on communication variables—to these distinct market segments.

Some authors have used the term product differentiation strictly in the third sense, as a communication strategy, and have presented it as a distinct alternative to market segmentation. This distinction is inherently confusing and implies, incorrectly, that the firm has the choice of either doing "real" market segmentation and physically differentiating products for each defined segment, or using communication to do the job. Seldom, if ever, is that approach a clear strategic choice for a given product. Some of these authors also imply that there is something bogus and misleading about using communication to create a distinct brand image when there are minimal product differences. There is, nevertheless, great value in a strong brand image for both the customer and the marketer, whether that brand is IBM, Budweiser, Du Pont, or Sony.

MARKET TARGETING: SELECTING MARKET SEGMENTS

Market targeting, illustrated by the Republic Airlines focus on young business travelers, is the process of selecting those market segments the company wishes to serve. It is the most important element in developing a business strategy, the heavy half of the statement of product/market scope. It is the first step in developing the value proposition.

The selection of target markets is a commitment of resources to delivering superior value to a specific set of customers. Who are those customers? How do we decide which set of customers to commit to? It is helpful to recall that the failure of the original marketing concept to address this specific issue—how does the firm decide which customers to try to satisfy?—was one of the major criticisms that diminished its acceptance and was addressed by the early forms of strategic planning. No firm can satisfy all the needs of all potential customers. Recognition of this basic truth is at the heart of market targeting.

For a new business, the entrepreneur's commitment could begin with the perceived needs of a set of potential clients or customers. Thus, a developer of educational software may begin, before there is a product, with a commitment to enhancing the learning of elementary school children in grades 1 through 4. More than one visionary has started a business or a not-for-profit undertaking because of a basic commitment to solve a particular problem.

More frequently, the vision of a business opportunity has its origins in technology, new or old, high or low, that creates the possibility for solving a problem better, for delivering superior value. Quite often, the business begins with a new product idea before there is a good sense of the scope and characteristics of the potential market. The entrepreneur or company believes that the new product concept has some inherent superiority based on the firm's superior knowledge, skills, and other resources.

Underlying the new product idea is, implicitly, the concept of distinctive competence, described in Chapter 3. The commitment to develop and maintain one or more distinctive competences must be made as specific as possible. The first and perhaps the most difficult step is to define the distinctive competence. What is the company really good at? What does it do, or what can it potentially do, better than anyone else in the world? The answer must go deeper than the current product form and identify the knowledge-based competences that will sustain the business.

Assuming that an answer to that question is forthcoming, then the even more important question might be phrased simply as "Who cares?" or "Who needs it?" In Chapter 3, the essential point was made that a distinctive competence cannot be defined except in the context of a market target. A distinctive competence is defined by the customer's perception of value. Thus, potential customers must value the knowledge and skill that is the basis for a distinctive competence before it becomes meaningful. How does it deliver perceived superior value to customers, in their terms? What markets does it provide access to? Having defined those potential markets and applications, the analyst must go back and look at the assumed or hypothetical distinctive competence and its related new product idea more carefully. For these specific customers, what are the purported benefits, and limitations, in the customers' product use system compared with alternative products and substitutes?

POSITIONING A PRODUCT TO A PROSPECTIVE CUSTOMER

Positioning is the development of the value proposition, the statement of how the firm proposes to deliver superior value to customers. Positioning is the communication about the product, not the product itself. This is evident in the classic definition of positioning by the authors who popularized the term, Al Ries and Jack Trout:

> Positioning starts with a product. A piece of merchandise a service, a company, an institution, or even a person. Perhaps yourself.
>
> But positioning is not what you do to a product. Positioning is what you do to the mind of the prospect. That is, you position the product in the mind of the prospect.
>
> So it's incorrect to call the concept "product positioning." You're not really doing something to the product itself.[3]

Developing a Positioning Statement—The "Value Proposition"

Positioning is the strategic decision making, the analytical, conceptual, and creative processes that lead to the positioning statement. The positioning statement, or what I prefer to call the value proposition, puts the concept into words and performs two critically important functions:

1. It becomes the selling proposition to potential customers, the reason they should do business with the company rather than its competitors.
2. It communicates to the whole organization a sense of specific purpose and direction, coordinating their efforts toward the overarching common purpose of creating a satisfied customer.

I prefer to call this verbal statement the value proposition for three reasons. First, it focuses on customer value and relates positioning to the value-delivery concept of strategy. Second, it goes beyond the somewhat limited notion that positioning is based solely on communication, which is a narrow definition of product differentiation, as discussed earlier. I don't disagree with Ries and Trout when they say that positioning is based on communication; the point of using the phrase "the value proposition" is that the benefits and attributes featured in the communication must have their roots in the company's resources, knowledge, and skills if they are to provide long-term, sustainable competitive advantage. Third, the positioning statement, as the phrase is commonly used, is aimed solely at customers. The value proposition is equally important for the organization that delivers the product. It keeps everyone in the value-delivery sequence focused on the customer. An important objective of the new Republic Airlines advertising campaign, for example, was to build organizational morale and to refocus service personnel on the needs of the business traveler.

Positioning and the development of the value proposition must be based on an assessment of the product offering and of the firm's distinctive competences *relative to competitors*. This is inherent in the notion that the customer defines value. The customer defines value by comparing the company's product offering with those of competitors in the context of his or her own needs, preferences, buying patterns, and use system. Thus, positioning is always done "relative to competitors." Ries and Trout pointed out that the phrase "product positioning" was incorrect; they might also have pointed out that positioning "relative to competitors" is redundant.

At the same time, it is helpful to look at competitors' positioning when developing the firm's own positioning and its value proposition. For example, Republic Airlines specifically considered a positioning based on their consumer research finding that Republic's flight personnel were friendly and helpful. That positioning was rejected, however, because United had already preempted the concept of friendliness as part of their positioning. Market pioneers often have the opportunity to protect their market positions based on preemptive communication.

Positioning: Who? What? Why?

The value proposition, or the positioning statement, has three parts:

1. Who is the target customer? We have already discussed the importance of defining the target customer as the first order of business.
2. Why should the customer buy it? The "Why?" part of the positioning statement is the familiar problem of defining the benefits for the customer, the reasons the company's product is better than competitor's offerings.

3. What are we selling? The "What?" part of the value proposition is the most basic, most challenging, and most interesting part of the problem—specifying the product concept, exactly what is being sold. This may be the most difficult part of the development of the positioning statement or value proposition. It must be defined from the point of view of the customer. It also defines the competition. We cannot get a clear definition of the relevant competitors until we know what we are selling.

The creative definition of a product concept is a great opportunity to redefine the competitive groundrules, even to devise entirely new markets. Federal Express did not present itself as another airfreight forwarder. Rather, it was an overnight delivery system for small packages and information. Tylenol wasn't just another pain reliever; it was a strong pain reliever for people who were worried about the negative side effects of taking aspirin.

The Ford Mustang has been one of the most durable models in the history of the automobile industry, and it provides an excellent example of getting the What right. The original concept for the car featured its Italian styling and American origins. It wasn't even called Mustang but "Torino by Ford—the brand-new import from Detroit." It was aimed at a younger customer who wanted an economical, yet high-performance "sports car" type vehicle. However, consumer research testing the product concept demonstrated that the potential market was much larger. It was renamed the Mustang and positioned as an inexpensive sporty personal vehicle offering economy and versatility (through a wide range of options for engines, transmissions, hard and soft tops, seats, wheels, upholstery, etc.).[4] The appeal of the initial Italian sports car positioning would have been much more limited.

Appropriate Positioning Creates Brand Equity

The concept of brand equity has become popular in recent years, replacing the older concepts of brand image and brand loyalty. A major reason for the new nomenclature is to recognize the financial value of a brand name. In the United Kingdom, accounting practice permits including the value of a brand on a company's balance sheet and depreciating it, like any other asset, over time. The prohibition of this procedure by accepted financial accounting practices in the United States became an important issue in the overheated merger and acquisition activities of the 1980s. It would have helped the acquiring firm's financial performance if it had been able to depreciate and take as an operating expense a portion of the "goodwill" paid for a firm with strong brand assets.

A strong brand is a major business asset. It typically represents the investment of millions of dollars in product development, advertising, sales promotion, after-sale service, and reseller support. The returns on those investments are earned over many years. For example, the dominant market shares in ready-to-eat cereals are still held by three of the oldest brands—Wheaties, Cheerios, and Kellogg's Corn Flakes.

While the term brand equity refers to the brand as a business asset, viewed from the perspective of the firm and its owners, the real meaning of the phrase resides in the minds of customers. Brand equity is based on the customers' knowledge of the brand—their ability to recognize it, to recall having seen it before, to associate it with various messages, attributes, benefits, and experiences, and to use this knowledge in decision making. In theoretical terms, there is a strong cognitive component to the concept of brand equity as well as a strong behavioral predisposition. These positive associations and predispositions in the mind of the consumer result in a more favorable response to the firm's marketing efforts for the brand, giving it a better return on its marketing expenditures.[5]

Thus, brand equity goes beyond the old concepts of brand image and brand loyalty, which referred strictly to the consumer's perceptions, without recognizing the brand's inherent strategic value. Brand equity incorporates the fundamental notion of the brand as a business asset. Brand loyalty referred to a not-so-easily defined notion of repeat purchasing—variously measured as proportion of product category purchases, probability of purchasing the brand on the next purchase, total brand units purchased by a consumer during a given period, and so on. Brand loyalty is a rather static concept when defined this way and doesn't facilitate considering the possibility of brand extensions—applying the brand to new products of the same or related type.

A strong brand is very close to a distinctive competence, but these are not the same thing. The distinctive competences are the underlying knowledge and skills on which the firm develops its brand equity. These competences might include the underlying technical knowledge (for example, expertise in ceramics chemistry and production technology) as well as advertising and promotion skills that led to the successful development of the Corning brand name for cooking ware.

The brand name, in creating a set of expectations for product performance, becomes part of the definition of quality by the customer. A strong brand creates high expectations. Consumers develop amazingly strong imagery around a brand name. You will never see a real model presented as Betty Crocker, the General Mills brand symbol. General Mills learned that no woman, not even a woman's voice or a pair of hands, could be convincingly presented as the "real" Betty Crocker.

Procter & Gamble was reminded of the strength of customer-defined brand equity when it changed Prell shampoo from a clear green gel to a reformulated blue variety that included a hair conditioner. As Jack Trout, the authority on positioning, commented: "Consumers thought Prell was the green stuff. The guys at P&G said, 'No, it's blue.' Challenging customer perceptions is very tricky, and is generally a mistake." Loyal consumers rebelled at the change and made their voice heard. Soon, new advertising appeared with the headline "Green is back! The original formula you've always loved." Loyal customers had a strong definition of value in their minds that did not include conditioners and the changed color. The new blue product was continued but appealed to a new market segment.[6]

Mercedes-Benz is about to test the strength and flexibility of this century-old brand name with their announced plans to introduce one or more models priced much lower than any previous model. It will be interesting to see whether these new cars carry the Mercedes-Benz brand name. It is a good bet that they will not. Two risks are involved—damage to the long-standing luster of the Mercedes-Benz name and the probability that no low-priced automobile will meet the expectations created by the name. On the other hand, if the Mercedes-Benz name is not used, the company faces the huge investment involved in establishing a new brand in perhaps the most competitive global market.

DEVELOPING THE PRODUCT OFFERING

Under the new marketing concept, the product offering flows from the value proposition, not vice versa. The value proposition establishes the firm's strategic direction. It is based on the selection of markets and customers to be served and a commitment to develop and maintain the distinctive competences necessary to deliver superior value to those customers. The product offering is a variable, to be tailored to the needs and desires, preferences, and buying habits of the chosen market target. Over time, the product offering must change as customer needs and preferences change. It is the value proposition that becomes the guiding star for continuous innovation in pursuing improved solutions to customer problems.

Getting from the value proposition to the actual product offering is a far from simple task. While the core product (again using Levitt's terminology) may be the starting point for developing the business, it is only the beginning. The next step is to understand the expected product, what it is the customer expects to be offered in terms of product performance, features, and service. This is the basis on which the customer will judge the quality of the product offering and be satisfied or dissatisfied. We can make a distinction between product features, those physical and service aspects that are part of the basic product offering, and additional services that add to the value of the product offering by enhancing the ease and utility of ordering, taking delivery, storing, using, and disposing of the product. This dichotomy is not a clear-cut distinction because of the ambiguous nature of the concept of a service, but we will try to make it understandable.

Before returning to product features and services as part of the product offering, two strategic issues in developing the product offering need consideration. First, there is the problem of defining what is required for a complete product offering. Second, there is the need to define the real customer for the product, the person or organization who will benefit most from the new product's capabilities, among all the interacting parties in the product delivery and use system.

Marketing an Incomplete Product: Why the Gould 4800 Failed

Failure to look at the product from the customer's viewpoint can result in going to market with an incomplete product. It is amazing how frequently this occurs. A classic illustration is provided by the Gould 4800, introduced in 1969 by the Graphics Division of Gould Incorporated as a key part of its drive to become an electronics company.[7]

The Gould 4800 was the first electrostatic, nonimpact printer developed for the computer. It had the remarkable ability to print up to 4800 86-character lines per minute, the equivalent of 60 sheets of 8½-by-11-inch paper, and it was very quiet. It also had excellent graphic output and plotting capability. When shown at an industry trade show, it solicited extremely positive feedback from those who saw it as a major technical breakthrough. Here was a printing device with the potential to bridge the huge gap between the incredibly fast calculation speeds of a computer and the archaically slow printing speeds of the old inked-ribbon impact printers, the fastest of which operated at only one-fourth the speed of the Gould 4800.

Several months later, not a single order had been received. Slowly, management at the Graphics Division of Gould Incorporated began to realize that they had gone to market with an incomplete product.

The Gould 4800 required a special coated paper, and Gould had built a pilot paper-coating machine to provide the necessary supply. Parts for building a larger machine were on order. Unfortunately, the paper was 8½ inches wide, whereas standard computer printer paper was 14⅞ inches wide and 11 inches high. The coated paper came in rolls, not sheets, and there was no provision for a hardware device to cut the paper into page-size sheets of the standard 8½-by-11-inch office size. Neither could the machine take preprinted forms or make multiple ("carbon") copies. To make matters worse, each sheet of paper cut to this size would cost 4.2¢ compared with the price for a standard 11-by-14⅞-inch computer sheet of only .14¢, 30 times more expensive. Finally, and perhaps most basically, Gould had developed none of the communications software to connect the printer to the computer. The apparent assumption was that the customers would be so excited about the performance and potential of this new technology that they would be willing to incur the expense of writing the software themselves or would put pressure on their computer vendors to do the necessary development. The latter outcome was highly unlikely because the major computer manufacturers also had their own printers for sale.

Although it isn't directly related to the central point about the dangers of going to market with an incomplete product, one other aspect of the Gould 4800 must be noted: Very few potential customers needed a machine that could print that fast. A machine with that printing speed needs constant attention just to take away the output. A roll of paper would be used up and need to be replaced every few minutes. It turned out that the really salable features of the device, which found a very limited market, were its noiseless operation, making it attractive for applications like brokerage houses, and its graphic plotting capability, which found use in process control applications.

The Gould 4800 is perhaps an extreme illustration, but not uncommon, and offers a useful lesson. The former President of Gould observed to me some years later that the principal contribution of the Gould 4800 had been as a training ground for several young MBAs who had been given the assignment, as part of their career development, of trying to turn it into a profitable business. It is a good example of technology-driven marketing as opposed to market-driven technology.

There are many other examples of incomplete products that went to market, such as raw materials without any provision for new product formulations or production processes, medical diagnostic technology without the necessary instrumentation, gardening equipment sold directly to consumers without any provision for repair service or replacement parts, and the Christmas nightmare of unassembled toys with no assembly instructions!

The Importance of Finding the Customer: Why Amicon's New Technology Floundered

A customer is someone or some organization willing and able to pay for the benefits delivered by the product. The identity of the customer is often far from obvious, especially when the value chain and marketing channel include many actors, some of whom are threatened by the new product and others of whom potentially can profit from it, depending on the arrangements negotiated for bringing the product to market.

Incomplete products result from a failure to understand how the customer will obtain and use them. At one level, the problem is simply not understanding the customer's knowledge level and use system. Few customers will be as technically sophisticated as the product inventor and developer. At another level, the challenge is to understand all the transactions, technologies, and economic actors in the value chain as the product moves from raw material through fabrication and assembly to incorporation into product systems that ultimately get used in some other system of production and consumption by the ultimate users.

Another case study illustrates this problem well. Amicon Corporation[8] owned the patent for a device incorporating a new membrane-based microfiltration technology with a specific application in human blood collection. In 1978, it was in the sixth year of the 17-year life of its patent and still did not have a product ready for the marketplace. The benefits of the new technology included the ability to return blood directly to the donor in a continuous filtration operation after the plasma had been removed for further processing. The procedure required less time than the old batch-collection process. It also allowed paid donors to contribute more frequently and had the potential to increase the total supply of blood plasma. Costs compared favorably with the old batch-collection and batch-processing technologies.

The new process was also much safer because it assured that the donor would receive back his or her own blood. Under the old batch process, blood was taken from the donor, centrifuged to remove the plasma, and then returned to the donor. There was a small but real chance of a mix-up. If the donor received another person's blood in return, the result could fatal. The ultimate beneficiaries, at least potentially, of the new technology were blood plasma recipients who would have an assured supply because of greater availability, the American Red Cross and hospitals who needed the plasma supply, and donors who would have less time commitment and greater safety.

The real problem was the complexity of the blood collection system in the United States. There are both commercial collection centers and noncommercial, nonprofit agencies, especially hospitals and the American Red Cross. National companies own and operate the commercial blood collection centers, supply the disposable products (catheters, tubing, storage vessels, and anticlotting chemicals, assembled into kits) used in the batch-collection process, and process the blood plasma into blood-plasma fractions. While there may be temporary shortages of blood of a given type in a specific geographic area, the amazing fact is that the blood supply is virtually always adequate to meet the requirements of those who need it. This brings us back to a basic question in market targeting, positioning, and the value proposition—Who needs it? In this case, the problem is to determine who in the total product delivery and use system will benefit most from the new technology and, equally important, who is most threatened by it.

Another way of stating the problem is as one of understanding how each of the interacting firms and organizations makes money. What is their strategy for profitability? The commercial blood collection centers proved to have little interest in the new technology because it could potentially lower their revenues by increasing the supply of blood and thus reducing its market price. Also, the new technology would somewhat increase their costs. This was especially a problem for the commercial centers owned by those firms that also sold the disposable supplies. The parties with the most to gain included the donors and blood recipients, neither of whom would be a significant factor because they would not directly purchase the product/service. In the strict sense, they were not potential customers because they did not have the ability to purchase the product.

The American Red Cross was a potential beneficiary of the increased availability and lower cost of blood plasma. (Even nonprofits have to make money and worry about both their costs and their revenues.) The Red Cross had recently built a new plasma-fractionating plant in collaboration with one of the major manufacturers of disposables that was also in the blood-fractionating business. The new technology could substantially lower the costs of blood collection, but the Red Cross also faced a major investment in new product development to bring the new technology into being, as there was still no physical product incorporating the new technology. Somebody still needed to develop the devices that would collect the blood and the instruments that would monitor the process. This provided a potential profit opportunity for the disposables suppliers, especially the one that had formed a strategic alliance with the Red Cross on the fractionating plant.

Once again, the Amicon example shows the need to develop a complete product offering before a new technology has economic value. It also illustrates the complexity of the product use and delivery systems that must be understood to develop a product offering that truly provides superior value to customers. Defining customers is not a simple proposition. In this instance, the actual customers for the technology, those who were willing and able to pay for it, were not those who were the ultimate benefactors, the donors and blood plasma recipients. Rather, the customers had to be economic actors in the value chain—processors, fabricators, and resellers who themselves had to add value before there was a complete product offering for the end user and who could see an opportunity to make money by helping to develop and promote the technology.

This set of costs and benefits, specific to each of the actors in the product delivery and use system, was critical to understanding the potential economic value of the new technology. The analysis of costs and benefits for each actor provided a basis for Amicon to select its potential partners and to negotiate licensing agreements that would result in the development of instrumentation and collection devices incorporating their membrane technology.

Developing the complete product offering requires knowing customers and their needs. Designing the product offering requires making decisions about product features that address specific needs and wants and offer superior value to the customer. It also requires knowing the total use and delivery system. Service is usually a critical part of the product offering.

Developing Key Product Features

Product features are part of the basic product/service offering. They are tangible and intangible aspects of the product that differentiate it from competitive offerings and add value for customers in the target market. They represent important "selling points" in the value proposition. For example, the Toshiba cardiovascular angiographic system is said to be superior to competition because it permits viewing multiple images simultaneously, its images can be enlarged, and it has computer-enhanced color to add increased information and diagnostic capability. Today, the standard product offering for many automobiles and light trucks includes a roadside assistance program as part of the purchase price, along with all the accessories and amenities from air conditioning and power windows to heated seats and rear-window defrosters. Many product features that used to be additional cost options on automobiles today come as part of the standard product offering, an example of how the augmented product of today becomes the expected product of tomorrow.

While continuous innovation and new product features can help sustain the life cycle of many products, service as part of the product offering is increasingly likely to be equally important in determining customer preferences and satisfaction.

Providing Service to Satisfy the Customer

The objective of every marketing program should be not simply to satisfy customers by meeting their expectations but to "delight" the customer's by exceeding those expectations. As noted in the discussion of total quality management, the best companies have defined quality not in terms of specific product features but as a way of doing business. The *expected* product includes essential service elements such as instructions for use and a guarantee of quality. Likewise, the key to the *augmented* product, the complete differentiated product, is often additional service, perhaps in the form of product upgrades as they become available, troubleshooting assistance by way of telephone, membership in a users group, and follow-up mailings with special promotional offers. The *potential* product is more likely defined by the opportunity to add additional services rather than physical product features.

In a broader sense, beyond the product itself, service includes all aspects of the customer's interaction with the company. The purchaser of a kitchen dishwasher hopes this investment will last for many years. The purchaser's "consideration set" of possible brands to purchase may be the result of many years of acquiring information about those brands from advertising, word-of-mouth from family members and friends, displays in stores, catalogs, promotional mailings, and other sources. When the person actually begins shopping, however, the retail clerk becomes the critical source of information and is part of the product offering. The clerk's approach to the prospective customer, including the quality of his or her product knowledge and attitude toward work, all become part of the customer's perception of the value of the brand. In a general sense, all products can be thought of as potential solutions to a problem. The salesperson determines the ability of the product or brand to solve the problem that the customer brings to the buying situation, both the purchase itself and the stream of benefits perceived to derive from the product over its lifetime.

The dishwasher customer may encounter several representatives of the company over time. At least two people will arrive to deliver and install the new appliance. What kind of an impression will they make? Even though they are the retailer's employees or contractors, they still represent the dishwasher manufacturer to a degree and they are also part of the product offering. The consumer who has questions or discovers a problem when using the unit for the first time, may call an 800 number, found in the owner's manual. How courteous and helpful is the person on the line? This customer service representative is also part of the company's product offering. Then there is the service technician, always expected to be there when needed. All these people define the augmented product and their ability to meet or exceed customer expectations is the key to quality.

In the total scheme of things, customer satisfaction is usually influenced as much by these human interactions as by the technical specifications and fancy features of the product itself. If your new car develops a problem on your first long trip, that is bad enough. What really makes you angry, however, is the bad attitude of the service manager and mechanic you encounter when you pull off the interstate highway into the local dealer listed in your owner's manual. That is the defining moment as far as you are concerned. Your impression of the airlines you fly with is almost completely determined by your interactions with the airline's employees—reservations clerks, baggage handlers, gate agents, cabin attendants, and the flight captain whose voice may be the only basis for your impression of him or her.

The quality of the service component of the product offering is a function of the care with which the company selects, trains, supervises, motivates, monitors, and rewards its service personnel. World-class service providers such as Disney, Swissair, McDonald's, and United Parcel Service are distinguished by the tight, efficient systems they have for directing their service personnel. They provide a model for all companies to emulate. The typical industrial parts manufacturer, for example, would do well to select, train, and manage telephone receptionists, order-entry clerks, credit personnel, customer service representatives, and anyone else who interacts with customers with the same care as Disney. Only then will it have a complete product offering with a high probability of exceeding customer expectations.

Many companies have defined quality service in simple terms, such as the number of times the telephone rings before being answered. This has the advantage of being measurable and can be monitored and reported back to those concerned on a regular basis. It is the kind of thing you do to win quality awards. Most customers however are much more likely to care about what they hear when the phone is answered. How many times have you heard:

> "We're sorry. All lines are busy now. Your call will be answered by the next available agent."
>
> "Your call is being answered by an automated answering system. If you are calling to report a problem, press #; if you wish to place an order, press 1. . . ."
>
> "Good morning. Would you hold please. . . ."
>
> "Our normal business hours are 9:00 A.M. to 5:00 P.M., Monday through Friday. Please call back then.
>
> "The guy you need ta talk wid ain't here right now."

So much for service. What you would really like to hear is:

> "Thank you for calling Centricut. This is Linda. How can I help you?"

Some of the best direct marketers (for example, L.L. Bean and Land's End) have excellent people supported by state-of-the-art customer information systems. After a prompt, courteous answering of the call, the representative will ask for either the identification number on the label of the catalogue you received or, if that isn't available, your last name and zip code. Instantly, the representative can bring up your name, address, and purchase record on a computer screen and proceed to say, for example, "Thank you, Mr. Webster. How can I help you today?" If you want to return merchandise, the employee can identify it in the purchase record and tell you how to return it. If you want to place a new order, that can be done quickly and your purchase record will be updated simultaneously. Your usual payment method is indicated on the screen, so you will be asked if you wish to use the same credit card. Once the call is completed, the updated customer information file becomes the basis for future mailings to you according to your indicated interests and purchase patterns and is available for immediate reference the next time you call.

Such sophisticated systems indicate what is possible in the realm of service as part of the product offering. Not just direct mail merchants but industrial companies such as General Electric, Hercules, Du Pont, and many others have learned how to use telemarketing and customer databases not just to lower their selling costs but more importantly to improve their customer service. Customers can call to place orders, to ask for technical assistance, to request a call from a field sales or serviceperson, or to ask about an invoice. Often, each customer is the responsibility of a single person who is the known contact, making the system almost as personal as a direct sales call. Many of these companies call their customers on a regular basis, say once every two weeks or every quarter, to see if they need anything. Information technology doesn't have to destroy the personal relationship. It can enhance it.

In the world of global markets, technological product parity, and the inevitable regression back toward price-sensitive commodity status for most products, customers are looking for reasons to prefer one company's products over those of another. The company that is easiest to do business with is likely to get the nod. Service as part of the product offering is where the competitive battles of the future will be won and lost. Service is likely to be the key to successful positioning and a complete value proposition.

Combining Product Features with Various Services: To Bundle or Not to Bundle?

Service as part of the product offering raises a number of important strategic issues, however, not the least of which is how to price it. Bundling is the process of incorporating product features and services in the product offering. While this may enhance the customer's perception of quality, it is also likely to increase costs. It is obviously essential that the customer place a value on the bundled product enhancements greater than the cost to the manufacturer of providing them. And the customer must be willing to pay for them.

Bundling decisions may be based on segmentation. Automobiles provide a good illustration. A particular model may come in several treatments ranging from a plain basic unit to a luxury style. Each treatment represents a distinct price point and has its own name designation:

- The basic model for the price-conscious shopper might feature vinyl upholstery, a four-cylinder engine, standard three-speed transmission, and an AM/FM radio.
- The next model might have cloth upholstery, an optional six-cylinder engine, four-speed transmission, AM/FM cassette player stereo system, rear window defroster, and special trim and wheels. This model might be aimed at a younger consumer, perhaps with a family with multiple drivers, who use the car mostly for local errands and trips.
- The top-of-the-line model might include as standard features a six-cylinder with a V-8 option, leather upholstery, AM/FM cassette and CD player stereo, four-speed automatic transmission, electric windows and seat adjustments, automatic door locks, and heated seats. The target market for this model would be a high-income older customer who uses the vehicle for longer trips.

Thus, there are distinct product offerings for distinct market segments with different price elasticities and different needs and wants.

For many products, the customer has the option of buying only the base product and then shopping for a better deal on the accessories, additional features, and services that are being offered as part of the bundled product. For example, the purchaser of a 35-millimeter camera has the choice of buying a complete kit or just the camera body. The kit might include a basic 50-millimeter lens, a flash attachment, and a carrying case. The kit will be priced at less than the prices of the individual items if purchased separately. However, the informed buyer may know that it is possible to buy the camera body separately and add lenses, a flash attachment, a carrying case, and other accessories of equal or better quality made by specialist manufacturers and sold at even lower prices than the bundled price of the brand-name camera manufacturer. These so-called after-market manufacturers are found in many industries from automobiles, cameras, computers, and diesel engines to elevators, machine tools, tractors, and plasma torches.

Any manufacturer who sells a product system is likely to face aggressive, intelligent price competition from "unbundlers," niche marketers who offer excellent substitutes for some part of the total product system at lower prices. It is likely that the marketing efforts of the systems marketers have educated customers over time to become sophisticated and confident enough in their product knowledge and use to make sound judgments of value. This creates the opportunity for the unbundler. Very often, the manufacturer of the bundled product system is a large corporation with layers of bureaucracy and administrative overhead costs that have to be covered by its pricing. How can IBM hope to compete with a specialty printer manufacturer?

The marketer who sells a bundled product offering usually must also make a significant expenditure for marketing communications to convey the concept of value designed into the product bundle. The luxury car model, the camera kit, the integrated computer system, the custom-built fire truck, must be promoted based on the value of the additional cost features. Brand image becomes a key part of the value proposition, and the total product concept must be developed in the customer's mind because, even though it is inherent in the bundle of specific product features and services, it may not be obvious from mere visual inspection.

Bundling makes sense economically and strategically when there are distinct market segments that need and value the performance provided by the bundled features. Bundling can be the key to product differentiation and augmentation. If customers come to expect the bundled product, this may make it more difficult for competitors to enter the market with a lower-price unbundled product. Or, if the real value is not there or has not been promoted adequately, it may *create* the opportunity for low-cost niche players to enter the market with one or more components of the total system.

One sophisticated economic model of the bundling decision concluded that bundling could be more profitable than selling unbundled components under the following conditions:

1. When profit margins can be maintained on the bundled components at levels greater than on the individual components.
2. When the firm's components in the bundled system are clearly superior to those of competitors.
3. When there are not distinct market segments that prefer to purchase components and construct their own systems, currently using competitors' components.

4. When the market is not growing significantly (which means that unbundling would merely substitute lower margin component sales for bundled systems sales instead of attracting new customers).[9]

As products mature, however, unbundling probably becomes increasingly common. Product knowledge becomes more generally shared and less proprietary, customers become more familiar with the technology, the industry converges on a common technical standard, and specialized components manufacturers with lower costs pursue increasingly small market niches. Customers become more knowledgeable and more confident as well as less willing to pay extra for service and unnecessary product features.

In some industries, the bundling function is typically performed by a distributor. In process control instrumentation, for example, a distributor commonly designs a system for a customer using components from several manufacturers. A similar situation is found in data-processing systems, with the well-known VARs (value-added resellers) who cater to particular end-user markets and assemble specialized hardware and software from multiple sources to fit the needs of these niche markets. Medical systems also are frequently sold through VARs. If distributors usually perform the bundling function, it might be unwise for the manufacturer to offer a bundled product unless it is marketed directly to end users rather than through distributors.

Information as Part of the Product Offering

In a general sense, every product is a bundle of information in that it contains the potential to solve a problem. You buy toothpaste for example based on your knowledge that toothpaste has the ability to clean your teeth, improve the health of oral tissues, prevent cavities, reduce halitosis, and so on. You cannot directly observe any of these benefits as an immediate result of using the toothpaste, but you are satisfied with the promise and potential of the product to produce these benefits. That information is what you are purchasing, not the benefits directly.

More specifically, many products are themselves pure information. The airline travel guide, the computer network, the cable television news service, and all financial services are pure information. As a product, information is very different from other products. Most products become less valuable as you use them. Many information products, such as telephone systems or computer networks, become more valuable the more users they have. The seller of an information product gives up nothing, as he or she still has the information (e.g., the airline schedules) even after selling it (e.g., to the travel advisor).[10]

Aided by the tremendous advances in information technology, more and more physical products contain an information component. The instrument panel of your new automobile may allow you to display such digital information as outside air temperature, speed, miles per gallon, miles since last stop, radio frequency tuned to, and whether any doors are not shut properly. Included with the owner's information is an 800 number to call for roadside emergency service, a list of all dealers in the United States and Canada (and perhaps Europe, if you purchased the car for European delivery). On the car are several microprocessors continuously monitoring the performance of all systems including ignition, fuel, lights, brakes, cooling, and ventilation. Information is a critically important part of the automotive product offering.

In industrial markets, information as part of the product offering is even more dramatically important. Customers of a major national chemical distributor chain have instant access via satellite hookup and computer terminals at their places of business to place orders, seek technical advice, check on the status of an order, schedule delivery, check on inventory levels and availabilities, or obtain information about hazardous materials and their handling.

Electronic data interchange (EDI) and computer-based order-entry systems are very common, linking customers to their vendors as part of a just-in-time inventory system. Especially for industrial raw materials, components, and subassemblies where technical product features offer minimal opportunity for differentiation, the only effective competitive weapon is skillful use of a superior information ability to enhance the relationship with the customer.

Even the most "low tech" company today must consider specifically the quality of the information component of its product offering to develop a complete concept of value for the customer. In many industries (e.g., hospital supplies, airlines, railroads, banking, drug wholesaling, snack foods, and credit cards), the fundamental key success factors in the business have been redefined around information technology and its capabilities. The value proposition is dominated by the information component of the product offering.[11]

COMMUNICATING VALUE TO THE TARGET MARKET

The value proposition must be communicated to the target market. Just as the product offering is tailored to the needs and requirements of the target market, so must the communication mix be responsive to the information requirements of the target customers and their characteristic reliance on various means and media of communication. Market targeting defines the audiences that communications must reach. Positioning defines the product concept and the benefits to be presented, explained, and developed by the marketing communication program. Positioning also implicitly defines "the enemy," that set of competitive product offerings and substitutes over which the company's product offering must achieve superiority in the perceptions and preferences of the target customer.

Managing Customer Expectations: Why Volvo's Advertising Backfired

Customer expectations are the standard against which the customer evaluates the product offering. Those expectations are developed in response to the customer's exposure to experiences and communications from many sources. A major objective of the marketer's communication program is to develop an expectation that its product will deliver superior value. This can be a two-edged sword.

Overpromising obviously can cause problems by creating expectations that cannot be met. Carefully defining the target market is the first step to avoiding overpromising. The market that is sought must in fact have needs and wants that are consistent with the company's ability to deliver superior value. Superior performance for one market segment may not be satisfactory for another. It is critically important that selling messages actually get delivered to the intended audience.

The second step in avoiding overpromising is to shun creative concepts with the potential to produce messages that result in unreasonable expectations. For many product categories, especially consumer packaged goods, it is quite common to rely on good old-fashioned boasting to help sell the product. Words like "super," "best," "world-class," "fantastic," and "beautiful" are used routinely to describe otherwise mundane products. Consumers are used to hearing this language and can put it into proper context. Such words do not imply specific claims about product performance, and there is no need to provide scientific evidence to support such boastful claims.

The problem of creative concepts that produce unreasonable expectations can be illustrated by the experience of Volvo automobiles in the 1970s in the U.S. market. Volvos were designed with an emphasis on safety and durability, supported by one of the best safety engineering programs in the world. Inspection of automobile registration data showed that 9 out of 10 Volvos registered in the United States in the past 11 years were still on the road. While this sounds remarkably good, it is in fact a claim that could be made for any brand. Volvo preempted the claim. This fact became the central theme of a major advertising campaign, directed at well-educated consumers with above-average incomes. The results were excellent as U.S. sales of Volvos more than doubled in a few years.

Like any car, however, most Volvos developed minor problems of wear and tear after years of heavy use, and indeed there was some evidence that Volvo owners really treated their cars as workhorses. Volvo owners had very high expectations for the durability and trouble-free operation of their cars, due in no small part to the advertising for the brand. Over time, many Volvo owners became dissatisfied and often complained loudly, through negative word-of-mouth comments to friends and acquaintances and even to consumer protection advocates and agencies. Volvo buyers had expected their cars to last forever. When they didn't, they were angry. The advertising program for Volvos was changed to an emphasis on the sensible nature of the person who bought a Volvo and the safety features built into the car.

Customer expectations are based on many sources of information other than direct communications from the marketer. Most important, of course, is the customer's prior experience with this and competitive product offerings. Repeat purchases of the same brand are based on strong expectations for continued superior performance. Every brand name is a promise. It stands for something in the prospective customer's mind.

Most products deliver performance that will be evaluated on multiple dimensions. Automobile and truck tires, for example, are expected to produce a comfortable ride, good gas mileage, safe stopping, sure gripping when cornering, easy steering, traction on wet highways, low road noise, and long life in terms of miles driven. Unfortunately, these features represent technical tradeoffs and no tire design can maximize more than a few of these parameters. If you want high mileage, you probably have to settle for a rougher ride and reduced traction in rain and snow. Seldom does the average consumer understand these tradeoffs. The person who buys a tire based on its claim of high mileage is likely also to expect superior performance on virtually all the other dimensions and is likely to be disappointed with the car's handling performance when driven aggressively.

Most industrial products, especially complex product systems, present a great challenge to create reasonable expectations. It is not likely that mass communications such as media advertising can do more than a small part of the job. Knowledgeable, skilled sales representatives must be assigned to target customers and they must be supported with carefully developed sales presentations and literature. Technical product information must be complete and easy to understand, and must specify the use conditions for which the product is, and is not, designed. This is a key step in managing customer expectations and a critical part of the equation of customer satisfaction.

Developing Value through Communication

While the value of the product offering must be inherent in the product itself, communication can nonetheless convey and enhance that value. For consumer goods and services, the principal communication methodology may be media advertising. For industrial products and services, customers may rely on the sales representatives, dealer personnel, and semitechnical printed materials of all kinds. As noted earlier, for many products and services, people who are part of the selling, delivery, installation, and repair process exert a major influence on the definition of value. They are part of the product offering.

Marketing communications that build brand equity increase the value of the brand for the consumer. When you receive a Cross pen and pencil set as a business gift, it has special value because of the brand name, which has acquired that value over the years, not just through its excellent design and materials but also from the advertising investments of the A. T. Cross Company promoting the product's durability, permanence, lifetime guarantee, and overall quality. The Kwik-Klik pen you received from another business acquaintance doesn't carry the same panache even though it writes just as well.

Brand equity is the return on investment in communications designed to enhance the value of the brand. Within marketing science, there is an ongoing debate about the relative profitability of advertising versus sales promotion expenditures. The latter are usually temporary price inducements of one form or another (coupons, trade discounts, offers of "free" merchandise, etc.) intended to produce incremental sales in the short term. It has been argued that these tend to diminish the value of the brand over time by creating customer expectations for lower prices. There is also the related issue of the extent to which consumers equate high quality with high price, using price as a key index of quality in the absence of clear visual and other product cues.

Because advertising is intended to produce positive effects on brand sales over the long term, usually a period of several years, it is much more difficult to measure the effects of advertising on sales and profitability. In a business climate that emphasizes short-term measures of business performance, advertising and other long-term marketing expenditures have been under pressure. There remains a basic research question whether advertising (and other forms of marketing communication designed to produce long-term results) really can enhance brand value as perceived by the customer and can build brand equity as measured by sales and profitability over multiple business periods.

While we cannot even begin to review this large and complex body of research here, we can cite a recent study that provides some evidence in support of the ability of marketing communications to build brand value for both customers and marketers. Boulding, Lee, and Staelin built a model of product differentiation and brand equity and estimated the effects of marketing communication using the PIMS database for consumer products. Their analysis looked at the combined effects of expenditures for advertising, sales force, and promotional activities on both durable and nondurable consumer products. They conceived product differentiation as an alternative to price competition (price cutting) and measured the effects of communication in terms of changes in consumer sensitivity to price differences. As expected, they found that expenditures for advertising and sales force activity *reduced* the consumer's sensitivity to price, while sales promotion *increased* it. From the perspective of the firm, advertising and personal selling expenditures reduce its vulnerability to price competition while sales promotion increases it.[12]

Obviously, it is assumed that the company's advertising and personal selling messages do not stress price competition. The low-price competitor that spends millions promoting low prices will undoubtedly increase the customer's sensitivity to price, not just for its specific products but for the whole product category.

The research does support the conclusion that marketers who stress product benefits for the consumer through advertising and personal selling can build brand equity through product differentiation that reduces its sensitivity to price competition. This is one more piece of evidence in favor of the value-delivery concept of strategy.

SUMMARY

Market segmentation, targeting, and positioning are the essential activities in developing a focused business strategy built around the firm's distinctive competence and its ability to deliver superior value to a well-defined set of prospective customers. Customers define the business by demanding that it commit its resources to doing certain things extremely well. Thus, selection of customers (not products) is *the* critical strategic choice for the firm. A critical function of the market targeting and positioning decision is to define those market segments where the firm elects *not* to compete.

Focused marketing, the hallmark of the marketing concept, means turning away certain potential customers and orders. For most managers, that is an extremely difficult decision, and in many firms, even whole industries, the sales concept still dominates. Under the sales concept, sales volume is the key to profitability and every customer is a good customer, every order a good order. The result is an operation loaded with barely profitable business.

Intelligent market segmentation, targeting, and positioning lead to the development of a value proposition, a product offering, and a communication strategy designed to deliver superior value to customers. These attributes assure that the product offering, including product features, service enhancements, and supporting communications, is complete. A major challenge of the market targeting process is to understand the complex systems of market transactions, marketing channels, and product delivery and product use systems within which the product offering will be developed and used. The problem is to find a real "customer," a person or organization that will value the product and will be willing and able to pay for it. We illustrated the problem with an example (blood collection and processing) where the beneficiaries of the technology were not the potential customers and the challenge was to *create* a customer that could derive economic benefit from the technology.

The markets of the 1990s are increasingly characterized by long-term relationships and temporary alliances among actors in the market system. Customers, suppliers, competitors, resellers, and manufacturers exist in evolving, interdependent relationships where distinct roles get blurred and where no firm performs more than a few specialized activities in the complex value chain. Developing a product offering that delivers superior value to end-user customers becomes an extremely complicated set of interdependent, interorganizational activities and relationships. Chapters 5 and 6 will examine this revolutionary development and the role of marketing within these new organizational arrangements and structures. In the old marketing concept, marketing was a management function within the firm. In the new marketing concept, marketing becomes a set of activities spanning the boundaries of many organizations.

5 RELATIONSHIP MARKETING

Buying and selling is essentially anti-social.

Edward Bellamy
Looking Backward, 2000-1887 (1888)

Until recently, the field of marketing was centered around the core concept of a market-based transaction. Reflecting its origins in economics, the study of marketing was concerned with the functions necessary to execute a transaction—sellers seeking buyers and buyers seeking sellers through processes of market information, providing assortments of merchandise, holding inventory, buying, selling, risk taking, transporting, providing credit, and so on. The marketing process was seen as ending when the sale occurred, when title to the goods transferred from producer (or reseller) to consumer. The sale was the objective and the end result of marketing effort.

Under the new marketing concept, the focus has shifted from one-time transactions to ongoing relationships. The sale is not the end of the marketing process but the beginning of a relationship in which buyer and seller become interdependent. The product or service enters the customer's use system, and the customer becomes a source of both financial support and ongoing requirements for the business. The purpose of marketing is not to make the sale; the purpose is to gain a customer.

Viewing the marketing process as one of building relationships is a logical outcome of the notion that every business is a service business.

When products are seen as bundles of benefits, when service becomes the critical component of the product offering, it is inevitable that we must focus on the ongoing relationship between the company and its customers. It is also logically consistent with the proposition that quality is defined by the extent to which the product or service, as it is used over time, meets or exceeds customer expectations.

In this chapter, we will look carefully at the evolution of marketing from a focus on transactions to an emphasis on long-term relationships and strategic buyer-seller partnerships. It will be helpful to take into account the specific differences between consumer products, including services, packaged goods, and durables, and industrial products and services. In consumer marketing, the relationship is with individuals; in industrial marketing it is with organizations, a fundamental difference. We will examine the role of information technology as a facilitator of relationship marketing and how it is redefining the key success factors in many industries. We will also consider how the nature of the marketing and selling process changes with relationship marketing. In Chapter 6, we will broaden our analysis to include all types of strategic alliances, not just those between buyers and sellers, and we will then consider how the role of marketing changes as companies shift their organizations from hierarchical structures to flexible networks of multiple alliances and strategic relationships.

THE ECONOMIST'S MARKETPLACE: TRANSACTIONS

The Pure Transaction

A pure transaction, the core concept with which this analysis begins, is a very rare bird. It is possible to describe one, however, even without ever seeing one. It is found frequently in the artificial world of the microeconomic paradigm, the basis of the economist's theory of the firm.

A pure transaction occurs in a perfect market, defined as one with a very large number of competing sellers, each selling an undifferentiated product, and a set of buyers who have perfect information about all product offerings, including prices. Consumer preferences are given, exogenous to the process. In this perfect market, no seller can influence the desires of any buyer. The only variable is price, and the buyer is a profit- or utility-maximizer, seeking the lowest price. Each transaction is a completely independent event, not influenced by consideration of past or future transactions. All that matters is price.

Every marketing manager (more generally, every businessperson) is dedicated to destroying every one of the economist's assumptions. The manager wants to create consumer preference, through product differentiation and marketing communications, for a product offering for which the consumer is willing to pay a higher price. Each competitor has attempted to position itself carefully in a segmented market where it has a virtual monopoly in its chosen market niche. Most markets consist of only a few sellers, each of which is watched carefully and responded to by the others. Consumers know these competitors, interact with them over a long period of time, and continually modify their buying preferences. Each firm's pricing actions and total product offering are monitored by the others, and competitors' actions directly influence their pricing, product, and promotion decisions.

In the pure version of the microeconomic paradigm, there is no product differentiation, no customer loyalty, no brand equity, no repeat purchase, no recourse to the seller, no service, no credit, and no commitment to future transactions. There is also no trust. Each party assumes the other is motivated by greed and self-interest and seeks to maximize only its own welfare in the transaction. The relationship is adversarial, mediated only by the price mechanism of the marketplace. *Caveat emptor! Caveat venditor!*

Perhaps the best example of a pure transaction in the real world is the purchase of agricultural commodity futures. Here the buyer buys only a contract, not the product itself. But even here, the buyer is likely to know personally the broker he or she does business with, and they are likely to have an ongoing business relationship.

The closest the average consumer comes to a pure transaction might be the purchase of unbranded gasoline at a self-service pump in a town the person has never visited before and to which he or she never expects to return, paid for by cash inserted through a slot in a bulletproof glass window in a kiosk located between the pumps. (You may have seen this place on one of your trips.) Here there is no brand recognition, no product differentiation, no familiar face, no credit card, no chance that the buyer will be back in the store. There is no possibility of a relationship.

Even here, however, the real-world consumer might have preferred a familiar brand name, a friendly clerk, some personal service at the gas pump, a rest room, a free cup of coffee in the store, and the opportunity to use a credit card. There is usually comfort and trust, albeit of a modest type, in a brand name, and the promise of a bit more customer satisfaction in a differentiated product, tailored to the needs of the individual.

The Sale as a Conquest

Pure transactions are rare and yet much of marketing thought and practice has been based on a transaction kind of mentality where the sale is a conquest and the relationship is adversarial. In the traditional view of marketing, the focus is on winning the next sale, not the last one. This is consistent with the old sales concept, not the new marketing concept. Under the sales concept, it is the sale that is important, not the customer. Marketers have characteristically devoted more energy and more promotional dollars to creating the next sale than to satisfying the customer they already have.

It is also fair to say that much industrial purchasing has been based on a similar set of assumptions. Purchasing managers have usually sought the lowest price by finding a large number of vendors who will offer a similar product, as undifferentiated as possible by means of concise purchase specifications. Industrial buying was typically adversarial and in many cases impersonal. In rigorously controlled purchasing procedures, as found for example in government procurement, all transactions were conducted based on a sealed bidding process and any attempt at personal influence was considered potentially unethical. Buying and selling were antisocial behavior, guided by the rules of the impersonal marketplace.

While the assumptions of the microeconomic profit-maximization model have served the field of economic theory well and produced an amazingly robust, rigorous analysis, they are increasingly less helpful as guidelines for the conduct of business. The narrow focus on transactions, on the sale as a conquest rather than on the customer as a long-term business asset, is potentially fatal.[1]

REPEATED TRANSACTIONS: CREATING A MORE ADVANCED MARKETPLACE

Differentiating Transactions

Most transactions occur as part of a stream, and because of their antecedents in prior transactions and consequences for future transactions, these repeated transactions are not pure and do not meet the assumptions of the economist's model. For any consumer or industrial purchase, there is almost always some prior knowledge of the characteristics that differentiate products and vendors, some previous contact, some information about competing products including their prices, and some possibility of future transactions between the buyer and the seller. Products are usually identified by their brand names or the names of their companies. Personal services are differentiated, by definition, by the personal characteristics of the service providers themselves—doctors, accountants, lawyers, insurance agents—even when they are closely controlled by regulatory requirements. Differentiation creates preferences, and preferences lead to repeated transactions.

Simple convenience is another cause of repeat purchasing. Customers who have processed available information and found an acceptable product offering may have little incentive to spend the time and energy required to evaluate alternatives. Increasingly, consumers find that time is their scarcest resource and saving time is a major motivator in the purchase decision process. It is easier, as well as reassuring, to buy a familiar brand and to shop in a convenient store. Familiarity is the first step away from the pure, stand-alone transaction toward a buyer-seller relationship.

Repeated transactions are common in the marketing of consumer packaged goods. Marketing effort is devoted toward differentiating products, building brand awareness, and creating brand preference and loyal customers. While for most consumer goods there is no direct personal contact between the buyer and the seller, no meaningful ongoing relationship, the presence of brand preference, customer loyalty, and repeat purchases shows that buyer and seller have progressed beyond the assumptions of the economist's model and the pure transaction.

With repeated transactions, a critical element enters the equation—*trust*. The familiarity of a brand name or a salesperson contains promise of consistent product and service performance, of a purchase experience that will meet expectations. Con- creatures of habit because of this; we have our favorite soft drink, snack food, convenience store, cash machine, and newspaper because we trust them.

The Value of Repeat Business

Repeat purchases and loyal customers are the main drivers of profitability for most businesses. It costs much less to service an existing customer than to create a new one. Studies suggest that to acquire a new customer requires spending about five times more than is needed to keep an old customer's loyalty.[2] Brand equity and loyal customers are valuable business assets representing the investment of large amounts of marketing dollars and effort. When former customers are lost, that investment goes with them. It isn't just the next sale that is lost; it is the profit on the stream of transactions that could have been expected if that customer had been satisfied.

An ongoing relationship with a loyal customer is valuable in several ways:

- There is the revenue and profit margin from the future sales of this product. The repeat customer may be willing to pay somewhat of a price premium and may need less price inducement such as special promotions, a point touched on in Chapter 4.
- There is the potential for additional revenue and profit margin from selling other products to the same customer. This is reflected in the concept of brand equity and the possibility of brand extensions to related products.
- There is the positive word-of-mouth generated by the satisfied customer and the sales generated from other customers as a result.[3]

For the large proportion of repeated transactions, however, there is no real *personal* relationship between the buyer and the manufacturer, although there may be some minimal amount of personal contact at the retail point of sale. Thus we do not characterize a series of transactions as a relationship. It is a basic fact of most consumer goods marketing that the specific identity of the customer is not known to the marketer, which disqualifies the stream of transactions with that buyer as a true relationship. You can't have a relationship with someone you don't know.

Furthermore, buyers of frequently purchased packaged goods don't worry about the welfare of the marketer to any great extent; they place virtually no value on the relationship with the manufacturer of the brand. Familiarity and repeated transactions stop short of being a real relationship.

ESTABLISHING BUYER-SELLER RELATIONSHIPS

A relationship is characterized by a stronger connection, usually personal in nature, that is ongoing and has multiple dimensions. In marketing, it means among other things that the buyer is known to the seller by name, that the buyer's geographic location and other identifying characteristics are known, and that the seller can communicate directly with the buyer. These are the essential characteristics of *addressability* at the core of marketing relationships. They are of sufficient duration to be referred to as *long-term* relationships, to differentiate them further from transactions. Providers of telephone service and banking services, for example, have always been involved in relationship marketing. They know the names and addresses of their customers, and maintain a record of their transactions over a long time period.

A relationship also implies a degree of interdependence as well as trust. The interdependence consists in part of the expectation of a string of future transactions as well as a degree of dependence on the other for providing resources (income for the seller, products and services for the customer) that are necessary for the ongoing operations of both. Each party to the relationship is specifically interested in ensuring the survival and welfare of the other.

Linked Operations and Interdependence between Customer and Seller

The two operations—those of the customer and those of the seller—become linked. This is true even at the household level. In fact, thinking of the household as a production system reveals some interesting marketing insights. In some sense, each household has the option of electing to produce virtually every purchased product or service themselves. While this is a little far-fetched in the age of supermarkets, cash machines, shopping malls, telecommunications, open-heart surgery, and two-income families, it is sometimes helpful to think of how consumers could produce the product or service we are selling. They can bake bread instead of buying it. They can write a letter or walk to visit their neighbors rather than use the telephone. They can pay cash rather than use credit cards. They can assume the risk of loss of income rather than pay for disability insurance.

It is also important to remember that every product or service must fit into the buyer's production system. If the customer buys a coffeemaker, it will have to fit into a system of equipment, kitchen space, and supplies for preparing food. As a timesaving device, the quality of the coffee brewed may be less important than the ease with which it can be filled, operated, cleaned, and stored as part of the morning routine in preparation for going to work. The alternative for the consumer may not be to purchase another type or brand of coffeemaker but rather to move the entire production system outside the home and purchase breakfast at McDonald's on the way to the office.

Relationships Create Expectations

In the world of relationship marketing, buyer and seller become interdependent. Relationships entail mutual expectations and obligations. You expect to be able to go to the local grocery store and find the fresh milk your children need, just as the store stocks it on the expectation that you will come in to buy it. That same storekeeper may set aside a copy of the Sunday *New York Times* for you, which you then have an obligation to pick up.

You may have a contract for the delivery of fuel oil to your home or your business. In both locations, you depend on the oil distributor for the flow of a material that is essential to your welfare. You may have paid in advance for the heating season's oil supply at a more favorable price. The distributor offered this discount to you in return for the certainty that advanced oil commitments to the distributor's suppliers, necessary for an assured supply during the winter months, would find a market.

Your operations and those of your grocer and your fuel distributor are linked and interdependent. They represent a relationship rather than a series of transactions because you are known by name, address, purchasing habits, and usage patterns. Each party has specific expectations for the other, and there are mutual obligations to buy and to sell.

Consumer durables represent a fertile ground for relationship marketing. If the product carries a warranty and the buyer registers a purchase with the manufacturer, the basis for a marketing relationship has been established. It is still remarkable, however, how few companies who request this information from customers use it wisely to build an ongoing relationship with the new purchaser. While appliance manufacturers routinely gather information about their customers, few of them use the information to build a relationship that could be the basis for future sales, even though a customer represents the potential for sales of an estimated $3,000 over a 20-year period.

Automobile manufacturers do a somewhat better job, perhaps because the value of a loyal customer has been estimated to be $150,000 over the customer's lifetime.[4] The auto manufacturers maintain a database with the names of every person who has purchased a new car, their address, the complete description and specifications of the vehicle that was purchased, and other information about the transaction and the buyer. The customer subsequently receives verification of the terms of the warranty, information about other product and service offerings, surveys of customer satisfaction with the dealer and the vehicle, follow-up on subsequent service visits and warranty claims, and notifications of product recalls if there are problems. Mailings to customers to follow up on service encounters and to promote additional sales of service and products frequently go to the customer over the dealer's signature. Customers expect to be supported with information and service by the manufacturer and the dealer as long as they own the car.

In industrial marketing and in the marketing of most personal services, especially financial services, relationship marketing is much more common than in consumer marketing. Personal service relationships are built on the expectation of integrity, professional competence and, usually, confidentiality in the relationship. Often, government and professional organizations set standards and monitor performance in ways that ensure maintenance of those standards of integrity, competence, and trust. The expectations are an essential feature of the relationship.

The industrial buyer-seller relationship entails a complex set of mutual expectations. Industrial customers become dependent on the vendor for the flow of materials and services into their operation. They need to know the vendor is a stable business that can provide acceptable products and services over the contract period. Customers also need to know whom to contact in the event of a problem with delivery, product performance, or billing and whether the vendor can react quickly if customer requirements change. The vendor, in turn, becomes dependent on each customer's taking the agreed-to volume (often a significant percentage of total plant capacity) and paying for it as promised. They are highly interdependent.

Negotiation as Part of the Relationship

In industrial marketing and in a good portion of consumer durables marketing, even when the marketer has a "list price," terms and conditions are agreed to by both parties based on negotiation. Prices for professional services, such as management consulting, accounting, and advertising creative services, are usually based on negotiations.

This is a critical difference from transaction-based marketing. In a transaction, prices are set in the market and are not subject to negotiation. In relationship marketing, especially in industrial markets, prices are set by a negotiation process that is part of the relationship. Price is determined by the process, not by the market alone, although the range of pricing alternatives is influenced by the competitive forces of the marketplace. The difference is critical to understanding relationship marketing: Price is an outcome of a negotiation process inherent in the relationship. Price is usually all wrapped up in a set of terms and conditions that are part of the total product offering. Price is part of the product offering.

The Adversarial Nature of Buyer-Seller Relationships

Even in the long-term buyer-seller relationship, however, both parties still traditionally view the relationship as essentially adversarial. Price negotiations often expose the adversarial nature of the buyer-seller relationship. There are many illustrations in both consumer and industrial marketing.

The automobile purchaser expects to have to bargain hard for a favorable price, and many customers probably regard the whole buying process as adversarial and distasteful. Only recently have some companies, especially Saturn, begun to address the selling process as part of the product offering. With a focus on the quality of the relationship with the customer, the company has encouraged dealers to follow a policy of adherence to low list prices and to avoid the high-pressure sales tactics that characterize the industry.

In industrial marketing, the tough-as-nails purchasing agent is still a folk hero in many companies, and industrial sales representatives approach the selling situation as a jousting match. From the perspective of the 1990s, the shortsightedness of a focus on price is now evident. In the days before the quality movement had become a driving force, good purchasing practice was defined as developing tight specifications and finding several vendors who were willing to bid, thus assuring that the procurement could be based on low price. It was common for manufacturers to have multiple vendors for every item, on the assumption (often not warranted) that their products were interchangeable. The lowest price bidder was awarded the largest portion of the company's requirements, with other vendors receiving smaller orders to keep them interested as potential bidders and to keep price pressure on the main supplier. Multiple vendors also provided some insurance against an unforeseen interruption in supply due to equipment failures, strikes, natural disasters, and so on.

Even though these business dealings meet the definition of a relationship, they were managed by the rules of the transaction. Most of the important information about a vendor's product offering was contained in the price, and the objective was to find the lowest available price. The result was often poor quality, poor service, production problems associated with changing vendors frequently, interruption in supply, and excessive inventories throughout the system. Low price did not always mean lowest total cost.

In this purchasing environment, the marketing and selling process was equally adversarial. Customers were given only the information they demanded, which was usually an attempt to justify the price being quoted. The supplier treated its manufacturing process and product technology as proprietary information. Any necessary negotiations to determine the terms and conditions of transactions were conducted on a "Win/Lose" basis. If the buyer gained something, the seller lost something in return, often in the form of profit margin.

Changing Your Attitude toward Customers—Viewing Them as Partners

Before discussing the operating requirements for relationship marketing, it is important to point out that this sales process is fundamentally a question of attitude. The customer isn't the enemy; he or she is a business partner. Under the new marketing concept, the company is expected to put the customer first, in all decisions, always. That means that the customer comes before the product. It also means putting the customer ahead of the sale. In fact, when compared with the company's capabilities, putting the customer first may require forgoing the sale. Some customer's requirements may be met only by compromising the firm's ability to satisfy other customers. Which customers come first? Those with which the firm has an ongoing relationship.

Under the new marketing concept, the relationship cannot be adversarial. It must be one of interdependence, trust, cooperation, and partnership. A direct implication of this requirement is that the company must choose its customers carefully. Not all potential customers are candidates for a long-term relationship, however. What can a relationship-oriented marketer do about a customer who is still committed to the old adversarial view of the world?

Good and Bad Customers

In relationship marketing, there are good and bad customers. The good customers are those who value what the company does well, who are attracted by its value proposition, who value the relationship they have with the company as an asset in their own business, and who are willing to pay fairly for the resources the company commits to solving their problems. The marketer has two potentially attractive options for those customers who do not value a long-term relationship. One is to do business, on a relationship basis, only with "good" customers. This may require some customer education, selling the basic value proposition including the value of the long-term relationship to the customer. The benefits of doing business on a relationship basis may not be obvious to the customer who has always treated the sale as a one-time transaction.

The other option is to develop a differentiated marketing strategy for distinct market segments, defined by the customer's preference for transactions or varying degrees of long-term relationship. A company that can learn how to deal profitably with customers who prefer a straightforward transactions orientation will find they are not necessarily bad customers. We will return to this idea shortly.

Implementing Relationship Marketing

For the industrial marketer, long-term relationships have several operational implications. The sale, the signing of the order, is just the beginning of the relationship. The buyer will probably issue multiple purchase orders over a period of months or years. There will probably be a contract spelling out the terms, conditions, and obligations of both parties although this will be subject to further modification as the relationship evolves. If the contract covers the purchase of a tangible product, a service bundle will also be required as part of the total product offering.

The buyer and the seller will engage in joint forecasting to assist in production planning. There will be several linkages between the buying and selling organizations at multiple management levels. For example, the two companies' chief executive officers may be involved in executing the final contract. The seller's applications engineers may interact with the customer's production engineering and product developers. The sales representative may have several contacts in purchasing, operations, and engineering. The seller's production supervisor and distribution manager may have regular contacts with the customer's production managers. The customer is purchasing not just the product but the total problem-solving capability of the vendor organization. All these contacts and activities must be coordinated and managed. The relationship will involve significant costs for both executing the contract, including selling and negotiating costs, and administering the ongoing relationship, including costs of coordination, monitoring, and controlling performance under the contract.

This process is far removed from the pure transaction. Pure transactions are very rare, although they are the basis for a view of marketing that focuses on the individual sale and sees it as a conquest of the customer. Most transactions occur as part of a stream of transactions, in which the sale is still a conquest, but the customer deals with the supplier based on familiarity, some preference, and a modest amount of trust. In repeated transactions, however, the identity of the customer is not known to the seller and the two parties still have no real relationship.

A buyer-seller relationship develops when the name and characteristics of the customer, including the history of transactions, are known to the marketer. The marketer can direct communications at specific individuals rather than at anonymous consumers in the mass market. Buyer-seller relationships involve mutual expectations and obligations and a degree of interdependence. And yet, even here, the relationship remains essentially adversarial, guiding by the transaction-oriented rules of the competitive marketplace.

True relationship marketing requires a fundamental shift in attitude, toward viewing the customer as a partner, a business asset to be managed for long-term profitability. The sale isn't a conquest and it isn't the end of the marketing process. It is the beginning of a relationship with the customer. The focus must be on the relationship, not the individual sale.

Here the road divides. Relationship marketing takes two different forms and directions, although the roads have some similar characteristics so exploring one will help us navigate the other. One road—the consumer marketing road—becomes a superhighway built on information technology. The other, much broader, road—the industrial marketing turnpike—accommodates the large, complex business-to-business relationships exemplified by just-in-time supply systems. We will first make a quick trip down the consumer marketing road; then we will come back to the intersection and explore the industrial marketing road. Both roads are equally important to understanding the fundamental changes that have occurred in the nature and scope of all marketing activities under the new marketing concept.

In both cases, information technology is an important facilitator. We will examine the potential of this technology in the context of consumer marketing and the practice of "interactive marketing." Although that discussion will be about the marketing of consumer goods and services, a large segment of industrial distribution is also being influenced and changed by this important development.

INTERACTIVE MARKETING: TREATING EACH CUSTOMER AS AN INDIVIDUAL

For the consumer marketer and the marketer of services, a commitment to relationship marketing is essentially a commitment to establish a customer database for developing and implementing all phases of marketing strategy, including product, pricing, and promotion decisions. There is a concomitant requirement for investment in an information system, including supporting technology. The winners in the consumer marketing wars of the 1990s will be those manufacturers, distributors, and retailers who make the necessary investments in information technology.

Such technology is redefining the key success factors in most businesses and has created a revolution by shifting the orientation from production efficiency back to customer needs. Because it permits direct, personalized communication with the individual customer, "high tech" becomes "high touch." It draws the customer closer to the company, builds a relationship, and reduces the probability that the customer will switch to a competitor. Companies in the future will see their best profit opportunities in exploiting their customer base, selling more products and services to their existing customers rather than trying to find new customers for their existing products.[5] The combination of customer loyalty and the large investment required to develop the necessary information capability can also provide an effective barrier to competitive entry.

In interactive marketing, each customer has a record in the database with information about the customer's personal characteristics, media usage patterns, and purchase history. The content of the data file will obviously depend on the specific needs of the marketer and the type of business involved. The fundamental shift is from mass marketing to individual marketing, from treating the unknown customers as anonymous units in the marketplace to treating them as individuals with unique needs, preferences, and requirements, and as unique business opportunities.

Building a Profile of Each Customer

This brings us back to the fundamental importance of *addressability*. Each customer becomes known as a specific individual at the first contact with the marketer. She might respond to an advertisement in a newspaper or magazine, dial an 800 number, or receive a personal call from a sales representative. She might join a buyer's club at her local supermarket or open an account with a bank, a car rental company, or a credit card company.

At that first contact, the marketer will request certain information, depending on the nature of the business, legal and credit requirements, and so on. That information will include at least name, address, and telephone number, and may identify type of residence, place of employment, age, education, income, marital and family status, and more. She may also be asked to indicate which magazines, newspapers, and other media she relies on, whether she likes to receive promotional offers such as cents-off coupons, and which recreational activities she enjoys. All of this gets entered into the database and becomes the basis for directing specific communications and product offerings at that particular consumer.

The database notes each contact with the customer. The company will know which communications have been sent and can subsequently judge whether they were effective, modifying its efforts over time to reflect what it has learned about the customer's interests and responses. The customer's purchases or requests are entered into the database, so a record of *transactions* accompanies the personal information. Using statistical modeling techniques, the marketer can begin to develop analyses that will lead to increasingly efficient decisions about product offerings, pricing, and promotional activities.

The most familiar examples of interactive marketing include:

- Consumer credit cards of all kinds including banks and oil companies.
- Catalog marketers such as L.L. Bean, Lands' End, and Spiegel.
- Frequent flyer and frequent traveler programs such as American Airlines AAdvantage Program and Holiday Inn's Priority Club.
- Videotext computer networking services such as Prodigy.

In each example, the customer is known as an individual with whom the marketer can communicate directly, using specific promotional messages and tailored product offerings. Each transaction is entered into the database—every charge card use, every telephone or mail order, every flight or overnight stay, every sign-on to the computer network and every piece of information accessed during that session. Every electronic communication device, including telephones, automatic teller machines and cash dispensers, home computers, cable-access home televisions, and point-of-sale charge card readers, has the potential to become a two-way terminal in an interactive marketing system.

How to Benefit from the Customer Database

The most sophisticated systems for interactive marketing are found at the supermarket checkout counter where countertop and hand-held scanners record the details of every single transaction—each product by brand, size, price, and so on—and enter that information into the database. The purchase information can be matched up with the customer's file which is identified by a credit card or buying club card presented at the same time.

Either immediately or following the store visit, the marketer (through sophisticated modeling and decision rules) can offer the customer special buying incentives and rewards based on purchasing behavior. For example, the computer might print out instructions for the cashier to give special discounts right on the spot. Or the consumer might receive coupons good for her next purchase. For example, Coca-Cola might offer a coupon good for a free quart of Coke to every consumer who has purchased a large Pepsi, or Frito-Lay may send coupons for a free bag of Munchos to everyone who buys Fritos Corn Chips. Consumers are rewarded for their participation in these programs by receiving these discounts and special promotional offers.[6]

Even more sophisticated are so-called single-source databases that match up the customer personal data file and the transaction file with information about that customer from other sources such as cable TV monitoring systems, newspaper and magazine circulation files, and consumer credit files. Thus, the marketer may be able to target TV ads to customers with specific demographic and shopping characteristics and to subsequently evaluate advertising expenditures by noting the individual purchase responses by customers in the database. The possibilities here are mind-boggling.

Potential Problems Related to Interactive Marketing

At these levels of sophistication, interactive marketing systems raise a number of important management issues. First, there is the matter of expense. These sophisticated information systems require huge investments in hardware, software, and modeling capability. They require massive expenditures to generate and maintain databases, whether developed on a proprietary basis or purchased commercially from vendors such as Dun & Bradstreet, Inc., Citicorp, TRW, and Information Resources, Inc.

Second, there is the issue of confidentiality and privacy. Consumers may not take kindly to marketers' having such detailed information about them. Opportunities for abuse exist, especially if there is unauthorized use of the information or if a careless provider releases incorrect information, for example, about a consumer's credit history. While these are legitimate concerns, there is also evidence that most consumers enter into such marketing relationships with enthusiasm. The vast majority of those offered participation in supermarket buying clubs, for example, elect to do so. Also, many customers may view interactive marketing as an attractive alternative to a flood of unsolicited junk mail and direct marketers' telephone calls during the dinner hour.

Third, there are issues relating to management, including developing the necessary statistical modeling capabilities within the firm to exploit the potential of interactive marketing and information technology. It is fair to assume that most marketing managers do not possess the necessary educational and technical backgrounds. Managers must be supported by a staff of analysts and programmers, representing a significant ongoing expense. Then, accounting systems must be developed for managing the database as a strategic asset.

Determining the Value of a Customer

With the interactive marketing capability in place, and with a customer database that is continuously updated and analyzed for new marketing opportunities, the company can place a specific value on a given customer. The value of that customer reflects the statistically determined value of the profit margins on a future stream of transactions with that customer. The data will allow the firm to compute the frequency and size of purchases by that customer and the expenses associated with communicating with that customer. Further analysis will place a value on the potential purchases of new products and services to be offered to the customer.

For the interactive marketer, the customer database becomes the single most important business asset, the most valuable part of the business. It is also its most important strategic resource. The product offering becomes a variable, changing to meet the evolving needs and preferences of the customers in the database. New products are a major tool for maintaining and enhancing the relationship with the customer.

Not every marketer is a candidate for a full-blown interactive marketing system based on sophisticated information technology. But the concept can be applied at a much more immediate level. While the most dramatic opportunities may exist for consumer packaged goods marketers who have the data available from millions of daily transactions recorded at the point of sale, virtually every business can learn the identity of its customers, develop a small amount of valuable information about them, and track their purchasing history. With that data, even the smallest marketer can tailor products, services, prices, and communications more efficiently.

The basic point of relationship marketing is one of attitude—treating the customer as a partner rather than an adversary. The opportunity is to enhance efficiency by focusing marketing effort on the existing customer base rather than using a shotgun to blast marketing dollars into the anonymous marketplace hoping that a few new customers may fall to ground. Interactive marketing binds the customer to the company and vice versa.

DEVELOPING MARKETING ALLIANCES

Out of a focus on relationship marketing (including but not limited to interactive marketing) comes another strategic development of the utmost importance under the new marketing concept: marketing alliances. It starts with the proposition that the firm's customer base is its most important and most valuable strategic asset. The question is how to develop and exploit that asset for maximum strategic advantage. The answer proposed in this book is that improving and broadening the product offering is the way to offer additional value to customers and strengthen the relationship. This approach binds the customer ever closer to the company and builds the value of the customer base itself.

But—this brings us back to the fundamental shortcoming of the old marketing concept, which failed to recognize that a commitment to customer satisfaction must be matched up with the company's capabilities. That issue was addressed by strategic planning. No company can be all things to all customers. How can we reconcile the need for continuous broadening of the product offering to serve the customer base better with the limitations that any firm faces in developing and delivering products and services? How do we integrate the concepts of distinctive competence, the value proposition, and relationship marketing?

There are two answers, and the first—which is not necessarily the best—is to *develop internally* the capability necessary to broaden the product line offered to the customer base. Thus, an airline may decide to start an insurance company to offer frequent flyer program participants death and disability coverage as part of the service they receive when booking on their flights. Or a catalog marketer may decide to manufacture certain products itself, such as the L.L. Bean hunting shoe or the Lands' End canvas luggage or the Orvis fly rods, in order to control the quality and availability of a key part of their product offering.

The danger to this do-it-yourself approach is that the company may not be able to develop the distinctive competences to be a truly viable competitor in this new business or the scope and scale of operations required to become an efficient producer. Airlines probably are poorly equipped to begin insurance companies; catalog marketers usually have limited manufacturing skills.

Increasingly, *marketing alliances*, the second alternative, are seen as the most effective and least risky path for expanding the product offering for the customer base. The marketer looks for partners who can provide products and services that will enhance its relationship with its customer base. The customer base remains the focus of its strategic intent and the source of its distinctive competence. For example, the Prodigy Service (which is itself a kind of marketing alliance as a joint venture of IBM and Sears, Roebuck) has a number of marketing alliances with providers of information services including an airline, hotel, and rental car reservation system through American Airlines' "EAASY SABRE" service, an encyclopedia from Grolier, an educational service from *National Geographic*, a travel guide provided by

Mobil, a bill-paying service in connection with Manufacturers Hanover Trust Company, and a fresh flower delivery service from FTD (Florists Transworld Delivery). Many United States airlines have entered into marketing alliances with foreign carriers to extend their routes around the globe. Mobil Oil Credit Company regularly offers merchandise from a variety of manufacturers at favorable prices and credit terms to its credit card members.

The relationship marketer has the opportunity to take multiple products and services, some of them actually produced by the marketer and the others purchased, and integrate them into a total system for the customer. This function is seen, for example, in the activities of so-called systems houses and value-added resellers in the computer field. The distinction between a manufacturer and a distributor becomes blurred as the firm committed to relationship marketing is likely to perform both sets of functions. The focus is always on the customer relationship, not on products or manufacturing plants.

Strategic marketing alliances also take other forms beyond broadening the product offering. In a general sense, all marketing-related combinations with other businesses are marketing alliances. These include the hiring of an advertising agency, contracting with a market research firm, and long-term relationships with resellers of all kinds. Chapter 6 returns to the subject of marketing alliances, with a look at strategic alliances and network organizations. The present chapter considers marketing alliances as a specific tool for enhancing the firm's ability to deliver a broader range of services and products to its base of customers. Marketing alliances are a logical result of a move toward relationship marketing.

We now go back to the intersection of consumer and industrial marketing and travel down the road of strategic partnerships in business-to-business buyer-seller relationships. Not all such relationships are true partnerships. The concept of strategic partnerships is uniquely applicable to business-to-business marketing.

BUILDING STRATEGIC PARTNERSHIPS

This chapter has progressed along a continuum from pure transactions to repeated transactions to buyer-seller relationships to strategic partnerships. The long-term buyer-seller relationship may take the form of a strategic partnership. While the distinction between relationships and partnerships is one of degree, the unique characteristics of a strategic partnership make it a more complete and totally involving relationship. These characteristics make the strategic relationship specific to industrial marketing, where both the partners are businesses or other types of organizations with strategic intent, a concept not highly relevant for consumers.

A key distinguishing feature then is the *strategic intent* of both the customer and the marketer. The buyer has assigned a key part of the value chain to a partner on whom the buyer will depend for the creation and delivery of value to his or her customers. These relationships have also been called "value-adding partnerships"[7] to capture this essential notion of the vendor as an integral part of the firm's value creation and delivery process. The concept of partnership represents a significant change from the adversarial nature of most buyer-seller relationships. Most strategic partnerships require that the marketer make investments specific to the relationship with this buyer, and they typically represent a significant portion of the marketer's total production capability. Business between the parties is conducted on the basis of terms and conditions specific to the partnership. It is organized and managed by a different set of rules than those that apply in normal, market-based relationships.

The concept of vendor partnering developed in the 1980s as a direct result of the quality movement and total quality management. The preponderance of pressure to move in this direction came from the buyer's side of the relationship as manufacturing organizations attempted to export their quality programs downstream into their vendors' operations. For this reason, much of the following analysis comes from the customer's perspective.

In the value-adding strategic partnership, the vendor's operations become an extension of those of the customer and the boundaries between the two organizations and their operations become blurred. Instead of simply awarding a portion of its requirements to various suppliers based on price, the customer is likely to evaluate vendors against multiple criteria. The customer is interested in the vendor's total capability for providing solutions that involve both products and services. Rather than develop a tight specification and ask several vendors to bid against it, the customer will ask the supplier partner to assist in the design of the product and the development of those specifications, to take maximum advantage of the vendor's technical competence. The design process is guided by the customer's definition of value and draws on the distinctive competence of the vendor organization.

Establishing Just-in-Time Supply Systems

Just-in-time supply systems are the epitome of the strategic partnership. Typically, these consist of a single vendor for a given part (although there could be more than one supplier) who agrees to provide 100% usable product to the customer in specified quantities, usually just enough for one production shift. Furthermore, these quantities must be delivered on a very tight schedule, with delivery times usually specified with acceptable variation of no more than several minutes. It is the combination of quality, quantity, and schedule that defines a just-in-time supply system.

Just-in-time systems were developed based on the model provided by the Japanese automobile industry, especially Toyota City, in what is called the *kanban* system. Toyota City is unique because the vendors have built supply facilities very close to their customer. Some of the just-in-time systems developed in the United States by Japanese automobile assemblers have also included new vendor facilities nearby. A unique feature of the Japanese *kanban* systems is the interlocking ownership patterns among customers and vendors, part of the larger *keiretsu* system of organization found in Japan. The simple idea behind *kanban* is to turn the operations of vendors and the customer organization into one large machine.[8]

Just-in-time systems have two inseparable objectives: lower inventories and better quality. Traditional production scheduling and inventory systems depended heavily on the presence of "buffer stocks" at several points in the production process to protect against the presence of defective parts and inconsistencies in the ordering and delivery of parts from several vendors. These buffer inventories were subject to shrinkage and deterioration over time from damage, theft, and exposure to the elements. Because not all vendors' parts were interchangeable and because designs might change during the production period, duplication and obsolescence were major costs. Under the old systems, it was common to talk in terms of "days" or "weeks" or even "months" of inventory on hand. In just-in-time systems, the measuring units are minutes.

It is said that Toyota's managers developed their ideas about just-in-time systems while visiting the United States. Much of the initial thinking at Toyota was stimulated by Eiji Toyoda's visit in 1950 to Ford's totally integrated River Rouge plant, although there was also a lot about that wholly-owned-by-Ford operation that the Toyota people thought needed improvement.[9]

Other Japanese production managers are reported to have drawn inspiration from the efficiency of the modern American supermarket. They were impressed by the fact that these large retailing facilities devoted virtually all their store space to actual shelf display of merchandise, with very little inventory sitting in the back room. This was in marked contrast to the Japanese system, which even today is characterized by small, inefficient grocery retailers with very broad but extremely shallow selections of merchandise and an equally inefficient pattern of wholesale distribution.

Quality and inventory control were totally interrelated. In the old production systems, extra inventories were needed because of the presence of unusable parts. Quality levels were stated in terms of defects per hundred or per thousand parts delivered. Incoming inspection was a major part of the supply process, but since it was seldom possible to do 100% inspection, some defective parts inevitably entered the production process. If an entire batch was defective and was not caught at incoming inspection, the problem was integrated into the system resulting in a whole production run that required rework at the end of the process or else was allowed to go into the field where customers would discover the problem.

Perfect quality, consisting of 100% usable product delivered on time in the necessary quantities, could eliminate the need for incoming inspection and substantially reduce the costs of inventory, production delays, rework, and end-user customer dissatisfaction. It was a basic lesson that had to be learned the hard way—from global competitors in the marketplace. While just-in-time systems in the United States were first developed in the automobile industry in response to market inroads by Japanese manufacturers, they soon spread out to the suppliers' suppliers and into other industries.

Using Sole-Source Procurements

The requirements of just-in-time supply systems created a strong leaning toward sole-source procurements. The demands of the system for integrated design, production, and logistics activities call for total integration between the customer and the supplier. They require extensive communications and multiple interpersonal relationships between the two organizations. Product, production, and distribution/logistics decisions must be made jointly and in unison. The relationship's time horizon is long term because the supplier probably will have to make extensive investments in plant, equipment, information systems, and organizational arrangements that are specific to this single customer.

In return, the customer may also have to make relationship-specific investments, in tools and dies, in shipping and handling equipment, and also in information systems. The two companies' operations become totally linked and interdependent. There is substantial risk for both of them, but each trades off the risk associated with market-based uncertainty for the risk that comes with resource dependency. Both trade off market control for administrative control over the buyer-seller relationship, which significantly increases their costs for executing and monitoring their transactions while reducing the costs associated with low quality, high inventory, price negotiations, production uncertainty, and market uncertainty.[10]

Underlying the entire relationship is the fundamental requirement for *trust.* Sole-source strategic partnerships are high risk for both parties. Each is totally dependent on the other for that part of their operation—the customer for an uninterrupted supply of a critical subassembly, component, or raw material, the marketer for a substantial portion of its total revenue for which it has made a substantial investment.

While strategic partnering has been most visible and most advanced in the automobile industry, it has spread quickly into a broad variety of businesses. Among the companies that have spoken publicly about their strategic partnering activities are the marketers GE, IBM, DuPont, Monsanto, and Honeywell with customers that include American Airlines, Ford, Milliken, Procter & Gamble, and the federal government.

A major source of the risk inherent in strategic partnerships is American companies' lack of experience in managing these arrangements. Whether they were aware of it or not, most American purchasing, sales, and marketing managers were trained and educated under the assumptions of the old transaction-based, adversarial model. Company policies and procedures reflected these assumptions. Strategic partnering requires cooperation, win/win negotiation, and joint problem solving, whereas the traditional sale-as-conquest approach calls for persuasion, bargaining, and compromise (win/lose and lose/lose negotiations), and the protection of individual self-interest (profit margins and proprietary technology). Strategic partnering calls for a new set of marketing skills and attitudes not readily found in many industrial firms.

Managing Strategic Partnerships

From the marketer's perspective, the move toward strategic partnering with key customers is a step in the implementation of the new marketing concept. As already observed, however, it also calls for a new set of management skills and it raises a unique set of management issues. These issues begin with the problem of selecting strategic partners. The next set of issues comes in the structuring of the relationship with the strategic customer partner. Then there follows the challenge of managing the evolving relationship. Experience has shown that strategic partnerships are extremely changeable as the relationship matures.

When to Partner: The Customer's Perspective

From the customer's perspective, the first problem is to determine when to rely on a strategic vendor for the majority or all of the firm's requirements for a given procurement. This decision depends both on the nature of the product being purchased and the availability of attractive partners for collaboration. The internal assessment would be based in the customer's quality management program and the opportunity to assign an important part of its value creation activities to an efficient specialist firm with the necessary capability and the willingness to make the commitment to this customer.

Choosing the Partner: The Customer's Perspective

Once the decision has been made to seek a vendor partner, the problem shifts to selecting the proper partner. Almost certainly, the firm will already have an established relationship with the potential partners, although this would not be true if the product was being produced internally. If the vendor is known, much of the required experience will exist throughout the customer organization in the knowledge of those who have worked with this vendor. Some of the most important information will be subjective and qualitative, having to do with the management knowledge, skills, and attitudes of the vendor firm. Professor Robert Spekman, an authority on industrial marketing, has proposed the following questions for evaluating a potential strategic supplier:

1. How early in the design stage is the vendor willing and able to become involved?
2. Does the vendor understand the level of commitment required to achieve the targeted gains in quality and does it have the resources required to sustain that involvement?
3. Will the supplier be able to grow with us and to continue to offer improved value in the future?
4. Does the vendor really have the necessary technical competence and will it be willing to contribute that expertise?
5. Does the supplier have a team approach to quality, purchasing, and production and a positive attitude toward cooperation and collaboration, including win/win negotiating?
6. Is the supplier's senior management committed to the processes of cooperation, collaboration, and conflict-resolution required for strategic partnering? What have they done to demonstrate that commitment?
7. How much future planning is the supplier willing to share with us? Is management willing to share the necessary proprietary information with us and, at the same time, treat our proprietary information in a confidential manner? Is there a fundamental level of trust in the relationship?
8. How well does the supplier know our business? Has its management made the necessary investment of time and effort to become truly knowledgeable about our operation and our problems?
9. Has the vendor demonstrated commitment in the past by willingness to make necessary investments in plant, equipment, and other resources? What has been the level of that commitment?

10. What will the supplier demand of us in return? What assurances and guarantees will this supplier require as a condition of partnering?[11]

When to Partner: The Marketer's Perspective

Strategic partnering calls for a significant investment in relationship building and management on the part of the marketer. The first requirement, however, is the commitment to a positive attitude toward relationship marketing, as called for by the new marketing concept, and the fundamental willingness to put the customer first, always, that is its hallmark. Thus far, this book has shown that profitability improves with a commitment to strategic partnering, from more efficient marketing expenditures and greater profit margins on sales to established customers. We need to balance our perspective with the caution that not all market segments, and not all customers within those segments, are good candidates for strategic partnership.

The customer, not the marketer, often will make the overture about partnering. In this case, the marketer must decide whether to make the necessary investments and commitments. As a first order of business, the company must decide whether it wants to do *any* business on a strategic partnering basis. Is partnering consistent with its business strategy? Is it consistent with its distinctive competence? Before deciding on a partner, the more basic strategic questions must be answered. An overture from an important customer may force the issue, but it must first be addressed at the strategic level. Examining the potential relationship with a customer who has raised the question of strategic partnering can be a useful first step in analyzing the general strategic issues, but they must be resolved in a strategic framework of market segmentation, targeting, and positioning.

A critical question is whether that particular customer is actually willing to make the required long-term commitment. Unfortunately, some marketers report very negative experiences in this regard. The customer brought the vendor into a strategic partnering arrangement, often as part of its quality program, only to revert to old buying tactics to drive prices down severely once the vendor was irreversibly committed to plant, equipment, and systems that made it virtually dependent for survival on that customer. It is a disturbing fact of commercial life that the customer can more easily monitor and verify the activities and performance of its suppliers to invoke contract penalties and rewards, than it is for the supplier to monitor and control the activities of its customers.[12]

As in the case of a customer looking for a vendor to partner with, the marketer must question the customer's motives and the nature of the commitment under consideration. The reader can easily turn the set of questions reviewed earlier into those that a potential vendor partner would ask about its customer, simply by substituting the word "customer" for "supplier."

In those cases where the initiative for strategic partnering will come from the marketer, there are two sets of decisions. The first is whether to pursue a relationship and partnership marketing strategy or to stay in a traditional old-fashioned transaction-marketing mode. The second set of decisions, given the decision to move toward relationship marketing as a strategy, is whether to treat all customers the same way or to define distinct market segments based on the nature of the buyer-seller relationship. In industrial marketing, the opportunities for such segmentation are greater than they are in consumer goods marketing, where it is more likely to be an all-or-nothing commitment, given the nature of the required investments in technology and supporting information systems.

For many industries, relationship marketing is not new. Most industrial marketing is relationship marketing, at least to a degree, because the customers are known by name, location, and operating characteristics; there are probably multiple personal contacts between the companies; and their operations become interdependent to a significant degree. In commercial banking, for example, where relationship marketing has been accepted business practice for decades, a given client will depend on the bank for a full range of banking services. Even here, however, some customers prefer to deal on an individual transactions basis and divide their business among several banks based on current pricing for cash management services and loans of various kinds. The interrelationships between customers and vendors in such industries as chemicals, paper, machinery, mainframe computers, and railroad transportation place them within the band of relationship marketing, rather than transactions, by definition. The preponderance of industrial marketing activity is relationship marketing. The real question is whether the marketer should move to the more advanced stage of strategic partnering with customers and assume its attendant commitments.

It is essential to look at the details of customers and competition in a given market segment. If there is little or no meaningful product differentiation, if multiple vendors are common, if prices fluctuate wildly depending on supply and demand, if customers are known to follow aggressive, transaction-oriented purchasing practices, then there would not appear to be great opportunities for strategic partnering, even when customers request it. On the other hand, if buyer-seller relationships tend to be stable, if service is an important part of the product offering, if substantial investments and other costs are associated with switching vendors, then the potential for strategic partnering is great. Strategic partnering is also favored when the customer depends on the vendor for substantial portions of its technology, as in the relationships between airframe and jet engine manufacturers and between computer chip manufacturers and their equipment suppliers.

Cautions about Strategic Partnering

Recent theoretical analysis suggests that, contrary to the popularity of the notion that strategic partnering is good business practice for both buyers and sellers, marketers should be very careful about entering into such partnerships. This analysis concluded that they make sense for marketers only when specific assets and uncertainty create the need for such practices. That is, if the vendor is required to make specific investments; if the customer is also required to make specific investments; if there is high uncertainty about both future market conditions, especially volume requirements, and technology—then there are incentives for both parties to develop a long-term strategic partnership.

Strategic partnerships are also favored when vendor performance requirements are both complex and ambiguous, in particular when many factors other than price are important, and when normal business practice favors long-term continuity. Finally, strategic partnerships make more sense when both parties benefit from joint forecasting and planning in R&D, engineering, and production.[13] Absent those conditions, strategic partnering may be a bad idea for the marketer, even when it is a good idea for the buyer.

Put simply, marketers must protect their investment. Strategic partnering is going to make sense when a marketer has reason to believe that the customer will honor its commitments over a long period of time and be willing to engage in collaborative action and joint problem solving. A field study of one manufacturer's collaborative relationships with a total of 46 supplier partners confirms this viewpoint. It was found that successful partnerships are based on substantial investments by one party that are specifically valued by the other. Each side must be convinced that the other faces high costs if it elects to exit the relationship. Also, each party must have access to alternative partners and strategies, so it does not have "all its eggs in one basket," so it cannot be "held hostage" by the other, and so it is not threatened by its dependence on the other. Even then, however, each party must continuously reconfirm its commitment to the other for the relationship to remain productive and stable.[14]

DEVELOPING THE PARTNERING STRATEGY

As noted earlier, not all customers are attractive candidates for relationship marketing, especially as the relationship progresses toward a true strategic partnership. One way to think about the problem of developing a partnering strategy has been proposed by James Anderson and James Narus.[15] Their approach integrates the issues of partnering addressed earlier with the broader strategic considerations of market segmentation, targeting, and positioning. It also uses the concepts of the augmented product and of product bundling to provide a comprehensive view of the strategic challenges inherent in buyer-seller partnerships. Their framework has six stages:

1. Market segmentation, placing customers on the continuum from transactions to partnerships.
2. Assessing the value of the product to customers in each segment.
3. Market targeting—selecting customers for specific types of relationships.
4. Developing relationship-specific product offerings.
5. Evaluating relationship outcomes and reassigning accounts.
6. Updating the relationship offering.

This framework is a useful way to summarize this discussion of strategic partnering.

Stage 1: Segmenting the Market

In every industry or market, customers will illustrate a wide range of preference and conduct when it comes to buyer-seller partnerships. Some will evidence a clear preference for low price and a transaction type of business relationship. Others will demand substantial service commitments from their suppliers, have a broader definition of quality, and expect to develop long-term relationships. The transaction customers will be interested in what can be essentially thought of as the core product. The relationship customers are interested in the augmented product. Partnership customers must also be interested in the potential product.

A marketer may face the full range of relationship possibilities in the firm's served markets. A large paper manufacturer, for example, may have customers in several industries such as newspapers, catalogs, magazines, book publishing, packaging, and envelopes. Each of these industry segments will include a broad variety of purchasing practices. In some industries, say envelopes, a transaction orientation may be common; in other industries, say newspapers, the emphasis may be on long-term relationships; in packaging, the customers may tend to emphasize strategic partnerships that draw on the paper manufacturer's full technical capabilities. In other industries, say magazines, the paper manufacturer may see a full range from transactions to collaborative partnerships.

Each customer industry or market segment is likely to contain subsegments of customers with similar buying characteristics. The segmentation exercise identifies customers for differentiated marketing effort, in terms of both the product offering and marketing communications.

Stage 2: Assessing Product Value to Customers

Buyer and seller seek the same objective from strategic partnering—superior value from using the vendor's products in the target application. At a given point in time, however, not all customers with potential for relationship or partnership marketing may be fully aware of the benefits. The marketer needs to assess the operations and management of candidates to understand the opportunities that may exist above and beyond the current methods of doing business. The customer's definition of value, as already noted, changes continuously. An enhanced product offering may be the key to moving the customer away from a transaction and price orientation.

An assessment of the potential for delivering superior value to a prospective customer must be based on a full understanding of the customer's operation and definition of value. What is the firm's strategy for making money? Is it geared to be a low-cost producer or does it go to market with a highly differentiated, high-quality product offering? Does the customer define cost in terms of purchase price for the core product, or does it have a total-cost-in-use view that looks at the total product offering, including service? How can our product deliver superior value: by offering a low-cost, low-price alternative—the core or expected product—or by offering an augmented product?

Again, a wide or narrow range of vendor relationships may characterize each market segment.

Stage 3: Targeting the Market

In determining the number of segments to target, the marketer making this critical management judgment must assess the firm's own capabilities. Does it have the capabilities required to compete in multiple market segments? Can the firm sell both a core/unbundled product and an augmented/bundled product offering? It may be very hard to keep products, strategies, and operations separate. Are there adequate marketing communications skills and resources, especially depth and breadth in the sales organization, to launch focused marketing efforts at multiple market segments?

The most sophisticated marketers will lean toward a "portfolio" of relationships, from pure transactions to strategic partnerships.[16] They will recognize the potential, over time, for upgrading customer relationships into higher value-producing opportunities. They will identify market segments that are relatively underserved by their competitors with less refined market segmentation, targeting, and positioning strategies.

Other firms, especially those in tightly focused market niches and possessing limited production and marketing resources, will elect to concentrate marketing effort on one or a few market segments where they can achieve unique and sustainable competitive advantage. These may be relatively small market niches that are not likely to attract larger, resource-rich competitors. With these focused segments, it is still possible to develop a range of relationships.

The last step in market targeting is to select specific customers. Once again, this calls for detailed analysis of each potential customer's use situation, production capabilities, definition of value, and relationship preferences. It is important to know their present suppliers and the nature of those relationships in deciding whether they are likely to be strongly satisfied with the existing arrangement.

Stage 4: Developing the Product Offering

Having targeted market segments and individual accounts in those segments, the marketer still faces the difficult problem of developing a product offering for those customers. Once the different types of customers and their definitions of value are understood, the company can refine its own value proposition: the reasons each type of customer should do business with that firm rather than its competitors. While there should be a strong bias toward relationship marketing and strategic partnering, it may also be that the best opportunities exist in unbundling the product, focusing on the core product, and offering the customer a very attractive price. For the supplier with the capability to be a low-cost producer, this can be an attractive alternative if the product is more or less like a commodity and if the customer doesn't have a real need for the high-cost service enhancements being offered by competing suppliers.

On the other hand, an enhanced service offering—giving the customer an augmented product rather than merely the expected product—is often the key to delivering superior value. In many industrial market segments, especially those with well established and limited competition, a new market entrant with a superior product offering may be able to change the key success factors by significantly increasing customer expectations.

A marketer who follows a strategy of differentiated marketing, as opposed to concentrated marketing in a single segment, will need to develop distinctive product offerings for each segment. Special care must be taken to ensure that the market segments are in fact distinct and to offer unique product bundles in each segment. Obviously, service, along with these unique features, will be a critical part of the total product offering.

Organizing to Implement the Relationship Product Offering

Equally important, it probably will be necessary to develop tailored marketing communications and distribution arrangements for each segment. In relationship marketing, the sales representative and the distributor become part of the product offering. Some customers may be reached through direct selling, either by a geographic sales force or by a sales force organized for key accounts, a particular industry, or a specific product offering. Others may be served through telemarketing or various types of resellers. If the company has identified multiple target markets with unique requirements, it will want to consider using several different types of marketing channels and sales approaches, in what has been called a "hybrid channel system."[17]

The sales force is especially critical as a tool for implementing a relationship or partnership marketing strategy. A market segment characterized by a transaction approach, a limited core product, and low price will require a different type of selling effort than a partnership-oriented segment with an augmented product offering at a higher price. Separate sales organizations may be required. The transactions customers may be reached through a nonspecialized geographic sales force calling on potential customers in several target industry segments. The selling task may involve mostly soliciting and responding to requests for quotations or taking orders from a standard product catalog.

The partnership segment may require a key accounts sales organization, perhaps with several sales representatives and managers from several functions assigned to each account, carefully managing the relationship in a negotiated, collaborative approach to addressing unique customer problems with special engineering and manufacturing solutions. Market segments receiving the standard product offering may be serviced through independent distributors who have the freedom to offer further price reductions to these transaction-oriented customers. The higher the value of the product offering in the customer's use, the more likely that customer should be targeted for relationship or partnership marketing and served directly through a product, market, and/or account specialized sales force.

The investment and expense involved in maintaining multiple sales forces and distribution arrangements are the major reasons the firm may decide to follow a strategy of concentrated marketing. Even if it has the resources for more than one approach, it may still think that the complexity of maintaining distinctively different marketing approaches will be a source of potential problems, especially if customers in one segment become aware of different pricing, product offerings, services, and sales coverage and distribution arrangements available to customers in another market segment. Most likely, customers in the augmented product (relationship) segments will demand the lower prices of customers in the core product (transaction) segments, whereas those enjoying low prices will demand higher service levels. Neither may be willing to give up what it is already getting, so simply reassigning them to another market segment may not be the answer. Customers don't always understand or care about the marketer's segmentation strategy!

Stage 5: Evaluating Outcomes and Reassigning Accounts

Not all customers targeted for a given approach will be responsive to it. Stable relationships require that both parties be comfortable with the approach adopted by the other. There will be obvious mismatches where the marketer tries a relationship approach and the customer responds in transaction mode or vice versa. There will also be instances where the customer would prefer a stronger relationship orientation and an enhanced product offering with better service while the sales representative, through ignorance and insensitivity to the customer's needs, continues to behave in transaction mode, pushing price and looking for the next order instead of concentrating on building a stronger relationship.

In the latter instance, the real problem may be a poorly trained and supervised sales representative rather than a strategic failure. The marketing strategy won't count for much if the sales force is not prepared to implement it in the field. The natural tendency of most industrial salespeople is to concentrate on getting the next order and to assume that the lower the price, the higher the probability of making the sale.

Other customers may respond positively at first and then modify their behavior over time. This is especially an issue in strategic partnering, where the vendor must make large initial investments and other resource commitments to become a strategic partner for its customer. Several studies have found that strategic partnerships remain viable to the extent that *both* parties have substantial and roughly equal dependence on the other. If the supplier has made the principal investment and committed a significant portion of its production capacity to the strategic customer while the customer has continued to maintain relationships with other vendors (perhaps on related product lines even if there is a sole source arrangement with the focal supplier), the relationship will be unstable.

Managing the Partnering Cycle

There appears to be a predictable evolution in strategic buyer-seller partnerships. After the initial courting period in which the parties make their mutual commitments and go through a "honeymoon" period, often characterized by public pronouncements about the path-breaking nature of the partnership, the collaborators settle down to do the work required in managing the partnership. There will be inevitable problems, misunderstandings, and disagreements, not all of which will be completely resolved to both partners' satisfaction. This can lead to growing dissatisfaction with the relationship, an active search for other partners, strained relations, and either reconciliation or dissolution of the strategic partnership.

This cycle can be anticipated and managed, in particular by knowing the signs of trouble to look for and having the necessary mechanisms in place for joint problem solving and conflict resolution. If the basic forces at work in the partnering cycle are ignored, problems are inevitable.

The basic weakness in strategic partnering comes from the relative lack of "market control." This is the negative side of the move away from market-based transaction orientation. In a transaction type of buyer-seller relationship, the customer has the comfort of knowing competitive product offerings and prices are available, which provide a handy reference for assessing the performance of the vendor (although, as noted earlier, it is harder for the supplier to monitor the customer's performance). Competitive bids are frequently solicited just "to keep the supplier honest." Similarly, the threat of a potential competitor can provide the necessary incentive for the vendor to strive to achieve cost improvements and product innovations.

In moving from transactions to strategic partnering, we substitute bureaucratic or administrative control for market control. The buyer's and seller's operations become linked as if they were part of the same organization, and their relationship is guided by internal communications, negotiated agreements, policies, and procedures as part of their joint understanding. Market forces have been largely removed from the relationship.

Experience suggests that this is a very fragile and tenuous arrangement, especially for buyers who are accustomed to doing business in the adversarial transaction mode. How can they be sure they are "getting the best deal" and being treated fairly by the vendor, especially in a sole-source procurement? How can they know that the product represents the supplier's best effort to find cost reductions and to make improvements? What incentive does the supplier have to make the necessary investments in research and development?

There may also be specific issues in the day-to-day relationship such as a quality problem or a late delivery or a personal disagreement between members of the two organizations that provokes an accusation of lack of commitment. It is almost inevitable that, for one reason or another, the buyer will be asking "What have you done for me lately?" and "How do I know that I can trust you to put my best interests first?"

One way for the buyer to try to get answers is to explore the market and initiate discussions with other potential vendors. This is most likely to take the form of simply looking for a lower price, without necessarily getting into the details of the competitive product and service offering. This not only will reveal new options from other marketers anxious to establish a new relationship but also is likely to introduce suspicion and distrust into the established collaboration. The buyer may decide to try to renegotiate the arrangements or may invite another vendor to provide a portion of the requirement. Sensing this possibility, the marketer may also be looking for new partners who will place a higher value on the commitments made in the form of production and service capabilities now being questioned by the existing partner. At this stage, the strategic partnership is in danger of breaking down as each side accuses the other of unfair dealing and violations of the agreement.

It is essential that the marketer committed to strategic partnering be sensitive to the issues raised by the absence of market control. Marketers must continuously monitor the relationship for signs of stress and have procedures that are clearly understood by members of both organizations to take care of the inevitable problems and disagreements. They must be sensitive to the buyer's need for frequent demonstration of satisfactory performance under the contract, and offer continuous improvements in the product and service offering.

In the final analysis, "What have you done for me lately?" is a legitimate question to ask of a vendor. As the customer faces changing requirements from its own customers, continued pressures for cost reduction, changing technology, and changing competition, it must depend on its strategic vendor partners for new solutions, and better and better definitions of superior value.

Having said that, however, it isn't ordained that strategic partnerships should last forever or that transaction customers cannot evolve into relationship and partnership prospects. As the customer's situation and definition of value change, so must the marketer's approach change. It is necessary to regularly evaluate each customer to be sure that they have been assigned to the proper relationship segment and then to modify the arrangements as necessary, reassigning accounts to different sales and distribution channels to match up the product/service offering and related marketing communications with the customer's way of doing business.

Stage 6: Updating the Relationship Offering

It was pointed out in Chapter 3 that continuous innovation is "the name of the game" under the new marketing concept. It follows logically from the commitment to putting the customer's interests first in all aspects of the business operation. If quality is defined as meeting and exceeding customer expectations, and if the customer's expectations keep increasing as the company improves its performance and competitors make promises of superior value, continuous improvement is an inevitable requirement for survival in the customer relationship.

These comments are made in the context of the relationship with individual customers, especially those who have been chosen as strategic partners. There is also the broader strategic issue, at the market segmentation and targeting level, of developing the product/service offering appropriate to each segment and modifying it over time as the strategic focus evolves and shifts in the changing market. In particular, as the company moves along the continuum from transactions to strategic partnerships, it will be necessary to augment the product offering and develop new bundles of product features and services.

At a given point on the continuum, let us say in normal buyer-seller relationships that are neither transactions nor strategic partnerships, there is also the dynamic transformation of the augmented product into the expected product. As product life cycles evolve and markets mature, the customer expects more for less. As often noted throughout this text, offering the augmented product has the effect of educating customers about the product and the market so that they can now concentrate more on finding the lowest price for the enhanced product offering. In a real sense, good is never good enough.

The marketer must systematically, from time to time, assess the adequacy of the product offering for a given market segment and adjust it accordingly. Given a thorough consideration of what is involved in the necessary improvement and upgrading, the marketer may decide that the cost of the next generation of product improvements is beyond the company's capabilities. The choices then are to exit the market or to unbundle the product and resegment the market. These may offer more attractive profit opportunities, especially for smaller firms following niche marketing strategies.

For example, consider a market in which a major competitor has made a huge investment in information technology. That competitor now offers every customer a computer terminal tied into a communication network that provides instantaneous information on product availability at multiple inventory locations, all pricing and credit terms, technical information on product features and use, electronic order processing, and overnight delivery anywhere in North America. Our marketer may correctly conclude that this has fundamentally changed the key success factors in the business. The best response for the smaller competitor may be to significantly reduce the company's technical service levels and prices and to focus on providing personal service to those customers in the nearby regional market who require standard products and whose firms are too small or otherwise unable to take advantage of the new technology.

Modifications to the relationship offering should be considered in both directions as the market evolves. There is a never-ending cycle in which differentiated products regress toward commodity status while commoditylike products are differentiated with new product features and services. At any point in the cycle, the marketer's strategic choices should be made in the context of its relationship marketing strategy and be guided by its strategy for developing and maintaining its distinctive competence. Market segmentation, targeting, and positioning remain as the essential strategic activities in developing the value proposition in relationship marketing. As the customer's definition of value keeps changing, so must the firm's value proposition. Value is defined in the marketplace, by the customer. That is the basic truth on which the new marketing concept is based.

SUMMARY

The old view of marketing that focused on the next sale is being replaced by a new view that centers on the customer as a long-term business asset. The economist's concept of the transaction occurring in a perfectly competitive market has been replaced by the concept of a relationship between the company and its customer. The purpose of marketing is not to make the sale but to gain a customer who will provide higher revenues and profit margins at lower marketing costs over the life of the relationship.

In consumer marketing, customer databases and interactive computer systems now permit the development of precisely tailored marketing strategies aimed at individual customers, who can communicate back to the marketer. In the age of addressability, interactive marketing replaces mass marketing. Marketing is driven by customer needs, not products and production requirements. When the company sees its customer base as its principal business asset, it may be more effective to rely on marketing alliances for broadening its product offering to these customers than to attempt to produce them internally. Growth comes from serving customers better and concentrating on the firm's distinctive competence.

In industrial markets, there is a similar evolution from transactions toward strategic partnering, often driven by the customers' total quality management programs. Here the drivers are the interlinked goals of higher quality and lower costs with both partners seeking enhanced value. The opportunities for more profitable and more stable long-term strategic partnerships are balanced by the higher risks associated with interdependence. Only if the investments and commitments of the parties are in reasonable balance and if both recognize and value the commitments that each has made for the other will these relationships remain stable.

Sophisticated marketers can think of a range of business relationships from transactions through increasingly complex buyer relationships to true strategic partnerships. Market segmentation, targeting, and positioning can yield highly differentiated marketing strategies for each of several distinct segments, taking full advantage of the different opportunities represented by customers who prefer to do business based on transactions, relationships, or partnerships. For all but the most sophisticated and resource-rich firms, the better opportunity may be to concentrate marketing effort on those market niches that are relatively underserved and where the company's distinctive competence can result in the best product offering.

In Chapter 6, we broaden our consideration to the whole range of strategic alliances that are available to the firm committed to delivering superior value to customers. As each firm defines its distinctive competences and decides which to develop most aggressively, it needs to find strategic partners who can assist it with their own unique capabilities. Strategic partnerships with customers are only one type of strategic alliance.

6 STRATEGIC ALLIANCES AND NETWORK ORGANIZATIONS

Corning is now what we call a "global network."

James R. Houghton (Chairman, Corning, Inc.)
"The Age of the Hierarchy Is Over," *New York Times*
(September 24, 1989, Sec. 3, p. 3)

For too long, bureaucracy, hierarchy, and multiple layers of middle management protected CEOs from their customers. Messages from dissatisfied customers, containing information on the nature of competition and changing customer definitions of value, seldom if ever found their way to the policy and business strategy level of the organization in a timely manner. The new product development process, the lifeblood of any business, was slowed down by the need for reviews across multiple business functions and approvals at multiple levels of the hierarchy. Hierarchies are governed by policies and procedures designed to preserve and protect the status quo, including managers and their departments. They tend to be internally focused, not externally driven. Values relating to entrepreneurship, flexibility, responsiveness, and innovation are not prevalent in most large, bureaucratic, divisionalized organizations. There are few advocates for change.

New organization forms are emerging with the potential to bring about a revolution in the conduct of business affairs as fundamental as the industrial revolution, which replaced craft production with machine production, and as significant as the development of the functional, divisionalized corporation, which replaced the owner-managed firm. These new organization forms, which we will rather imprecisely call "network organizations," are driven by customer orientation, the quality imperative, the quickening pace of technological change, the convergence of multiple technologies in a given area, and the overriding need for responsiveness and flexibility in the intensely competitive global marketplace. Network organizations consist of multiple strategic partnerships and alliances, as well as wholly-owned subsidiaries and divisions. Traditional organization forms are modified, supplanted, integrated into the new structures, or replaced altogether.

The much publicized downsizing, delayering, and disintegration of such corporate giants as General Motors, IBM, Boeing, Sears, Roebuck & Company, Eastman Kodak, Xerox, and United Technologies, to name a few, must be seen in this light. The reporting often concentrates on what is disappearing, usually referred to as "lowering overhead" (getting rid of layers of management and unneeded production capacity, including labor) without also telling what is being created in its place. As the bureaucratic hierarchies come apart, network organizations evolve to perform the required functions of value creation and delivery more efficiently.

Network organizations have pervasive implications for the role of marketing in the organization. Exploring those implications is the purpose of this chapter.

Network organizations represent a fulfillment of the twin mandates of the marketing concept—*customer orientation* and *innovativeness.* In contrast to the old marketing concept, however, they address specifically the strategic issue of matching up customer needs with the firm's distinctive capabilities. Network organizations are constantly redefining how the company can participate with multiple partners in the development and delivery of superior value to customers. They are defined by their customer base and their knowledge and skills, not by their factories and offices. Network organizations are the hallmark of the new marketing concept of the 1990s.

STRATEGIC ALLIANCES

Chapter 5 examined two types of strategic alliances: strategic partnerships with major customers (or with vendors, from the buyer's perspective) and marketing alliances in which the firm seeks a partner in a related business who can help complete the product offering or who can offer a needed marketing skill, such as advertising creativity, distribution, or marketing research. Other types of strategic alliances include:

- Partnerships with real or potential competitors for the development of a new product.
- R&D partnerships focused on achieving a desired technical breakthrough (usually involving two distinct but related technologies).
- Manufacturing joint ventures to own a facility that produces products to be sold separately by the partners.

One of the most familiar forms of strategic alliance is the *joint venture,* in which the partners combine resources to produce some tangible result such as a new product. Joint ventures are the most complete and complex form of strategic alliance, usually resulting in a new company that can itself begin to enter into other types of strategic alliances. In contrast to other forms of strategic alliances, joint ventures have their own capital structure, with the partners as shareholders.

Strategic alliances—a tool for achieving the strategic objectives of the partners—can be defined formally as a strategic collaboration among partners involving the commitment of assets and management resources with the objective of enhancing the partners' competitive positions. Each element of this definition is important. The collaboration must have the strategic intent of enhancing the partners' competitive positions. There must be a commitment of assets, in the form of investments or facilities. And there must be a commitment of management time and personnel to the venture.

Among the most common objectives for strategic alliances are exploitation of the potential inherent in related technologies, new product development, building an efficient production facility, entry into a new market (either a foreign country or a new industry), increasing global service capabilities for global customers, and the outsourcing of manufacturing to a more efficient competitor. The following widely publicized examples illustrate the many forms that strategic alliances can take:

- General Mills has combined with Pepsico Inc. to create a joint venture to market their snack foods in Europe. General Mills has also formed a 50-50 joint venture with Nestlé to sell General Mills cereals everywhere but in North America.

- Ford Motor Company teamed up with Mazda Motors Corporation, of which it owns 25%, to create 10 new cars including the Ford Explorer/Mazda Navajo, built by Ford; the Ford Probe/Mazda MX-6; the most recent Ford Escort/Mercury Tracer; the Festiva; and the Mazda 323. A new Mazda pickup truck will be built by Ford. Ford, when building its Hermosillo (Mexico) assembly plant, said to be the most efficient in the world, modeled it after Mazda's Hofu (Japan) plant. Ford also partnered with Volkswagen to create Autolatina to produce cars in Brazil.
- IBM and Apple Computer have an extensive agreement to collaborate in developing new products in several areas including hardware, software, and networking. The agreement calls for two new companies to develop multimedia software and a new operating system, cross-licensing of technology, and shared facilities and personnel. IBM has over 400 other strategic alliances, especially with software developers, whom it calls "business partners."
- AT&T joined the Dutch firm Phillips to sell telephone switching equipment to government-owned telecommunications companies in Europe and to manufacture circuitboards in Holland.
- Texas Instruments and Hitachi teamed up to develop a new generation of computer memory chips.
- Motorola and Toshiba have a similar collaboration.
- First Boston Corporation and Crédit Suisse formed a joint venture to strengthen their positions in the Eurobond market, the former bringing its skills in new product development and the latter offering access to European investors.
- General Electric Company has formed eight joint ventures in such areas as lamps and factory automation, with partners in Europe, South Korea, and Japan.
- Inland Steel and Nippon Steel cooperated in building a new continuous cold steel mill in New Carlisle, Indiana.
- Corning, Inc., which has redefined itself as a network of strategic alliances, has started 38 joint ventures in 12 countries since 1924;

they now account for over half its annual profits. Partners have included PPG Industries in glass; Dow Chemical in silicones; Asahi Glass for television tubes and computer displays; Genentech and Eastman Kodak in industrial enzymes; Siemens in fiber-optic cable; and Ciba-Geigy for blood and urine analyzers.

- USAir and British Airways have entered into a strategic alliance, through British Airways' purchase of 19% of USAir stock, that will feed passengers between their systems, giving each entry into the other's domestic market.
- Northwest Airlines and KLM have also entered into a strategic alliance involving flight code sharing within printed schedules and computer reservations systems, allowing passengers to fly on both airlines as if they were a single system.

As many of these examples illustrate, strategic alliances are often the best answer to the strategic problem of entry into a foreign market, as a means for overcoming political and cultural barriers. Most strategic alliances involve the sharing of technology, either product or process technology and often both. By allowing the partners to share and jointly develop technology, a strategic alliance can speed the new product development process and substantially reduce the cost. Strategic alliances are a virtual necessity if a firm wishes to compete in the global marketplace and faces competitors from Europe and Japan that are following global strategies.[1]

Strategic alliances are certainly not a panacea. Many studies, by both academic researchers and management consultants, have found that the chances of a strategic alliance succeeding are less than 50/50, where success is defined as meeting the partners' objectives.[2] The problems usually result from interorganizational conflicts between the partners, including incompatible expectations, often rooted in very different corporate cultures. It helps if the firms are of roughly equal size. It has also been found that alliances between a strong firm and a weak firm have a lower probability of success; they should be based on mutual strengths rather than being intended to overcome a strategic weakness. The strategic rationale for the alliance usually proves to have been sound, however, even if the alliance fails. That is, most alliances fail because of bad implementation and management, not because they were bad ideas in the first place. As more companies gain experience with strategic alliances, and as their experiences become the basis for more research and writing on the management of alliances, the chances for success will continue to improve.[3]

Our purpose is not to assess the management issues involved in strategic alliances but to recognize their strategic importance, the way they are changing the shape of many organizations, and the new requirements for marketing management that result from these organizational arrangements.

THE VALUE CHAIN REVISITED

The Evolving Concept of the Marketing Value Chain

In Chapter 3, we introduced the concept of the value chain, that set of linked activities from raw material to end use by the consumer involved in developing and delivering value. It includes the extraction of the raw materials and their processing, research and development activities, the design and production of goods and services, the assembly of products, their promotion and distribution, the combination of products and services into systems, pricing, customer service, and all the support functions such as advertising, sales promotion, market research, transportation, credit and financing, and public relations and publicity (see Figure 6–1). Today, the concept of the value chain must also go beyond customer use and look at the consequences of consumption and the activities necessary to deal with them, including recycling, recovery, and reclamation of waste products.

Obviously, no single economic actor is able to perform all the functions along the value chain efficiently without help from other organizations and economic actors (not even the fabled Ford Motor Company and its fully integrated River Rouge plant supplied by Ford's own mines, steamships, railroad, wool farms, and power plants). An important contribution of this concept is that it looks at the firm from the outside, as part of a total value chain, not as a separate entity isolated from the rest of the competitive world. The fundamental strategic issue for the firm is how to get the necessary functions performed most efficiently.

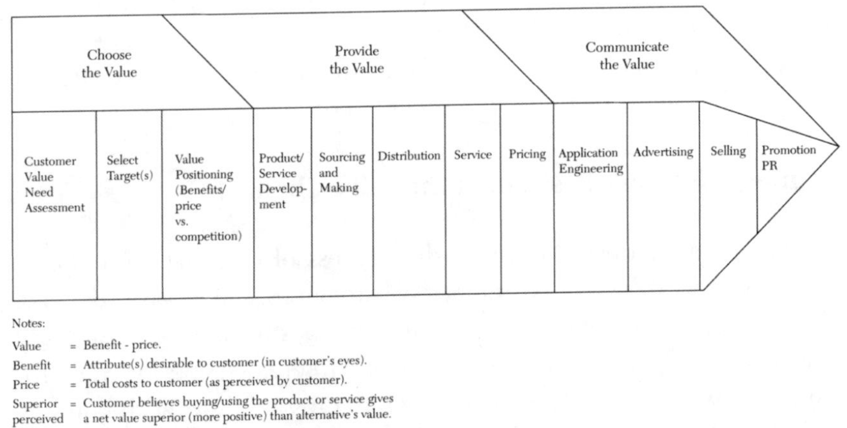

FIGURE 6–1. The marketing value-chain. *Source:* Cathy Anterasian and Lynn W. Phillips, *Discontinuities, Value Delivery, and the Share-Returns Association: A Re-examination of the "Share-Causes-Profits" Controversy,* Research Program Monograph, Report No. 88-109, (Cambridge, MA: The Marketing Science Institute, October 1988), p. 8. Reproduced with permission.

Under the old model, based on a transaction orientation as reviewed in Chapter 5, the choices for the firm were cast as a dichotomy. Either the firm could perform the function or activity itself, trying to achieve efficiency through internal, administrative, bureaucratic controls and functional specialization, or it could purchase the required product or service from an external specialist in a market-based, adversarial transaction guided primarily by the price mechanism of the competitive market. Keeping competitive pressure on external providers was a key to efficiency. Chapter 5 reviewed in detail the shortcomings of this worldview.

Every firm makes a number of strategic choices about those parts of the value chain that it will perform internally and those for which it will rely on outside suppliers and other partners. Because of the need for flexibility in responding to a changing competitive environment and the customer's continuously evolving definition of value, more and more firms are shifting their bias from owning and making to sharing assets and buying. As the firm tries to define its distinctive competences and to develop its unique value proposition for the customer, it must make a conscious strategic choice about those activities it will perform itself and those it will turn over to others. For most firms in the 1990s, this means becoming much more focused on a small set of activities where it is, or has the potential to be, the best in the world.

Defining the Firm's Position in the Value Chain

Marketing was defined earlier as the process of defining, developing, and delivering value to customers. Customer orientation leads to a value-delivery concept of strategy for the business. Every company must be clear about the functions required to create superior value for customers, where it has the competence to do something at the quality level of the best competitors in the world, and where it must depend on other partners for *their* distinctive competence, now and in the future.

We come back to the basic proposition that the customer defines value. Selection of customers, based on the firm's unique abilities to serve a particular set of market needs better than its competitors, is the first order of business in developing strategy. The firm must have done the analysis necessary for market segmentation, targeting, and positioning before it can refine its value proposition, and then decide where it must concentrate its investments in developing the resources and skills necessary to maintain its distinctive competence. The concepts of strategic focus and strategic partnering are inseparable; you can't have one without the other.

Prahalad and Hamel have developed the concept of "core competence," referred to in this book as "distinctive competence," and its relationship to strategy.[4] This concept was introduced in Chapter 3, as part of the discussion of quality and the need for continuous innovation. It is fundamental to the development of a strategy for delivering superior value to customers and to the development of strategic alliances for creating and delivering superior value. Prahalad and Hamel make the point this way:

> Nor is it possible for a company to have an intelligent alliance or sourcing strategy if it has not made a choice about where it will build competence leadership.[5] . . . How can a company make partnerships intelligently without a clear understanding of the core competencies it is trying to build and those it is attempting to prevent from being unintentionally transferred?[6]

Certain strategic alliances will be based on the need to "import" the partner's distinctive competence (one that the firm does not have and does not wish to develop itself), in order to build an up-to-date and complete product offering. This might lead to a strategic alliance with a vendor of a critical component, for example, such as the laser for a computer printer, or with an independent distribution organization in a foreign country. In this type of strategic alliance, the partners are operating at different points in the value chain; such arrangements can be called "vertical" alliances. (Marketing channels involving manufacturers and resellers at various stages have been called "vertical market structures" in the academic literature.) Corning, for example, often prefers to develop a core technology, such as ceramic filters, and to then find partners that will develop and market specific end-use products such as automotive emissions-control devices.

Other strategic alliances are created for the codevelopment of a technology that is central to the distinctive competence and strategic commitment of both parties.[7] These can be called "horizontal" alliances. In this instance, both partners are operating in the same range on the value chain. They are competitors, at least potentially. Both parties are committed to achieving and sustaining competence in that area and see the alliance as the best vehicle for maintaining it. In such alliances, developing terms for sharing the new technology poses one of the larger challenges in forming and managing the alliance.

One of the reasons for strain in strategic alliances is that, over time, vertical alliances may begin to look more horizontal as a partner that was joined because of competence at a different point in the value chain begins to move into the firm's position. A specific illustration is provided by the American firm that formed a marketing alliance with a Japanese distributor. Over time, the Japanese company gained familiarity with the American firm's product technology and became interested in manufacturing products for sale in Japan. At the same time, the American firm began to develop its own sales and service organization in Japan, creating the distinct impression that it was planning to compete with its partner. The strategic alliance ended with the firms positioned as competitors.

Marketing channels are a well-known example of strategic alliances. In this sense, strategic alliances and network organizations are not new. Partnerships between manufacturers and distributors have been around for centuries, beginning in the United States when Cyrus McCormick created a network of dealers for his mechanical reaper. The extension of similar partnership arrangements to other types of companies in the value chain is a strikingly new idea, however. It is common now to find strategic partnerships with multiple parties at several stages of the value chain, reaching backward to raw materials, core technologies, and component parts as well as forward to the last stages of distribution and the end user.

WORKING WITH RESELLERS AS PARTNERS

Marketing channels provide a prototype for strategic alliances between partners at different points in the value chain. With few exceptions, American and European firms have tended to be specialists in either manufacturing or distribution. Automobile, farm equipment, and truck manufacturers, for example, have always relied on independent dealers while large retailers such as Montgomery Ward and JCPenney have rarely owned their own factories, relying instead on manufacturers, over whom they were often able to exercise considerable influence and control. The integrated petroleum companies provided something of an exception as many did own their marketing and distribution organizations, but these were separate companies, many of which have now been sold off or shut down.

Services companies provide a more complicated situation. Insurance companies, for example, tend to be divided between those who sell their products through independent agents and those who go to market through their own sales organizations. Airlines, car rental companies, hotels, and cruise lines rely heavily on travel agents to market their products but, at the same time, maintain their own reservations, sales, and marketing organizations. Strategic marketing alliances have become common in the travel industry, bringing airlines, car rental firms, and hotels together to offer a packaged product to the traveler.

The Impact of Megaretailers on Marketing

In the United States, the past decade has been characterized by the decline, if not the demise, of the traditional, large retailing organizations, such as Sears, W.T. Grant, Montgomery Ward, and Macy's, and the emergence of new, huge, superefficient retailers, such as Wal-Mart, Kmart, Toys "R" Us, Home Depot, Price Club/Costco, and Circuit City. These "megaretailers" feature very large stores, low prices, limited selections of brands, and highly efficient ordering and supply systems. In strategic alliances with manufacturers of well-known brands, these megaretailers represent a powerful force for change and create superior value for the customer. They represent a significant shift in market power from manufacturers and their brands toward the retailer, who has become the "channel captain" in many instances.

These large retailer partners become the voice of the consumer to the manufacturer, doing research with their customers to guide product development and using sophisticated information systems to track product movement in their stores. Like manufacturers in strategic partnerships with other manufacturers and tied into their just-in-time supply systems, companies that wish to distribute through the large retailers must develop sophisticated order-processing and delivery procedures that offer quick response throughout the retailer's operations.

The ability to provide quick and superefficient response to inventory requirements becomes at least as important as the manufacturer's brands to the retailer. The manufacturer must develop and manage huge, complex systems to be an effective partner for a Wal-Mart or a Price Club/Costco. While the manufacturer's brand names are still valued by the retailer, they are not the critical issue in many manufacturer-retailer partnerships.

Low prices, based on world-class efficiency and low cost of purchases, are the critical strategic variable for the giant retailers. Studies have estimated that average prices in these stores are as much as 25% lower than those in traditional retailing outlets. They sell at "everyday low prices," rather than offering frequent price reductions and promotions at the point of sale. Manufacturers such as Procter & Gamble have encouraged the movement to everyday low prices throughout their supermarket customer organizations and have substantially cut back on their trade and consumer sales promotions. Excessive promotional activity was generally believed to detract from the brand equity created through image-building advertising. Not all retailers have responded positively to these moves, although the megaretailers distinctly favor the everyday-low-pricing approach.

Who "Owns" the Customer?

Many of the large retailers may stock only a single brand of a given product. The manufacturer is in the perhaps enviable position of being the sole supplier. There is a tremendous volume of business to be gained by becoming sole supplier to one of the megaretailers. Is that really such a great position to be in?

A shopper who goes to Wal-Mart expects to find the lowest prices anywhere. The customer needing disposable diapers frequently will buy whatever brand is offered. It is to the retailer's advantage if the consumer recognizes and values the manufacturer's brand, because this helps fulfill the promise to the customer of delivering superior value. But almost any recognized brand will fill the bill, from both the consumer's and the retailer's perspectives, as long as the price is low and the shelves are kept stocked. If a well-known brand name is not available at low prices, the retailer may find it quite acceptable to offer a store brand. The consumer's relationship is with the retailer, not with the brand manufacturer. The shopper came looking for price, not a brand name.

The manufacturer has suffered significant loss of market power under these new relationships. The retailer calls the shots. The retailer owns the customer. Procter & Gamble is valued as a supplier by Wal-Mart for its efficiency, not primarily for its brands. The consumer, while happy to find P&G brands at Wal-Mart, is probably not shopping there for that reason. Being closer to the customer, the large retail organizations are probably in a better position to determine and track changing consumer needs and preferences. Their ability to demand the lowest prices from their suppliers, as well as special services of all kinds, makes them very tough customers.[8] (Some buying practices border on being cantankerous—Wal-Mart telephones its suppliers collect!)

These retailer-manufacturer power struggles will be played out in the 1990s, and it may be a decade or longer before winners and losers can be declared. The odds, however, seem to favor the retailers. They have the relationship with the customer as well as the market power to shift billions of dollars of revenue among manufacturers. They are the voice of the consumer in the evolving network organizations. The consumer goods manufacturers who survive in this environment will be those who can modify their own organization structures to become effective partners in the consumer marketing network.

DEFINING THE CUSTOMER

Defining the customer becomes a key strategic issue for the players in a network organization. Who is Procter & Gamble's customer: Wal-Mart or the shopper who buys the diapers? Can it be both? These are critically important questions, given the basic principles of the new marketing concept:

- Customers define the business.
- Customers define value.
- Customer-orientation should be the driving force in every business.
- Marketing must move from a transactions- to a relationship-orientation.
- Information about customer needs, preferences, and buying patterns is the most important input to all business decisions.
- The firm should be committed to continuous innovation to offer superior value to customers.

The definition of the customer must be found in the concept of *partnership*. From the manufacturer's perspective, the brand name represents a promise to the consumer or end user of consistent product quality and performance. Because that has value for the consumer, it also has value for the reseller. But as discussed in Chapter 5, if the consumer is not known to the manufacturer, there is no possibility of a relationship between them. If there is no brand identification, the question is moot; if the customer can't identify the manufacturer, there can be no relationship.

Even if their customers are not known to the manufacturer of the branded product, they frequently *are* known to the reseller. Some retailers such as Sam's Club (an affiliate of Wal-Mart), are "for members only" and charge an annual membership fee. Others such as JCPenney establish a relationship with customers through credit cards and charging privileges. Buying clubs are the basis for relationship building in supermarket chains that have adopted scanner technology and built customer databases. In these instances, it is the reseller who "owns" the customers and who has the relationship with them. The manufacturer is a partner with the reseller in delivering superior value to customers, embodied in the branded product and supported by efficient systems for order processing, delivery, and in-store stocking.

Partnership is the key concept. All the partners in the network organization must share a common commitment to delivering superior value to the ultimate customer, and the work of each partner is not done until the end user is satisfied.

Whose customer is it? There are two answers:

1. The customer "belongs to" the company with the customer database and therefore the opportunity to build a relationship. With that ownership of the customer goes the awesome responsibility for keeping the rest of the network organization informed about the customer's evolving definition of value.
2. The customer belongs to the entire network organization. He or she isn't really "our" customer or "your" customer. Rather, all firms in the network are engaged in the joint pursuit of satisfying the customer by delivering super value. Anyone who is not committed to that basic objective cannot be an effective partner. Once again, adversarial, transaction-oriented thinking is out of place.

For the manufacturer of consumer packaged goods, the most important relationship is with its resellers. The reseller company and its buying and operating personnel are the names in the manufacturer's database, the customers with whom it is in daily contact, the ones who tell it what it must do to be an effective partner in the relationship.

For the industrial supplier, the manufacturer-customer is the focal point, but here too the vision of the total network organization must extend out to the consumer end user. The manufacturer of textile fibers, as it tweaks molecules and extrusion processes to create its yarns, must look beyond its immediate customer—the fabric manufacturer. It must be able to look out past the garment designer and manufacturer, through the fashion retailer, to focus on satisfying the consumer, who wants durability, color fastness, easy laundering, moisture wicking and quick drying, and a subtle look of worn-out elegance!

CREATING A "BOUNDARYLESS" ORGANIZATION

A network organization, then, is a set of interlinked, interdependent companies, each concentrating on a fairly narrow range of economic activities where it strives to achieve best-in-the-world performance, collaborating with the other partners to deliver superior value to end-user customers. The partners deal with one another through long-term commitments and relationships supported by contractual agreements and facilitated by processes for mutual problem-solving and conflict resolution. These relationships are *collaborative* rather than adversarial, focused on maximizing the *long-term value* of the relationship to both parties rather than the value of each individual transaction for each of the partners. Each partner, ideally, understands its distinctive competences and is committed to maintaining them while relying on the partners for their distinctive competence, constantly challenging them to do a better job.

The *Keiretsu* Model

The network organizations evolving in the United States are in some respects similar to the *keiretsu* organizations in Japan. These are interlocking networks of companies from multiple industries, often linked primarily through buyer-seller partnerships and distribution arrangements. The keiretsu are usually headed by a large bank or manufacturer, which often serves as a source of "patient capital" for other companies in the network. Among the best-known keiretsu are those of Mitsui (which includes Toyota), Mitsubishi, Sumitomo, Sanwo, and Dai Ichi Kangyo. These long-term relationships among companies are typically supported by linked ownership, with each partner owning a small number of shares, usually less than 1% of the total, in the other partner. The objective of share ownership is to symbolize the mutual commitments within the keiretsu, not to exert any kind of control. The keiretsu usually functions on the assumption that the partners will not do business with competitors outside the network.

The American network organizations differ in a number of important ways from their Japanese counterparts:

- Banking regulations keep banks separate from manufacturing in the United States.
- The American networks have much more limited share ownership among the partners, although in some instances a major firm may buy interest in a smaller supplier, for example, to provide the capital for a major R&D project or plant expansion needed to become a just-in-time supplier.
- The power of the leader of the network to dictate terms and to control the operations of its suppliers is much more limited by both law and culture than is the case in Japan. Supplier firms in the United States may be both as large and as innovative as their industrial customers, whereas in Japan the large parent/customer company provides the leadership on technical innovation.

American firms must learn the attitudes and behaviors of cooperation and collaboration that are characteristic of Japanese business if they are to be effective participants in network organizations. The relatively poor success record of strategic alliances in the United States is due in part to strong values of independence and the old adversarial tactics and distrust that have characterized market-based transactions-oriented relationships.

The network organizations evolving among American companies are really a new and distinct organization form, neither hierarchies nor markets.[9] Prices are determined not by the impersonal market but as an outcome of negotiation processes and joint problem solving focused on delivering superior value to customers. Price is an output of, not an input to, the buyer's and seller's decision processes. But, unlike hierarchical organizational structures, the partners maintain their freedom and flexibility for dealing with those economic actors who are most efficient and most responsive to changing market conditions. Decision makers can focus on externally driven definitions of value and efficiency, not internal mandates of policy, procedures, and protocol designed to protect the hierarchy and defend the status quo.

The Demise of Hierarchy

While elements of hierarchical organization forms will remain in most companies for the foreseeable future, it is the modifications and transformations of hierarchies that should attract our attention. In the words of James Houghton, Chairman and Chief Executive Officer of Corning, Inc., "The age of the hierarchy is over."[10] A recent article in *Business Week* identified five characteristics of the new organizational model, each of which has been analyzed in this chapter or in Chapter 5 and compared it with the traditional corporate form as follows:

1. *Excellence.* The commitment to a focus on core competences versus the attempt to be "best of everything."
2. *Information Technology.* Linking independent and geographically separated companies in common purpose versus the practice of bringing everything "in house," usually in large factories and office buildings.
3. *Opportunism.* Flexible definition and redefinition of partnering arrangements in response to changing market conditions versus persistence in maintaining the existing organization structure, size, and procedures.
4. *Trust.* Relationships based on mutual commitment versus the old assumptions of arms-length, market-based, adversarial transactions.
5. *No Borders.* Organizations based on cooperative relationships among independent actors versus the old organizations depicted by boxes, lines, and pyramids defining precise arrangements of authority and responsibility, evaluation, and control.

Business Week called this new organization form "the virtual corporation," adopting a term already in use by several consultants, authors, and management gurus.[11] This name would seem to overlook the fact that the new organization is not a corporation but an interlinking of separate companies. It is an appropriate term, however, from the point of view of the focal firm, the company that is reconfiguring its operations around partnering. In fact, each company might be seen as a participant in multiple networks, some of which it controls and others in which it has a supplier position. This raises some interesting issues, as previously noted, about the leadership of the network. As a general pattern, the company in the buyer's position within the network, and the focal point for organizing the value-creating capabilities of the others, can be expected to be the leader.

Others have called these networks "boundaryless" organizations. Once again, General Electric Company may be leading the way with a new concept of management and organization, as it did with the original marketing concept, strategic planning, and the PIMS studies. Although GE management would probably not claim to have created the concept of the "boundaryless" organization, it appears to have coined the term and has been its most vocal advocate. In GE's 1990 *Annual Report,* Chairman and CEO John F. Welch commented:

> In a boundary-less company, suppliers aren't "outsiders." They are drawn closer and become trusted partners in the total business process. Customers are seen for what they are—the lifeblood of a company. Customers' vision of their needs and the company's view become identical, and every effort of every man and woman in the company is focused on satisfying those needs.
>
> In a boundary-less company, internal functions begin to blur. Engineering doesn't design a product and then "hand it off" to manufacturing. They form a team along with marketing and sales, finance, and the rest. Customer service? It's not somebody's job. It's everybody's job.[12]

As Mr. Welch points out, the concept of the boundaryless company as part of a network has clear implications for the traditional functional form of organization. Functional specialization and autonomy are relics of the past. Separate departments and staff functions, the well-known functional "chimneys" or "silos" of management, with their hierarchical reporting and approval processes, are simply too slow and too complicated for the new organization. It takes too long for the required levels of authority to approve decisions and then communicate them back down and out to the parts of the organization that will have to implement those decisions.

In place of functional organizations, teams of people with the knowledge and skills necessary to address and resolve a particular problem are created, managed, and then disbanded as problems are resolved and new opportunities and challenges emerge. In Chapter 3, we saw that teams are a key part of total quality management and can bring the relevant skills from multiple disciplines into a coordinated response to a customer's problem. In network organizations, the team members may come from several companies. Such cooperative endeavors are the essence of network organizations.

Within General Electric, a process called "Work Out" has been underway for several years with the objective of breaking down traditional functional barriers and hierarchical decision processes and creating flexible, team-based mechanisms for customer-focused problem solving. The GE process is guided by a value-delivery concept of strategy, focused on understanding customer needs, with a goal of becoming the most efficient producer in the world in its chosen businesses.[13]

With this strong focus on customer needs and creating superior value for customers, network organizations represent a fulfillment of the promise of the original marketing concept. Profit is a reward for creating a satisfied customer, for having matched a set of customer needs with the firm's unique resources and skills. Strategic partnering and relationship marketing configure the firm's capabilities with those of other economic actors to create the best, most efficient, solutions to customer problems in a competitive marketplace.

Consistent with the value-delivery concept of strategy, the shared problem for all the players in the system is to keep focused on the customer's constantly changing definition of value. This poses a fundamentally new challenge for marketing management in the context of network organizations.

THE ROLE OF MARKETING IN NETWORK ORGANIZATIONS

The network organization is centered around the firm at the hub, what we will call the *core firm,* the leader of the network (see Figure 6–2). The core firm is defined by its core competences and its customer base. Its knowledge of its customers, its relationships with them, and their trust in the company make up one of its core competences. To

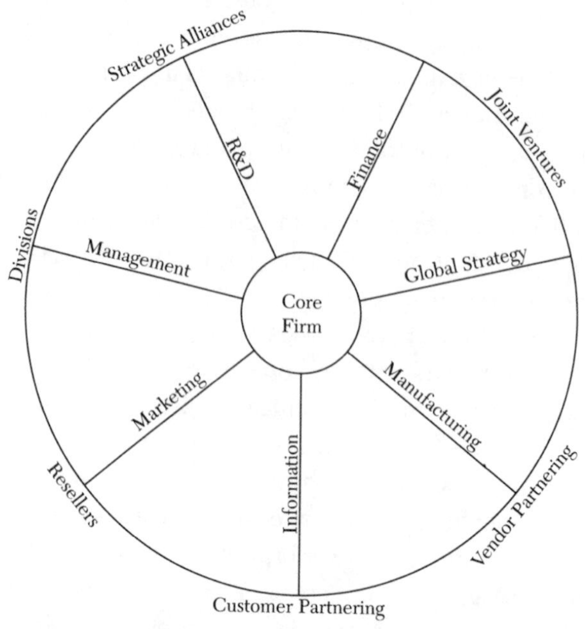

FIGURE 6–2. The network organization.

the maximum extent possible, this competence should be databased, embedded in a customer information file that is computerized and available to all participants in the network. The network organization consists of the core firm plus its resellers, customer partners, vendor partners, joint ventures, and other strategic alliances as well as its more traditional divisions and other strategic business units. The traditional management functions are the knowledge and skills that hold the network together—marketing, finance, manufacturing, information management, and general management. These management functions represent knowledge and expertise, but the boundaries between them become permeable and the organization functions as a team. The functions are bound together in the context of a global strategy that defines markets globally and is built on sound information about customers and competitors.

The essential role of marketing in a network organization is to keep all the partners and business units focused on customers and their changing definition of value in the competitive marketplace.

Marketing's responsibility can be thought of as being "expert on the customer." Marketing's principal activity is providing information to decision makers throughout the organization, and this is the main justification for maintaining marketing as a separate and identifiable business function. The marketing function needs to be supported by a highly competent management information capability and the appropriate investments in information technology. The overarching objective of all marketing activity should be ongoing assessment of customer needs and the company's product offering compared with those of competitors, defining new ways to deliver superior value to customers. The product offering is a variable, subject to continuous improvement.

A related responsibility for marketing management, in conjunction with top management of the corporation and of individual business units, is to be an advocate for the customer throughout the organization. It will be recalled that one of the shortcomings of the original marketing concept was that it was frequently not supported by top management, who continued to put the shareholders' interests ahead of the customers'. Chapter 7 describes in greater detail the problem of developing a customer-oriented organizational culture and also traces its positive impact on profitability.

Marketing at the Corporate Level

At the corporate level, which is to say at the hub of the network and from the point of view of the core corporation, the strategic problem is to define what business the company is in and to determine the mission, scope, and structure of the firm, specifically its position in the value chain and its distinctive competences. As part of corporate management, the basic responsibilities of the marketing function fall in five areas: (1) customer advocacy, (2) market structure analysis, (3) positioning in the value chain, (4) professional development, and (5) strategic partnering.[14]

Customer Advocacy

As just noted, marketing must be an advocate for the customer. Marketing managers must take the lead in making sure that all business decisions take the customer's point of view as the starting point. The very best customer information must be available throughout the network to enable consensus about the performance variables that are important to customers and the attributes of the product offering that will serve those interests best. At the top management level, corporate leaders must be able to explain to other constituencies, especially owners and suppliers, why their interests are also ultimately best served by putting the customer's interests first.

Market Structure Analysis

Marketing should also be responsible for market analysis as the key input to strategic planning. At the corporate level, the central question is what businesses (product/market combinations) to be in. The marketing task is to understand the structure of the market in terms of the strategic market segments defined by sets of customers with common needs and buying patterns and sets of competitors serving those segments with differentiated strategies. The market position, resources and skills, and distinctive competences of each major competitor must be analyzed in detail. As a prelude to a decision to enter or to exit a business, it is essential to understand the key success factors in that business. How do customers define value and how do competitors provide it? Can our firm establish a leadership position in this market with a distinctive and superior product offering? Of particular importance is developing an understanding of the strength of the relationships between competitors and major customers in their served markets.

Positioning in the Value Chain

Although the development of the value proposition is a strategic problem that must be addressed at the level of the business unit, a prior set of issues needs to be addressed at the corporate level, namely the positioning of the firm in the value chain. Marketing plays a key role here because the task must be approached from the perspective of the customer, whose definition of value must be translated into specific capabilities and activities. Performing those activities involves specific skills and resources that the firm must either develop and maintain internally or acquire through strategic partnering. Where in the value chain will the firm attempt to establish a unique and sustainable competitive advantage?

Professional Development

At the corporate level, and in conjunction with human resource management, the marketing manager must ensure that there are programs for recruiting, developing, and deploying professional marketing management talent throughout the organization. As a starting point, marketing management must be recognized as a distinct and important management competence, not simply as a reward for a successful sales management or strategic planning performance—although such experience can be helpful. Marketing people must be selected for their analytical skills and their understanding of the marketplace, especially customer needs and buying patterns, relationships with distributors and other key partners, and competitors' business strategies and product offerings. In a large corporation, marketing management at the corporate level, again in conjunction with the human resource professionals, should also have responsibility for developing and delivering training programs to nurture an understanding of marketing and of the marketplace throughout the organization, across all disciplines and functions, at all levels of management.

Strategic Partnering

At the corporate level, marketing management should have central responsibility for designing, developing, and managing strategic partnerships with key customers, resellers, and vendors. These partnerships are a direct outcome of the definition of the firm's position in the value chain. Contractual relationships with these partners should be designed specifically to ensure maximum value for customers, including clear statements about new product development activities and responsibilities, expectations about cost- and price-reductions, and criteria for assessing performance. In most companies, marketing management should be the repository of the highest levels of experience and skill in designing and managing strategic partnerships, including the necessary skills in negotiation.

In the traditional sense, marketing management does not "do marketing" at the corporate level. Rather, the function of marketing at the corporate level is that of advocating for the customer, representing the customer's viewpoint in the strategic planning process, positioning the firm within the value chain and creatively defining its distinctive competences, developing marketing management competence throughout the organization, and developing the firm's strategic partnering arrangements.

In network organizations, marketing management has a critically important role to play with dimensions that differ significantly from traditional corporate responsibilities. Defining the firm's position in the value chain and guiding the development of strategic alliances to offer superior value to customers are unique responsibilities in network organizations. Marketing management's fundamental and essential responsibility is to keep the whole network focused on the customer by designing a corporate-level strategy, and organization structure and culture, appropriate to the firm's value-delivery mission.

This task does not call for a large marketing staff at the corporate level. Rather, it requires experience, expertise, and sophistication in understanding customer needs and communicating this understanding throughout the organization. It would be a mistake to have marketing become a bureaucratic enclave, but it would be equally disastrous to skimp on commitment of resources necessary to attract and retain the most competent marketing management personnel.

Marketing at the Business (SBU) Level

At the corporate level, the strategic question was "What business are we in?" At the level of the individual business unit, the strategic question is "How should we compete?" The tasks for marketing management at this level are:

- Market segmentation, targeting, and positioning.
- Developing the value proposition for the business.
- Developing the partnering strategies for the business unit.

The value proposition becomes the basis for communicating with customers and for focusing the entire organization, including strategic partners, on delivering superior value to customers. Once again, the key responsibility for marketing management, this time at the business unit level, is to be expert on the customer and to communicate that knowledge throughout the organization.

Market Segmentation, Targeting, and Positioning

The analytical work of marketing managers at the corporate level concentrated on understanding market structure, clusterings of customers and competitors into market segments. At the business unit level, the problem is to understand each segment in detail, to select those segments that the firm will focus on—a task which usually calls for some resegmentation of the market and presents the opportunity to define new segments, and to develop the firm's positioning relative to competition in those segments. The discussion of these subjects in Chapter 4 was aimed primarily at this management level.

Developing the Value Proposition

The value proposition summarizes the firm's business strategy at the business unit level. In a network organization, it performs the essential function of focusing all the partners on common definitions of value for the customer and coordinating their efforts in the work of delivering superior value.

Developing Partnering Strategies

As the individual business unit defines its distinctive competences (a subset of the distinctive competences of the larger corporate/network organization), and specifies its position in the value chain, it identifies the need for partners to deliver a superior product offering to customers. Those partners include resellers of various kinds, partners for the codevelopment of technology and new products, critical vendors for goods and services that help to complete the product offering, and partners with related product offerings that can be packaged into larger systems of solutions to customer problems. A defining characteristic of a network organization is that virtually every activity, function, product component, and service is analyzed in terms of whether it should be provided by the core firm or by a strategic vendor. The "make versus buy" question—whether something is to be obtained through transactions, relationships, alliances, or internal production—is part of every strategic decision and is recognized as an option for the performance of every step in the value chain. This analysis includes all the services performed by the marketing organization, including advertising, sales promotion, personal selling, distribution, package design, and publicity, as well as all product components and materials. Marketing management guides the search for answers to that question by defining the customer's best interest for all the parties involved, by looking at the product offering through the eyes of the customer, and by knowing the competitive options available to customers in the marketplace.

Marketing at the Tactical Level

At the tactical level, we are back to the traditional role of the marketing function—decisions about product, price, promotion, and distribution required to implement the business strategy. This is the level of *functional* strategy as distinct from corporate and business level strategies. At this level, the organization requires functional specialists in the individual business units including sales managers, product managers, pricing specialists, sales promotion experts, advertising managers, and so on, to decide on and deliver the specific product offering for the customer. They too must be "expert on the customer" and guided by the overarching value proposition. They can also be controlled and evaluated by specific budgetary objectives and other quantitative and qualitative measures of customer satisfaction and business performance, including sales volume, market share, and profitability. Their mandate is to obtain maximum returns from the financial resources that they are given as part of the budgeting process.

Even at the tactical level, however, marketing takes on new forms in network organizations. The focus shifts from transactions to relationships and alliances with customers. Long-term goals and measurements become more important relative to short-term gains in volume. Marketing managers do more of their analysis using the customer database that is developed as part of relationship marketing, providing the opportunity for analysis with real customers about the possible impact of virtually every marketing action.

Regis McKenna, a well-known marketing consultant, author, and lecturer, has articulated the changes in marketing management in a fashion that fits nicely with Jack Welch's concept of the boundaryless organization:

> The marketer must be the integrator, both internally—synthesizing technological capability with market needs—and externally—bringing the customer into the company as a participant in the development and adaptation of goods and services. It is a fundamental shift in the role and purpose of marketing: from manipulation of the customer to genuine customer involvement; from telling and selling to communicating and sharing knowledge; from last-in-line function to corporate-credibility champion. . . .
>
> The relationships are the key, the basis of customer choice and company adaptation. After all, what is a successful brand but a special relationship? And who better than a company's marketing people to create, sustain, and interpret the relationship between the company, its suppliers, and its customers?[15]

An important detail of McKenna's comment is that marketing is equally responsible for guiding relationships with suppliers and customers, as part of its responsibility for value delivery. The vendors become part of the company's product offering and part of the relationship with the customer. Under a value-delivery concept of strategy, the relationship between the company, its suppliers, and its customers is seamless (see Figure 6–3). Marketing is the management function responsible for defining, developing, and delivering superior value to customers.

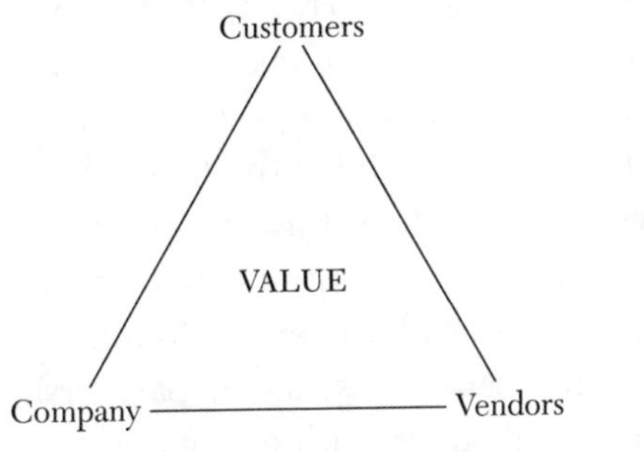

FIGURE 6–3. Partnerships in a value-delivery concept of strategy.

SUMMARY

Organization forms are evolving rapidly, from hierarchical, bureaucratic divisionalized pyramids into networks of strategic partnerships along with more traditional business units. The objective of this organizational evolution is to respond more quickly and effectively to changing customer needs. The new organization forms offer more flexibility and help the firm focus on its distinctive competence while it depends on partners for their distinctive competences as necessary to complete the product offering to the customer.

Providing superior value to the customer is the purpose of the network organization. In network organizations, the most important business asset is the customer base and the ongoing relationship with those customers. Customers define the business because they define value. As their definition of value changes, so must the business change.

Within these new organization forms, the role of marketing must be redefined. At one level, marketing is no longer a functional specialty because the entire organization and all the individual actors must take responsibility for delivering superior value to customers. However, professional marketing managers are necessary at both the corporate and business unit levels to provide information and expertise about customers and to implement the firm's business strategy with product, pricing, promotion, and distribution strategies and policies. Marketing strategy must guide the sales function.

The key marketing function in the network organization is to manage the relationship between the firm and its customers (and information about them) and to keep the entire network focused on the customer's definition of value. Marketing represents the customer to the company as well as the company to the customer. At the corporate level, this calls for advocacy on behalf of customers; analyzing market structure to determine which businesses to be in and how to position the business within the market; defining the firm's distinctive competence; developing a partnering strategy for delivering value; and developing qualified marketing management throughout the network organization.

At the business unit level, the strategic role of marketing shifts to that of developing and managing strategic partnerships, including long-term relationships and alliances with customers, suppliers, and technology providers; market segmentation, targeting, and product positioning;

and developing and communicating the firm's value proposition throughout the network. At the tactical level, marketing managers within the business unit must design and implement the marketing mix (decisions about product, price, promotion, and distribution), with a focus on long-term customer relationships as appropriate.

In the network organization, the boundaries separating the company from its customers, suppliers, distributors, and even its competitors (as potential partners for the development of technology) break down. Likewise, within the organization, old functional boundaries give way to cooperation and teamwork, focused on finding the best solutions to customer problems, reducing the time and cost required to create and deliver a complete product offering. Network organizations are a tool for achieving customer orientation and represent a fulfillment of the marketing concept.

7 ORGANIZATIONAL CULTURE AND CUSTOMER ORIENTATION

We exist to provide value to our customers, which means that in addition to quality and service, we have to save them money.

I know most companies don't have cheers, and most board chairmen probably wouldn't lead them if they did.

Sam Walton
Made in America (Doubleday, 1992, pp. 10, 157)

The new marketing concept calls for putting the customer first—always. At its heart, the marketing concept is a statement of corporate or organizational culture, a set of values and beliefs relating to the importance of serving the customer. To repeat, from Chapter 1, a statement by the father of the original marketing concept, Peter Drucker:

> [Marketing] encompasses the entire business. It is the whole business seen from the point of view of its final result, that is from the customer's point of view.[1]

Adoption of the marketing concept as a management philosophy is a shared recognition that everything that happens within the company must be focused on creating satisfied customers and maintaining a commitment to continuous improvement on behalf of the customer. This notion of a shared viewpoint is at the heart of most definitions of organizational culture. Following a definition proposed by Stanley

Davis,[2] organizational culture can be described as *the pattern of shared values and beliefs that help the members of an organization understand its functioning and provide them with norms for behavior in the organization.* Thus, implementation of the new marketing concept calls for understanding corporate culture and managing it with the objective of focusing everyone's attention on their role in delivering value to customers.

ORIGINS OF THE "CORPORATE CULTURE" IDEA

In the 1980s, corporate culture became something of a fad among business commentators and management experts. The concept of culture was simultaneously applied to nations, companies, and groups within organizations. Japanese companies were said to derive some of their competitive edge in the global marketplace from unique characteristics of the Japanese national culture, including cooperativeness, commitment to the larger group, and a strong work ethic. While national or "background" culture is an important consideration, it is distinct from the concept of organizational culture.

At the corporate level, the successes and failures of companies as diverse as Apple Computer and IBM, Wal-Mart and Sears, EDS (Electronic Data Systems, founded by Ross Perot) and General Motors, and Reynolds Metals and Bethlehem Steel were attributed by some observers to their underlying organizational cultures. Yet it is an open question whether all organizations have identifiable, strong cultures, and whether the culture, as expressed by the values of the founders, is the same as the culture practiced by current organizational members. Many authors, such as Wilkins and Ouchi[3] and Martin,[4] have argued that a strong corporate culture is an exception rather than the rule and that multiple cultures may exist in any organization, often in conflict with one another.

Some experts argue that strong culture is more often found at the level of the work group, in what might be called "clan" or "group" culture. For example, a strong professional identity shared by a group of functional specialists in a field like engineering, chemistry, or actuarial science may be thought of as a type of organizational culture. Within a given company, the superior performance of a particular department, project, or team is often believed to reflect a strong *subculture* shared by the group that distinguishes it from other groups within the organization. Such attributions abound in stories of successful new product developments, for example, encapsulated in phrases like "skunkworks," and in the mythology of superperforming districts within a sales force.

It has become apparent that culture means different things to different people. The scholarly literature on the subject of corporate or organizational culture contains many varied and even conflicting concepts of culture, making it difficult to test some of the basic assertions about the relationship between organizational culture and business unit performance. Only recently has significant progress been made in understanding how organizational culture, and customer orientation as part of corporate culture, relates to such measures of performance as profitability, rate of sales growth, and market share.

In this chapter, we will first consider the relationships among business strategy, organization structure, and culture in the implementation of the new marketing concept. We will then quickly review several different views of corporate culture. While the argument about the correct definition of corporate culture is far from resolved, we will examine a view of culture as organizational knowledge or "cognition" that has proven to be helpful in assessing differences in the extent to which a firm is focused on its customers and how that, in turn, relates to performance. Finally, we will look at some research studies that have produced interesting evidence of the connections between corporate culture, customer orientation, and business performance.

HOW STRATEGY, ORGANIZATION STRUCTURE, AND CORPORATE CULTURE RELATE TO THE MARKETING CONCEPT

Implementation of the new marketing concept requires management attention at three levels: strategy, structure, and culture. Previous chapters have stressed that the company's business *strategy* must be focused on creating customer satisfaction through delivering superior value. The *structure* of the organization must be designed to implement the business strategy and to work with business partners to create and deliver superior value. Finally, the underlying values and beliefs of the entire organization must put the customer first in all organization activities. Studies of business success and failure have strongly suggested that *culture* is often at the roots of strategic outcomes and that, of all of the variables, culture is the hardest to manage and change.

At the *strategic* level of the new marketing concept, the challenge is to develop a business strategy around market segmentation, targeting, and positioning, one that clearly defines the value proposition of the company and its unique competitive advantage over the competition. The definition of market segments and target customers and the requirements for satisfying those customers, including investments in innovation, distribution, and promotion, should be at the center of the business plan. Financial goals should be seen as outcomes of successfully meeting market-oriented objectives, not as objectives in themselves.

Organization *structure* is the second element in the implementation of the new marketing concept. In traditional, hierarchical organizations, the marketing department was a separate management function responsible for product, pricing, promotion, and distribution policies. Such a view of the marketing function within the business is obsolete under the new marketing concept. Even in traditional, hierarchical organizations (which are, after all, still the norm), the marketing function must be decentralized away from the corporate level and out into the operating units of the business. At the business unit level, marketing responsibility and sensitivity must be dispersed through the organization so that everyone knows customer satisfaction is their overriding job goal.

In the new network organizations, the challenge for the marketing professionals at the hub of the network is to be expert on the customer, providing customer information to decision makers throughout the organization. Marketing management must also take the lead in advocating for the customer with business partners throughout the network. The overriding objective is to keep all efforts focused on the customer, putting the customer's interest ahead of those of *all* the other resource providers, including owners/shareholders, management, suppliers, and the employees themselves. It is the customer's willingness to pay that ultimately determines the value created for the owners of each of the individual business units and the welfare of the other claimants on these firms and their resources.

Every manager is familiar with the mandates of strategy and organization structure. Organizational *culture* is a less familiar concept. While everyone talks about organizational culture, there is seldom any depth of understanding of its sources, components, and influence. It is hard for managers to make organizational culture explicit and to discuss it analytically because it is both pervasive and elusive, multifaceted and intangible. These characteristics are at the heart of the very nature of organizational culture.

This essential feature of culture, its simultaneous ambiguity, pervasiveness, and intangibility, has been captured in the definition of culture as "the things people take for granted," the underlying set of common assumptions that make all other forms of interaction, social exchange, and joint action possible. One of the most significant challenges in implementing the new marketing concept, then, is to make the assumptions of corporate culture explicit, to be sure that everyone understands and is committed to the importance of putting the customer first. In this sense, the problem is to make the "intangible" values of a customer-oriented culture tangible in the form of specific words, symbols, behaviors, processes, and other actions.

THREE DEFINITIONS OF ORGANIZATIONAL CULTURE

Looking at organizational culture in different perspectives helps demonstrate the depth, complexity, and richness of the subject. Scholarly researchers, struggling to develop a reasonable definition of the concept that will facilitate studies of the formation and functioning of organizational culture, have followed several different research traditions from the fields of anthropology, sociology, and social psychology. Martin, for example, identified three very different concepts of culture as *integration, differentiation,* and *fragmentation* and then examined the same company using these different perspectives, in a manner reminiscent of the fable about the blind men and the elephant.

In the *integration* perspective, culture is what people share, implying there is an organizational consensus about certain important issues. The integration perspective would seem most appropriate for considering culture at the corporate level, from the point of view of top management. The new marketing concept requires that such a perspective be developed—that a commitment to customer orientation, value delivery, and quality be accepted as a basic set of norms throughout the organization, at all levels of the organization and across all functions.

In the *differentiation* view, culture is what makes people different from one another, and can be the source of conflict within an organization, as seen in the tension between business functions such as marketing and engineering. Those using this perspective find it not surprising that the values and viewpoints of top management often differ from those of people at lower levels of the organization. They are supported by the researchers who argue that a strong corporate level culture is more the exception than the rule. Subcultures may be much stronger within the organization. In this sense culture, or more accurately subcultures, can be a problem for the manager committed to the new marketing concept as different business functions and management levels will likely disagree about the value of putting the customer's interests first. The marketing people, advocates for the customer, may have to battle a top management committed to putting the shareholders first, R&D managers who want to pursue technology for its own sake, and manufacturing managers who want to produce large runs of standard products with cushions of a large order backlog and work-in-process inventories.

In the *fragmentation* perspective, culture is multifaceted and ambiguous, neither a monolithic shared consensus nor a distinct set of well-defined viewpoints. Rather, in the fragmentation viewpoint, culture is a dynamic concept reflecting changes in group composition, organization structure, and the external environment. People may be members of multiple subcultures within the organization and their self-concepts are likely to change rather frequently. The agenda of the organization changes continuously as the firm senses changes in the external environment and responds to them. Coalitions form and dissolve as people address the changing set of issues, and organizational culture changes accordingly. The ability to track and understand organizational culture is very limited in this view. Ambiguity is seen as *the* defining characteristic of culture. The fragmentation perspective would distrust organizational culture studies that focus on areas of consensus, arguing that these may be least important and of little use to organizational actors who are trying to deal with real, pressing, immediate problems in their jobs.[5]

These three different views of culture are interesting indeed, but each seems to offer only a partial view of culture based on limited aspects of the overall concept. Furthermore, the attempt to make these views relevant at all levels of the organization, rather than differentiating among the corporate, group, and subgroup levels, may create something of a strawman. For an in-depth understanding of an organization, it is probably useful to employ all three points of view, using the integration perspective to analyze the total organization as viewed by top management and employing the precepts of the differentiation and fragmentation perspectives to analyze conflict and disagreement at lower levels.

Implementation of the new marketing concept calls for an integrated perspective, a top management commitment to putting the customer first that pervades the organization. Overcoming barriers to its acceptance requires understanding the conflicts and ambiguities that exist at the operating levels of the business, guiding people away from traditional functional management viewpoints toward a consensus that puts the customer's interests first. The integration perspective on corporate culture should be the goal—a single, pervasive commitment throughout the organization, guided from the top, that gives primacy to satisfying customer needs and expectations. The differentiation and fragmentation perspectives define the problems managers must address in pursuing the goals of customer orientation. The latter two viewpoints can be useful management tools, however, sensitizing management to the issues that must be resolved in developing customer orientation throughout the organization.

FIVE PERSPECTIVES ON ORGANIZATIONAL CULTURE

From the point of view of top management policy makers, there are still many different ways to think about organizational culture.[6] While all these viewpoints have primarily an integration perspective, each comes from a different research tradition in the social sciences and is potentially useful for understanding a set of issues important to marketing managers. The five different viewpoints have been very effectively summarized by Linda Smircich:[7]

1. Comparative management.
2. Contingency management.
3. Organizational cognition.
4. Organizational symbolism.
5. Structural psychodynamics.

These five perspectives differ in terms of whether culture is seen as external or internal to the firm, whether culture is an input to organizational decisions and actions or an outcome of them, and whether the perspective sees culture as a part of the organization and a variable that can be measured and managed, or as a metaphor for the organization itself. Thus, we can characterize each viewpoint as to whether it sees culture as external or internal, input or outcome, variable or metaphor.

Comparative Management

For many managers, the comparative management view of organizational culture is the most familiar. It was popularized in the 1970s and 1980s by a number of books on Japanese management and other studies of cross-national differences in company performance and competitive effectiveness.[8] Obviously, this perspective treats national culture as a major determinant of corporate culture; it sees culture as *external* to the firm. Culture is an input to the firm's decision-making processes and a major influence on the behavior of organizational actors, and it is a variable that can be studied by academics and consultants although not controlled directly by managers.

Students of Japanese management have been impressed by the extent to which Japanese firms seem to focus on the customer although marketing departments as they are known in the United States are virtually unheard of in Japan. The Japanese language *kanji* characters for the word "customer" are literally translated as "honored guest." If Japanese companies are, in fact, characteristically customer oriented, it may be because Japanese customers are notoriously demanding in terms of quality and service. Long-term customer relationships are extremely important in the Japanese culture.[9] Perhaps one of the unique features of corporate culture in Japan is that it is so strongly influenced by national culture. It is an open question whether national culture exerts an equally strong influence on organizations in other countries. It is inappropriate, however, to equate national background culture with the unique culture of an individual organization.

Contingency Management

Like the comparative management approach, the contingency management perspective also treats culture as a variable that can be measured and as an input to management action. However, in contrast to the comparative view, it sees culture as *internal* to the firm, something that managers can direct and influence, if not strictly control. In this view, culture develops within the firm and is unique to it. It is called a "contingent" perspective because it sees performance outcomes as dependent on cultural variables. Culture is defined as a set of values, beliefs, commitments, and meanings shared by the members of the organization. This viewpoint was captured in such well-known books as Peters and Waterman's *In Search of Excellence*[10] and Deal and Kennedy's *Corporate Culture.*[11] Successful companies were believed to be characterized by such cultural attributes as teamwork, customer focus, employee empowerment, and a commitment to excellence.

In both the comparative and contingency management perspectives, culture is seen as a tool that can be taken into account and managed, at least to a degree, in ways that will enhance organizational performance. In both cases, the management task is to find consistency among strategy, structure, and culture. Thus, the strategy that worked well for a business unit in North America may have to be modified substantially to fit with the Japanese subsidiary's culture.

A concern for finding the proper fit of culture, strategy, and structure created a boom industry for management consulting in the mid-1980s.[12] More recently, the hiring of Louis Gerstner from RJR Nabisco to replace John Akers as chairman and CEO of IBM has been widely cited as an example of the need to bring in an outsider with a new set of values at the very top of the organization if a fundamental change in corporate culture is the objective. This has been said to be the specific intent of the Gerstner hiring—to start the process of changing IBM's corporate culture.[13] Although altering the pervasive, complex, and ambiguous nature of corporate culture takes more than a change at the CEO level, that can be an important and symbolic beginning.

These first two views of corporate culture, the comparative and contingency management perspectives, treat culture as a *variable* to be considered and, if possible, manipulated, in developing business strategy and organization structure. Culture is seen as one part of the organization.

In the next three perspectives on organization culture, culture is treated as a *metaphor* for the organization itself, another way of thinking about what the organization really is. A metaphor is a figure of speech or a symbol applied to something that it does not literally denote, to suggest a meaningful comparison and to further understanding of the concept. In explaining the ambiguous and complex concept of culture, the metaphorical approach has real value. Three different perspectives have been identified in which culture is a metaphor for the organization. In these views, culture isn't a *part* of the organization, it *is* the organization.

Organizational Cognition

Organizations can be viewed as systems of meaning and knowledge. In the organizational cognition model, culture is the *shared knowledge, rules, and understanding* that provide direction for members of the organization. Culture defines what constitutes appropriate and inappropriate behavior, what it means to be a "good" member of the organization. Culture also describes what is unique about the organization, how it distinguishes itself from other organizations. It helps members understand why things happen the way they do in the organization.

The organizational cognition view of culture has been used to study and classify different types of organizations, such as "entrepreneurial," "scientific," and "humanistic," and to compare them with one another.[14] The concept of organizational knowledge systems also recognizes that firms are more than the sum of the individual members' knowledge, values, and beliefs. It has been pointed out, for example, that no one person has all the knowledge necessary to launch and recover a space shuttle, but the NASA organization can now do it routinely. Organizational knowledge, skill, attitudes, values, and so on persist while the membership changes. This notion helps to get at the pervasive nature of organizational culture and how it is handed down from one generation of management to the next.

The view of organizations as systems of "shared cognitions" is also captured in the concept of managers' "thought worlds," an idea used by Dougherty to explore the conflict between marketing and R&D departments within companies.[15] Here the organizational cognition model is applied to subcultures. As noted in earlier chapters, even when various departments share a commitment to the customer, they may have vastly different definitions of what constitutes the customer's best interest. These managers live in fundamentally different "thought worlds," with different values, beliefs, cognitions, and rules for behavior—that is, different cultures. The organizational cognition view can be a useful tool for studying organizational conflict.

The organizational cognition perspective also helps explain a basic attribute of culture: It is a mechanism used by organizational members to resolve conflict. At the same time, this view recognizes that there might be multiple "types" of cultures within an organization, not all of them shared with equal loyalty by all the members. We can characterize organizations by their *dominant* organization type without saying that it is the only type. We will use an organizational cognition perspective to examine a "competing values" model of organizational culture later in the chapter, when reviewing a study of the relationships among corporate culture, customer orientation, and business performance.

Organizational Symbolism

A second metaphorical view of organizational culture sees organizations in terms of their *prevalent symbols and rituals,* as systems of symbolic discourse among their members. This view of organizational culture is especially clear in companies that have strong, long-standing cultures and familiar and easily observed behavior patterns. The presence of a strong dress code (white shirts and dark suits in the case of IBM, the absence of same at Apple Computer), company songs, even characteristic ways of speaking, come to identify members of the organization.

Language is the most obvious symbol system. To quote an article in *The Wall Street Journal,* "Like other tribal entities, corporations develop their own dialects as a way of linking members of the tribe and delineating their ranks." Walt Disney Company, the entertainment giant, was cited as an excellent example. Disney employees refer to one another as "cast members." They see themselves as "onstage" while working and "backstage" when on a break. Something positive that happens is called "good Mickey" while the opposite is "bad Mickey." Cheering up an unhappy child in a theme park is called "sprinkling pixie dust." Disney management obviously sees the strong culture and its symbols as an essential determinant of the quality of their product and the success of their business strategy.[16]

Most organizations have myths, rituals, and symbols that are important to the members and create a strong sense of belonging. Many companies consciously teach their members these aspects of culture through orientation sessions, seminars, regularly scheduled meetings, and social gatherings of all kinds. Company songs, cheers, slogans, and conventions for behavior are highly visible aspects of organizational symbolism, the patterns of symbolic discourse that provide the background against which members organize and interpret their experience within the organization. Conscious attention to organizational symbolism is undoubtedly helpful to managers trying to create a customer-oriented enterprise.

Structural Psychodynamics

Many companies have been described as virtual extensions of the personalities of their founders and early chief executives. Walt Disney, Henry Ford of Ford Motor Company, Edwin Land of Polaroid, Thomas Watson of IBM, and Sam Walton of Wal-Mart are among the most familiar examples. This view of corporate culture is captured in the structural psychodynamics perspective, which is rooted in the disciplines of anthropology and the study of social structure and transformational organization theory.[17] It sees an organization as a *metaphor for the unconscious mind of the founder,* an extension of that person's presence throughout the organization, as if people always ask "How would ______ expect me to approach this situation?"

How does a manager or a researcher identify, observe, and take a measure of an "extension of the personality of the founder"? The structural psychodynamic perspective is the hardest to understand and to make operational as a method for studying organizational culture. The most common way researchers use a structural psychodynamic perspective is to record the myths that organization members tell about the founder. In one well-known company, managers shared a perception that there were two distinct cultures: The first group consisted of people who were hired by and worked with the founder and the second culture was shared by those who came later. Recall that the first two paradigms treated culture as a variable that could be measured and managed; since the structural psychodynamic perspective is least easily translated into things that can be measured and managed, it is therefore of most limited usefulness.

Comparing the Various Perspectives on Organizational Culture

Each of the five perspectives on organizational culture offers a unique insight into the concept. For the manager interested in developing approaches for implementing the new marketing concept within a company, each viewpoint provides something to think about:

1. What is the influence of *nationality* on the willingness and ability of my organization, with its global subsidiaries and business partners, to focus on customers and a value delivery concept of the business? (Comparative management)
2. How is the performance of my business units influenced by *differences* in their cultures? What are the predominant *values* in those units and how does customer orientation fit into those values? (Contingency management)
3. How do different business units, functions, and levels of the organization view customers and their demands relative to those of other stakeholders? How do different organizational actors process and respond to information about the changing market environment? What are the basic *conflicts and disagreements* among different parts of the organization and how do they work themselves out into some form of organizational consensus for delivering value to customers? (Organizational cognition)
4. What are the important *symbols and rituals* in this organization? How do they help people find meaning in their work and develop shared understandings? How can those symbols and rituals be used to create a customer-focused, market-driven business? (Organizational symbolism)
5. What is the *legacy of the founders* and of earlier generations of management? How does their historical presence influence the ability of managers to respond to a changing market environment? What things are held to be most important and why? Are these the correct values for this company in the competitive marketplace? (Structural psychodynamics)

These are only a few of the many productive questions raised by the five different perspectives. The basic point is that organizational culture is important in designing and implementing business strategies that are consistent with the new marketing concept. Against this background of the nature of organizational culture, we now come back to the specific question of how culture, and customer orientation as part of the company's culture, influences profitability and other measures of business performance. The following section examines the theoretical construct of customer orientation and how it relates to corporate culture.

CORPORATE CULTURE, CUSTOMER ORIENTATION, AND INNOVATIVENESS

The original marketing concept stated that every business had only two basic functions: *marketing* and *innovation.* Marketing was defined as the process of listening to customers, understanding and satisfying their needs and wants, and putting the customer at the center of all of the firm's planning and operations. The marketing concept really describes a corporate culture, a basic set of values and beliefs that puts the customer first, always. But in defining and describing the concept of organizational culture, we have seen that it is ambiguous, complex, and multifaceted. It is time to make a clearer distinction between customer orientation and corporate culture.

Corporate culture is a much broader concept than customer orientation. Customer orientation is the business of putting the customer first in everything the company does and organizing all activities around the basic objective of delivering superior value. It begins with a set of values and beliefs, subscribed to by members of the organization, that recognizes the primacy of the customer's interest. As part of the company's value system, it is part of the company culture. Obviously, however, there can be strong corporate cultures that do *not* put the customer's interests first.

One of the most important questions to ask is simply, *Does it make any difference if a company is customer oriented?* Does customer orientation translate into enhanced business performance, especially in terms of profitability, growth, and market share? A related but different question is, *Does the type of company culture influence business performance?* There is also the question of the extent to which customer orientation is consistent with, or a part of, various types of corporate culture.

Only recently has there been serious study of the concept of customer orientation itself. In prior writing, the concept was often described and debated but there was little attempt to define it in rigorous ways that would permit careful measurement, a necessary first step in evaluating its usefulness and impact on business performance. Three recent studies have each developed more precise definitions of customer- or market-orientation, and in two cases specific measurement scales and other research instruments to determine the strength of the orientation in a given business.

The Market (Customer) Orientation Construct

Kohli and Jaworski set out to understand the construct of market orientation, its causes, components, and outcomes, and to develop a set of testable propositions about them. They wanted to know the meaning of market orientation, the factors that foster or discourage it, the consequences of it, and situations in which it might be more or less important. They began by reviewing the literature on the subject and concluded there was a consensus among authors in the field that market orientation (the phrase they used, not "customer" orientation) had three distinct components:

1. Customer focus.
2. Coordinated marketing.
3. Profit orientation—managing for profitability.

These are the key ideas of the marketing concept as described in earlier chapters.

The researchers then developed an interview guide to explore how managers view these elements of the concept of market orientation and how they turn these three ideas into practice. In-depth interviews were conducted with 62 managers in four cities. The respondents unanimously concurred that customer focus was the central idea in a market orientation.

Managers felt strongly that customer focus is more than a philosophical commitment. It requires information about customers' needs and preferences. Even that is not enough, however. Using current customer opinion to determine what is to be produced and sold is incomplete and inadequate. These managers advocated a broader strategic concept of market intelligence that included going beyond customer opinion to a deeper understanding of customer needs and wants, anticipating how those will change in the future, and analyzing the impact of a changing market environment. This finding is consistent with the notion that the customer's definition of value is constantly changing.

The concept that Kohli and Jaworski labeled "coordinated marketing," is similar to our concept of integrated marketing, the assertion of the marketing concept that each element of the marketing mix—product, price, promotion, and distribution policies—should be managed in the context of the overall strategy. However, their manager respondents saw it somewhat differently, as the proposition that all parts of the business had to be customer oriented and that market intelligence should guide their activities. It is significant that the managers, not the researchers, pushed the concept in this direction. Coordinated marketing is nothing more nor less than the application of market intelligence to decision making throughout the organization, making sure that all functions are guided by the customer.

A similar conclusion was reached with respect to profit orientation. The researchers presented profit orientation as the objective of a business guided by market orientation, the notion of managing for profitability rather than sales volume. Managers saw it differently. Without exception, managers saw profit as a *result* of market orientation rather than as part of it. In fact, the managers' interpretation would appear to be loyal to the original statement of the marketing concept by Peter Drucker that profit is a *reward* for creating a satisfied customer.

Thus, the concept of profit orientation, like that of coordinated marketing, devolves back to the fundamental concept of customer focus, with an emphasis on market intelligence and management response to changing customer needs and preferences. This central tendency was captured by Kohli and Jaworski in their summary definition of market orientation as ". . . the organizationwide *generation* of market intelligence pertaining to current and future customer needs, *dissemination* of the intelligence across departments, and organizationwide *responsiveness* to it."[18]

With the definition of the construct pinned down, Kohli and Jaworski then developed a total of 25 propositions to guide future research. These research propositions look at the influence of senior management, interdepartmental dynamics, and organizational systems on the development of market orientation, how it is influenced by structural factors on both the demand and supply side in the market, and how a market orientation influences customers, employees, and business results. This research program is now underway. While no results have been published, Jaworski reported at a recent conference that an early research finding is that top management support and market-based managerial reward systems are two variables that appear to have a significant impact on market orientation and business performance.[19]

The fundamental contribution of the Kohli and Jaworski research is that it validates the basic proposition that customer orientation is the key idea in the marketing concept and that its implementation is a matter of managing market intelligence. Their research shows that managers interpret the concept in ways that have specific implications for managerial actions, that the marketing concept is in fact a useful one. This supports the assertion that the principal responsibility of the marketing department, and the only justification for maintaining it as a separate business function, is to be "expert on the customer." Their research also begins to pave the way for careful study of the relationship between customer orientation and business performance.

Effects of Market Orientation on Profitability

Narver and Slater have also reported some interesting research on the composition of the market orientation construct and its impact on business performance.[20] Their research venue was the forest products operations of a large western corporation. They initially approached managers in 140 separate business units, including distribution businesses (paper merchants), producers of specialty products such as cabinets, doors, and roof truss systems, and commodity products such as dimension lumber, plywood, wood chips, and logs. Their final analysis was based on the responses of more than 400 managers from more than 100 business units.

Like Kohli and Jaworski, Narver and Slater also used the term "market orientation" for their central construct. In their review of the literature, they found five ideas associated with the concept:

1. Customer orientation.
2. Competitor orientation.

3. Interfunctional coordination.
4. A long-term horizon.
5. A profit focus (see Figure 7–1).

To develop their research instrument, a questionnaire with statements with which respondents were asked to indicate the extent of their agreement, the researchers asked a panel of leading academic experts to assess the relative importance of these components to a definition of market orientation and to suggest additional items. This revised set of items was submitted to a second group of three academic experts. Those items considered by this group to be consistent with a market orientation were included in the final questionnaire. The resulting questionnaire was used with the manager-respondents, who were asked to indicate the extent of their agreement or disagreement with each statement.

The most reliable measurements were those relating to what the researchers called the "behavioral" components of the market orientation

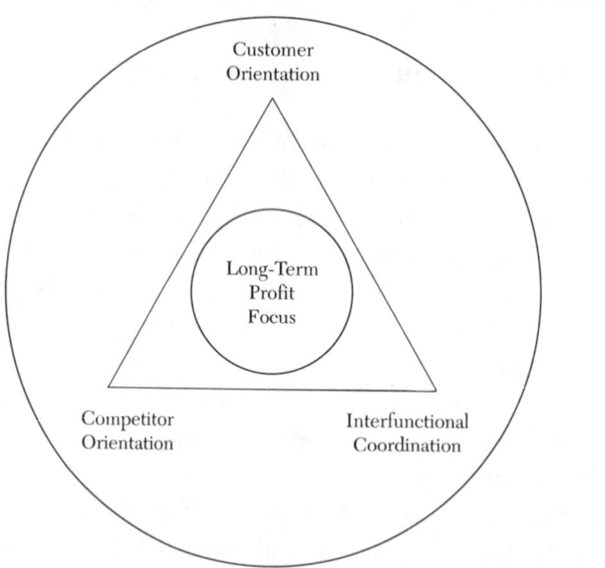

FIGURE 7–1. The components of market orientation. *Source:* Stanley F. Slater and John C. Narver, *Superior Customer Value and Business Performance: The Strong Evidence for a Market-Driven Culture,* Report No. 92-125 (Cambridge, MA: The Marketing Science Institute, September 1992).

construct—those that imply specific management behaviors or activities: customer orientation, competitor orientation, and interfunctional coordination, with customer orientation being the most reliable. This is very reassuring as it indicates that customer orientation is indeed a valid and important part of the market orientation construct. Competitor orientation and interfunctional coordination were also highly reliable. However, items relating to "long-term horizon" and "profit emphasis" were below the minimum acceptable statistical levels for reliability and were excluded from the analysis. A given business unit was assigned a score for market orientation based on an average of the scores of each of the manager-respondents from that unit on each of the three measurements: customer orientation, competitor orientation, and interfunctional coordination. Table 7–1 indicates the specific components of each of the three constructs.

In comparison with the Kohli and Jaworski study, Narver and Slater's work finds that *interfunctional coordination* and the idea that

Table 7–1. Items Used to Measure the Market Orientation Construct

Customer Orientation
Customer commitment
Creation of customer value
Understanding of customer needs
Customer satisfaction objectives
Measurement of customer satisfaction
After-sales service
Competitor Orientation
Sharing of competitor information by salespeople
Rapid management response to competitors' actions
Discussion by top managers of competitors' strategies
Targeting opportunities for competitive advantage
Interfunctional Coordination
Interfunctional customer calls
Information shared among functions
Functional integration in strategy
Contributions to customer value from all functions
Sharing of resources with other business units

Source: Adapted from John C. Narver and Stanley F. Slater, "The Effect of a Market Orientation on Business Profitability," *Journal of Marketing*, Vol. 54 (October 1990), pp. 20–35, based on their Table 1, p. 24.

marketing is a *companywide responsibility* are key parts of market orientation. Both studies place heavy emphasis on the customer information or market intelligence dimension. Narver and Slater's view of market orientation is somewhat more consistent with a value delivery concept of strategy, with its integration of competitor orientation into their measures, recognizing implicitly that customers define value by comparing the company's product offerings with those of competitors.

The results of the Narver and Slater investigation of the relationship between market orientation and business profitability are interesting but complicated. Profitability was defined as the performance of the business unit in comparison with that of its major competitor in its principal served market, as judged by the unit's top management team, on return on total assets, return on net assets, and return on investment. This relative measure of business unit performance is consistent with that used in the PIMS studies, discussed in Chapter 2.

The overall general result of the Narver and Slater analysis can be stated first: Market orientation *does* have a significant, positive impact on business profitability. For the noncommodity businesses (including distribution and specialty products), the relationship was "monotonic"—as market orientation increased, profitability increased. For commodity businesses, the relationship was more complicated: All businesses with a high market orientation score were on the high end of the profit measure. However, not all of the more profitable businesses had high market orientation scores; some of them had low scores on market orientation. For firms with market orientation scores at the median level or below, there was no consistent relationship with profitability.

Interpretation of this result suggested that it might be a case of the well-known "stuck-in-the-middle" idea that the least profitable businesses are those that have neither a differentiated, market-niche strategy nor a low-cost, low-price strategy.[21] According to this view, differentiation and low price are two generic strategies that can produce above-average profitability. Firms that have neither a differentiation strategy nor a low-cost strategy have below-average performance. The commodity businesses that were above average in profitability appeared to be those smaller businesses that had successfully positioned themselves as suppliers to large customers and were benefiting from long-term relationships and good records of customer retention.

This result underscores the assertion in Chapter 5 that it is usually more profitable to serve existing customers well than to devote major resources to finding new ones. It also refutes a popular belief, consistent with the old adversarial model of buyer-seller relationships, that large customers, who have more buyer power, produce less profitable results. Rather, it appears that a small, responsive supplier of a commodity product (who may be very service oriented, a source of differentiation), can achieve above-average profits even when working with large and powerful customers.

Narver and Slater recognized that profitability reflects many factors, not just market orientation. Among other variables, they examined:

- The size of the business in terms of total sales volume.
- Its market share and cost position relative to its major competitor.
- Industry structure variables including rate of market growth, industry concentration, entry barriers, buyer and seller power, and rate of technological change.

An interesting finding was that the smaller commodity businesses tended to be more profitable when the market was growing rapidly in the short term. This appeared to create an opportunity for small businesses that were responsive to their markets. Larger businesses, low in market orientation, suffered decreased profitability when their markets were experiencing short-term growth, reflecting their inability (or perhaps management unwillingness) to respond to changing market conditions. This finding of the importance of responsiveness is consistent with the Kohli and Jaworski definition of market orientation, which includes responsiveness to market intelligence.

Although Narver and Slater had no specific measures of company or business unit culture, they used the concept of culture to interpret some of their results. They made a distinction between those businesses with a strong market orientation and those dominated by a "product/technology-oriented culture." They saw the latter type of culture as a barrier to the adoption of a market orientation. A positive aspect of their research is that by focusing on a single corporation they could control for the effects of corporate-level culture. However, they could not assess its impact. It is commonsensical to equate differences in market orientation to differences in business unit and department "subcultures," but they could not do so rigorously, given their research design. In general, one must be cautious about projecting their results to other companies and other industries.

It is necessary to distinguish between customer orientation and corporate or organizational culture. Culture, as previously noted, is a broader concept. The strength of customer orientation is one dimension of an organizational culture. Since there are multiple types of organizational cultures, it remains an open question whether customer orientation is more consistent with some types of cultures than others. This was one of the questions addressed in the following research study.

How Customer Orientation, Innovativeness, and Corporate Culture Affect Performance

Deshpandé, Farley, and Webster (DFW) were also interested in understanding the fundamental relationship between customer orientation and business unit performance. Their conceptual model also incorporated innovativeness, picking up the other dimension of the marketing concept—innovation in the sense of continuous problem solving on behalf of the customer. Like Narver and Slater, they also developed a scale for measuring customer orientation. But they went further and developed and used a model of corporate culture to help clarify the relationship between customer orientation, innovativeness, and profitability.

The DFW Customer Orientation Scale

DFW saw customer orientation as a combination of market intelligence, a focus on customer service and operational measures of service levels, responsiveness to the customer, and acceptance of the proposition that the customer comes first. Table 7–2 indicates the statements used to measure customer orientation, based on a review of the literature and the Kohli and Jaworski and Narver and Slater studies. These nine items are a subset of a larger group of 30 questions originally tested in a small sample of firms. The nine measures used are those that proved to be statistically most reliable as measures of customer orientation. They were combined into a summary measure used to describe the customer orientation of each firm studied.

Table 7–2. Items Used for a Customer-Orientation Scale

1. We have routine or regular measures of customer service.
2. Our product and service development is based on good market and customer information.
3. We know our competitors well.
4. We have a good sense of how our customers value our products and services.
5. We are more customer focused than our competitors.
6. We compete primarily based on product or service differentiation.
7. The customer's interest should always come first, ahead of the owners'.
8. Our products and services are the best in the business.
9. I believe this business exists primarily to serve customers.

One version of these questions was used with two managers from the marketer-company. A modified version was used with two managers of a customer company, in which the first person pronoun (we, our, I) was replaced with the phrase "The supplier" and so on.

The DFW Sample: A Quadrad Design

The DFW study used a unique "quadrad" design. Two managers from a supplier company were interviewed and asked to indicate three important customers. On a random basis, one of these customer organizations was contacted and two purchasing managers from the customer organization were interviewed using the same research instruments as used with the supplier firm's managers. Customer respondents were asked to evaluate the supplier's organization, not their own. Thus, there were a total of four managers' responses for each subject firm—two from the firm itself and two from the customer organization. These two pairs of respondents or "dyads" were combined into a "quadrad." This design permitted DFW to compare a firm's assessment of its own customer orientation with that of a major customer. Which would you expect to have a stronger association with profitability, sales growth, and market share?

DFW used professional market research companies to interview managers in Japan, Germany, France, England, and the United States. A total of 160 firms were examined, with a total of 640 managers interviewed. Appropriate care was taken in preparing questionnaires for use in each country, using back-translation to ensure that consistent meanings were maintained in all countries.

The DFW Innovativeness Scale

This study also measured the innovativeness of the firm as one determinant of its performance. The researchers borrowed a scale from an earlier study.[22] On a five-point scale from "Never" to "Always," respondents were asked to indicate:

In a new product or service introduction, how often is your company:

- ☐ First to market with new products and services.
- ☐ Later entrant in established but growing markets.
- ☐ Entrant in mature, stable markets.
- ☐ Entrant in declining markets.
- ☐ At the cutting edge of technological innovation.

A single innovativeness score for each supplier firm was created by averaging the responses of the dyads. The resulting innovativeness score was very high on a statistical measure of reliability giving the researchers confidence that they had a good measure of innovativeness.

The DFW "Competing Values" Model of Organizational Culture

The DFW study is believed to be the first to use rigorous modeling and measurement to study organizational culture within the field of marketing. To measure culture, they used a scale adopted from Cameron and Freeman[23] and Quinn,[24] researchers in the organizational behavior area, which is based on an organizational-cognition type model of organizational culture. The model is shown in Figure 7–2.

This "competing values" model is based in the organizational cognition tradition in that it looks at the culture of the organization as a mechanism for processing, and acting on, information about the changing market environment. It uses two fairly simple dimensions that can be thought of as the extent to which the organization tends to be more internally or externally focused and whether its responses to change tend to be flexible and spontaneous or tightly controlled and orderly. Using this simple two-by-two matrix, it defines four types of organizational culture: Clan, Adhocracy, Hierarchy, and Market (see Figure 7–2). It is called a "competing values" model because it

ORGANIC PROCESSES (flexibility, spontaneity)

INTERNAL MAINTENANCE (smoothing activities, integration)	EXTERNAL POSITIONING (competition, differentiation)
Type: Clan Dominant Attributes: Cohesiveness, participation, teamwork, sense of family Leader Style: Mentor, facilitator, parent-figure Bonding: Loyalty, tradition, interpersonal cohesion Strategic Emphasis: Toward developing human resources, commitment, morale	Type: Adhocracy Dominant Attributes: Entrepreneurship, creativity, adaptability Leader Style: Entrepreneur, innovator, risk taker Bonding: Entrepreneurship, flexibility, risk Strategic Emphasis: Toward innovation, growth, new resources
Type: Hierarchy Dominant Attributes: Order, rules and regulations, uniformity Leader Stule: Coordinator, administrator Bonding: Rules, policies and procedures Strategic Emphases: Toward stability, predictability, smooth operations	Type: Market Dominant Attributes: Competitiveness, goal achievement Leader Style: Decisive, achievement-oriented Bonding: Goal orientation, production, competition Strategic Emphasis: Toward competitive advantage and market superiority

MECHANISTIC PROCESSES (control, order, stability)

FIGURE 7–2. A "competing values" model of organizational culture types. *Source:* Rohit Deshpandé, John U. Farley, and Frederick E. Webster, Jr., "Corporate Culture, Customer Orientation, and Innovativeness in Japanese Firms: A Quadrad Analysis," *Journal of Marketing*, Vol. 57 (January 1993), pp. 23–37, at p. 25. Reproduced with permission of the American Marketing Association.

recognizes that any organization is likely to contain multiple sets of values and beliefs, as proposed by the differentiation view of culture. However, an integration view is also achieved by combining these multiple viewpoints into a kind of organizational consensus around the types of values likely to be dominant in a conflict situation.

The model sees culture as a mechanism for resolving organizational conflict. Culture becomes an influence when members disagree about what action to take, expressing itself in statements such as "That is not the way we do things around here!" A simple example of such a situation would be an organization where a contingent of managers argues for protecting the employment status of department members and rewarding their loyalty (a "Clan" type culture), whereas others argue for reorganizing the department and moving quickly to respond to the changing market (an "Adhocracy" type culture).

Thus, cultures can link competing viewpoints, balancing internal and external forces in ways that guide people in making the difficult choices that characterize business decision making. Virtually every organization faces the challenge of finding the proper balance between stability and change, the need for order and continuity on the one hand and for flexibility and responsiveness on the other. Because it captures this tension, the competing values model has a good measure of "face validity" in the real world of management.

The information-processing approach of the competing values model of organizational culture is entirely consistent with the Kohli and Jaworski definition of market orientation, with its focus on market intelligence—the gathering and dissemination of market information and the organization's responsiveness to it. We would expect to find some consistent relationship between organizational culture type and extent of customer orientation.

The four types of organizational culture are defined by the members' shared beliefs about four characteristics of the organization: its dominant attributes as an organization (e.g., cohesiveness, entrepreneurship, orderliness, or competitiveness); its leadership style; its bonding mechanisms; and its strategic emphases. Each type of organization is described by a set of adjectives on each of these four dimensions.

Respondents were instructed to divide 100 points among four statements about their organizations on each dimension. For example, on leadership, respondents were asked to distribute 100 points among these four statements:

1. The head of my organization is generally considered to be a *mentor, sage,* or a *father or mother figure.*
2. The head of my organization is generally considered to be an *entrepreneur,* an *innovator,* or a *risk taker.*

3. The head of my organization is generally considered to be a *coordinator,* an *organizer,* or an *administrator.*
4. The head of my organization is generally considered to be a *producer,* a *technician,* or a *hard-driver.*

A sum of all the points assigned to the "A" responses provided a score for the Clan type culture, the "B" responses for the Adhocracy, "C" responses for the Hierarchy, and "D" responses for the Market type culture, according to the individual respondent. The scores of both members of the dyad were averaged to produce a score for the supplier. Customer purchasing managers were administered the same questionnaires, with appropriate small changes in language to make it clear that they were evaluating their supplier's organization; these answers were scored and summarized in the same fashion.

The Four Culture Types in the DFW Model

Clan. Clan type cultures are focused on the internal maintenance of the organization but tend to make flexible and spontaneous responses to the changing environment. Leaders are facilitators and mentors, parent figures for organization members. The bonding mechanisms of the organization emphasize loyalty, tradition, and cohesiveness. Strategic emphasis is on developing the human resources of the organization and maintaining employee commitment and morale. Journalistic accounts of the Apple Computer organization suggest that it fits this type of culture, with its popcorn machine in the lobby, Friday afternoon beer fests, open lounge-type offices, and casual dress. Clans value cohesiveness, teamwork, a sense of family, and participative decision making.

Adhocracy. Adhocracy type culture also values flexibility and spontaneity but is more focused on the changing external environment. The strategic emphasis shifts from human resources to products, innovation, market and sales growth, and the requirements of the changing marketplace. Leaders exhibit entrepreneurship and innovativeness and are risk takers. The bonding mechanisms likewise emphasize entrepreneurial skills, risk taking, and innovation; members who exhibit these characteristics find mutual affinity. General Electric is reported to be striving to achieve this type of culture through its "Work Out" program, with its emphasis on entrepreneurship and risk taking, a conscious move away from the competing values of the hierarchy culture.

Hierarchy. Hierarchical cultures are internally focused and deliberate and cautious in their response to a changing environment. Hierarchical values compete with those of the adhocracy. General Motors is probably a good example (historically, at least) of a hierarchical culture. Hierarchies place an emphasis on rules, order, policies, and procedures as their dominant attributes and their bonding mechanisms. Traditions and past practices provide strong guidelines for behavior. The organization rewards people for being good soldiers or for what one manager referred to as attendance rather than achievement. Leaders are coordinators and administrators; risk taking is not rewarded and might even be actively discouraged by the strategic emphasis on stability, predictability, and smooth transitions. Hierarchies are least responsive to a changing environment; they are internally focused and value control over flexibility.

Market. Market-type culture combines an external focus with a planned, coordinated, and controlled response. It provides the competing values for the clan culture. Market cultures value competitiveness, goal setting, and achievement over cohesiveness and teamwork. The leaders are decisive and achievement-oriented rather than being mentors and process-oriented facilitators. Members bond through striving for productivity, goal achievement, and competitiveness. The organization is focused strategically on maintaining its competitive advantage and market superiority. Pepsico has been described as a market-type culture, in which managers are encouraged to be aggressive and competitive and guided by rigorous goal setting and evaluation processes.

This brief review of the four types of culture underscores the competing-values approach by noting that the diagonals of the matrix in Figure 7–2 point to competing frameworks that might exist within a given organization. No organization will exhibit only a single type of culture. The determining factor in defining culture is the relative strength or saliency of each set of values, especially as it is expressed when the organization must resolve a dilemma.

The DFW Organizational Climate Scale

The research questions asked of managers in the DFW study also included items to measure organizational climate. Culture and climate are related but distinct concepts (although some scholars argue that this is a distinction without a meaningful difference). Organizational climate is the way in which culture is expressed, the ways in which managers make operational the themes of the underlying culture. Climate is expressed in the members' behavior that is rewarded, encouraged, supported, and expected. Organizational climate can be thought of as the answer to the question, "What happens around here?" whereas culture answers the question, "*Why* do things happen the way they do?"[25]

The scale used to measure organizational climate had been developed and tested before, in the same study that provided the DFW innovativeness scale.[26] It consisted of the eight items in Table 7–3, to which respondents indicated their agreement or disagreement, using a five-point scale.

Organizational climate captures a firm's decision-making style. It is concerned with the extent to which people feel encouraged, supported, secure, trusted, independent, and yet involved in the organization. Where these attributes are prevalent, members are more likely to engage in entrepreneurial and risk-taking behavior. Thus, organizational climate, like customer orientation and innovativeness, should have a positive impact on business performance.

Table 7–3. Items Used to Assess Organizational Climate

1. Our organization has a strong tendency toward high-risk, high-return investments.
2. We are always trying out new ideas.
3. Excellent performance is rewarded in our organization.
4. In our organization, there is excellent communication between line managers and staff people.
5. People trust each other in this organization.
6. Decision making in our organization is participative.
7. A friendly atmosphere prevails among people in our organization.
8. In our organization, people feel they are their own bosses in most matters.

The DFW Measure of Business Performance

Like many other researchers who have attempted to analyze the determinants of business performance, DFW measured it *relative to the largest competitor.* Managers were asked to assess their own company's performance on four dimensions—size (sales volume), market share, profitability, and growth rate—in terms of whether it was greater, equal to, or less than that of the major competitor. The measures on these four dimensions were summarized and averaged for the two managers who responded for each supplier firm to produce a single index of business performance.

The tremendous amount of information gathered by Deshpandé, Farley, and Webster presented a huge analytical challenge. They had measures of organizational performance, innovativeness, customer orientation, four types of organizational culture, and organizational climate from over 600 managers for a total of 160 supplier firms and an equal number of customer firms in five different countries. Sophisticated statistical analysis is required to bring together the responses of the four members of the "quadrad" into a single measure or to compare the responses of the individuals in a given quadrad with one another.

Another fundamental problem is the need to determine whether a given variable, such as customer orientation, has its influence on business performance directly or through its effect on one or more other variables, such as organizational climate or innovativeness. At this time, only preliminary results can be reported, but they provide some provocative and interesting suggestions about the relationship between market orientation and business performance. (These are only preliminary findings and should be regarded as tentative.)

Performance Is Related to Organizational Culture

It is the unique concern of the DFW research to try to understand the influence of organizational culture on business performance. Using the statistical technique of discriminant analysis, businesses were divided into high-performing and low-performing groups. The researchers had expected that the best performing culture type would be Market, followed by Adhocracy, Clan, and Hierarchy. For the whole sample, involving all supplier businesses in the five countries studied, the best performing cultures were Adhocracies, not Markets, which were the second best performing. The worst performing cultures were not Hierarchies, as had been expected, but Clans. Adhocracy and Market cultures had positive impact on performance, whereas Hierarchies and Clans had negative impact.

Thus, one important and general conclusion is that organizational culture does make a difference, and in the predicted direction . . . if no other factors are taken into account! Looking only at corporate level culture is a useful exercise, but we must remember that it is preliminary and incomplete. The external orientation of the Adhocracy and Market cultures produces positive results on performance whereas the internal focus of the Clans and Hierarchies has a negative impact.

This can be interpreted as a strong vote in favor of a market orientation which is, by definition, external. The superiority of the externally focused Adhocracy culture over the Market culture, which is also externally focused, might reflect the positive impact of organizational flexibility and responsiveness to changing market conditions by Adhocracies compared with the more careful and controlled, planned, and monitored response of the goal- and achievement-oriented Market culture. This interpretation would be consistent with both the Kohli and Jaworski definition of market orientation, with its emphasis on organizational responsiveness, and the Narver and Slater conclusion that market orientation has a positive impact on business performance.

As a test of the basic validity of the "competing values" model, these results are also encouraging. In the model, the competing cultures are the Adhocracy versus the Hierarchy and the Clan versus the Market: external focus and flexibility versus internal focus and control; or flexibility and internal focus versus control and external focus. Indeed, the statistical results show that Adhocracy and Hierarchy are strongly negatively correlated as are Clan and Market. However, Adhocracy and Market type cultures are also strongly negatively correlated, indicating that they are not likely to be found in the same company. Mechanistic processes for maintaining order, stability, and control would appear to be antithetical to flexibility and spontaneity, even when there is a common external orientation. This conjecture is supported by a very weak, albeit negative, correlation between Hierarchy and Market type cultures.

The Relationship Varies across Countries

These generalizations about the influence of culture types on performance soon get more complicated when we look at individual countries, as shown in Table 7–4. There appears to be a strong interaction between the national background culture and the corporate culture in determining the impact of a given culture type on business performance. The analysis described here looks at all European companies together, a total of 60 supplier firms divided evenly between France, Germany, and England, in order to have a large enough sample to permit valid statistical analysis. (A more detailed country-by-country analysis is planned for a later date.) It compares U.S., European, and Japanese companies with one another in terms of the relative influence of culture type.

In the U.S. companies, the best-performing cultures were Adhocracy and Market, although the statistical association with performance was quite weak. The worst performing U.S. company cultures were Hierarchies and this was a stronger statistical result. There was no measurable impact of Clan culture on performance in the U.S. companies. These results are generally consistent with the findings for the total sample—external orientation is better than internal focus. However, in the United States, except for the negative effect of Hierarchy, corporate culture doesn't appear to make much difference.

The Japanese companies showed a pattern consistent with the researchers' original prediction: The best performing corporate cultures were Market type, followed by Adhocracy, both of which had a positive influence. The Clan and Hierarchy cultures had a negative influence on performance, the last being the worst. Market type cultures may be

Table 7–4. How the Influence of Culture Type on Business Performance Varies by Country or Region

	Rank Order and Direction[1]			
Culture Type	**Total Sample**	**Japan**	**U.S.**	**Europe**
Adhocracy	1+	2+	1+	1+
Market	2+	1+	2+	3−
Hierarchy	3−	4−	4−	2−
Clan	4−	3−	3[2]	4−

[1] "+" = positive, favorable impact; "−" = negative, unfavorable impact.
[2] No impact either positive or negative.

more effective in Japan than elsewhere because their tight control is consistent with the national background culture of Japan with its emphasis on respect for authority, paternalism, and coordinated behavior and the dominance of enduring vertical relationships based on power throughout the social structure. In support of this suggestion, another research team has reported that Japanese distributors place a higher value on their relationships with American companies that use more authoritarian methods in dealing with them, because Japanese managers are more comfortable with the exercise of social power in any form.[27]

Perhaps the biggest surprises are found in the European results, which are in general *not* consistent with the results of analysis of the overall sample or those from the United States and Japan in particular.[28] In Europe, the one finding consistent with the overall result is that Adhocracy has a positive relationship to performance, in fact the strongest association found in any of the comparisons. The kicker is that the Market culture has a *negative* association with performance. Furthermore, the influence of Hierarchy is very small although it remains negative. Another surprise: the impact of Clan type culture in Europe is extremely negative, whereas it had no impact in the United States and a much smaller negative impact in Japan.

What is happening here? We can only guess at some of the possible connections between national background culture and corporate culture that would explain these different relationships across countries. Although we are dealing with conjecture, and perhaps with national stereotypes, rather than with reliable data about national cultures, it is interesting to speculate about the ways in which corporate culture type exerts its influence in different countries. These conjectures will produce more questions than answers.

One place to look for an explanation for the observed differences is to ask if a particular type of corporate culture is more or less prevalent in a given country, in comparison with the total sample. This analysis is presented in Table 7–5. In interpreting these data, take care to note that they describe the distribution of companies *in the sample,* not all companies in the country, and the sample in each case is too small to be considered representative of the country at large.

Hierarchical culture has a negative effect on performance in Japan and the United States but virtually no impact in Europe. Could that be because the dominant national cultures in Germany, France,

Table 7–5. Dominant Organizational Culture Types, by Country

	Compared with the total sample, the proportion of this culture type among companies in this country is:				
Culture Type	**Japan**	**U.S.**	**France**	**England**	**Germany**
Adhocracy	Fewer	Same	Same	Same	More
Market	Same	More	Same	Same	Fewer
Clan	More	Same	Fewer	Same	Same
Hierarchy	More	Same	Same	Same	Same

(To be read as follows: In Japan, there are fewer Adhocracies and more Clans and Hierarchies than in the rest of the sample of companies.)

and England are also hierarchical? On the other hand, the data in Table 7–5 show that Hierarchy cultures are no more prevalent in the European companies in our sample than in any other part of the world. Notice that Hierarchies are, however, more prevalent in Japan than elsewhere.

Why did Adhocracy have such a positive impact in Europe? Perhaps the German data dominated the results in Europe, and Adhocracy is more prevalent in the German sample companies than elsewhere. The flexible response of these Adhocracy firms to a changing market perhaps gives them a decided competitive advantage in the marketplace against their more traditionally oriented, slow-to-respond rivals, assuming that Hierarchy is the dominant form in the traditional national cultures of Europe.

Then why does Hierarchy have such a negative effect in Japan if authoritarian social structure is also part of the national culture there? And if cooperation is truly a basic value in Japanese culture as it is said to be, then why do Clan type corporate cultures have a negative impact on business performance there? Answers to these questions may come out of more detailed analysis of the DFW data, but they more likely require other studies that attempt to measure national background culture more carefully and to relate it more precisely to corporate level culture and organizational subcultures.

On a positive note, however, corporate culture can make an important difference in business performance, especially in terms of the responsiveness of the business to a changing market environment. But responsiveness is only one part of a broader concept of market orientation, and it is distinct from the more fundamental notion of customer orientation that is the hallmark of the marketing concept.

The Influence of Customer Orientation, Innovation, and Organizational Climate

We have two basic questions to answer. First, does customer orientation have a positive impact on business performance as called for by the new marketing concept? Second, how does the influence of customer orientation depend on the nature of corporate culture, if at all? These were the two fundamental questions motivating the DFW research project.

Customer orientation is positively related to business performance, but not as strongly as expected. For the suppliers' own assessment of their customer orientation, the relationship with performance was somewhat stronger than for the customers' assessment of their suppliers' performance, except in Japan where it was the customers' assessment that was more strongly associated with business performance. Innovativeness always had a stronger influence on performance than did customer orientation. These results are summarized in Table 7–6.

A simple conclusion from these findings might be that actions speak louder than words, that the new product development activities of the business and the decision-making and risk-taking propensities of its management count for more than the philosophical nuances of customer orientation. It might just be that customer orientation is a necessary but by no means sufficient condition for above-average business performance. Furthermore, initial analysis of the DFW data does not show particularly strong relationships between customer orientation and culture type. Initial predictions were that customer orientation would be strongest in Market and Adhocracy type cultures and weakest in Clans and Hierarchies. The actual results confirmed some of these

Table 7–6. Relative Influence of Customer Orientation and Innovation on Business Performance

	Rank in Order of Importance			
	Total Sample	Japan	U.S.	Europe
Innovation	1	1	1	1
Customer Orientation				
Self-assessment	2	2	3	2
Customer assessment	3	1	2	3

predictions but completely refuted others. Using simple correlation analysis yields the results shown in Table 7–7.

Some of these findings are reassuring, but not all of them. It is encouraging that customer orientation is significant in its positive relationship to the Adhocracy type culture and its negative relationship to the Hierarchy type culture. This is what we would predict, and it is consistent with the findings about organizational culture and performance. But the finding that customer orientation is *negatively* related to the Market type culture is counter to our expectations and significantly so. Likewise, the positive association between Clan type culture and customer orientation is not what we would have expected.

Again, what appears to be at work here is the importance of the positive external focus of the Adhocracy and the negative internal focus of the Hierarchy. It might be that the Adhocracy is more focused on the customer in its external orientation, while the Market type culture, although its orientation is also external, is more focused on competitors. The strategic emphasis of the Market type culture is on competitive advantage and market superiority. Perhaps this conflicts with the more basic assignment of delivering value to customers. Finally, the positive association between Clan culture and customer orientation (although not significant) might reflect a tendency to think of customers as "part of the family," which lacks the external market focus and so does not get translated into strong business performance.

One other important finding from the DFW study is that organizational climate has a strong, positive impact on business performance. The influence of climate is almost as strong as that of innovation. While

Table 7–7. Customer Orientation and Culture Type

		Association with Customer Orientation		
Culture Type	**Predicted Direction**[1]	**Rank**	**Actual Direction of Influence**	**Signif. Level**
Adhocracy	Positive	2	Positive	(.01)
Market	Positive	3	Negative	(.05)
Clan	Negative	4	Positive	(NS)
Hierarchy	Negative	1	Negative	(.01)

[1] All associations were expected to be statistically significant.
NS = Not significant.

the relationship between climate and culture needs exploration in greater depth, it appears, in fact, to be a distinct and separate phenomenon. Also needed is additional research on the relationship between organizational climate and customer orientation and innovativeness. Common sense suggests that there should be a strong relationship between innovation and organizational climate, as both are related to the risk-taking and decision-making styles of the organization.

IMPLICATIONS OF THE STUDY OF CORPORATE CULTURE

The Deshpandé, Farley, and Webster study of the relationship of organizational culture to customer orientation and business performance has opened some important doors. Its basic contribution is that it shows the importance and relevance of trying to understand organizational culture in order to improve business performance in the marketplace. The significant analytical results when the total five-country sample is used to examine differences between high-performing and low-performing companies show that the competing values model of organizational culture provides a useful and valid framework for marketing researchers. It offers a model that can be used in a global context and suggests that the general model of culture types can be universally applied even though there will be important differences across countries.

The research also shows that the best corporate culture in terms of business performance is likely to vary from country to country, under the influence of national background culture. The nature of those important differences is not understood and requires further research. What works best in one country may not work well in another. Managers must be wary of trying to apply lessons learned about corporate culture in one country to their operations elsewhere. Students of "Japanese" management or "American" management, looking for "best practices," should beware of these pitfalls.

Customer orientation has a positive influence on business performance, but not a strong one in the general sense of a set of values and beliefs about putting the customer first. Rather, customer orientation must be combined with innovation and with an organization climate committed to entrepreneurial risk taking and decision making if it is to be translated into business performance. This conclusion from the

Deshpandé, Farley, and Webster study, although based on tentative statistical findings, is consistent with the conclusions of the Narver and Slater study that the three behavioral components of market orientation—customer orientation, competitor orientation, and interfunctional coordination—were the significant influences on business profitability.

The overriding conclusion from the DFW study is that it is an external market orientation that produces superior performance, not an internal focus on the cooperation, coordination, and control mechanisms of the organization itself. Advocates of the new teamwork models of management would be well advised to be sure that the team's efforts are guided by market intelligence, customer and competitor orientation, and a value-delivery concept of strategy.

Managers need to manage customer orientation, corporate culture and climate, and innovation simultaneously. It is undoubtedly a mistake to concentrate on only one of these important ingredients in business success, although we need more research to understand their complex interactions and interdependencies.

SUMMARY

Customer orientation describes a corporate culture, a set of values and beliefs that focus on the customers' needs and expectations, and their satisfaction. But customer orientation is only one aspect of a corporate culture. After examining several different views of corporate culture, we settled on one that looks at organizations as knowledge systems, the "organizational cognition" model that is concerned primarily with how organization members gather and respond to information about a changing external environment. This view of organizational culture is consistent with a definition of market orientation that focuses on the gathering and use of market intelligence to guide all parts of the business in developing and delivering value to customers.

The concept of market orientation is broader than a focus on the customer and proves to be more powerful in predicting business performance. Customer orientation must be combined with competitor focus and interfunctional coordination if it is to enhance profitability. The firm doesn't just need customer focus; it needs to respond to the customer with strategies and product innovations that are responsive to changing needs and preferences.

A specific model of organizational culture, the "competing values" perspective, which is a type of organizational cognition model, was developed and used to examine the relationships among customer orientation, corporate culture, innovativeness, and organizational climate. Using two dimensions—external versus internal orientation and flexible versus controlled response to information about the changing market environment, four types of organizational culture were defined and examined in detail: Adhocracy, Market, Clan, and Hierarchy

Some preliminary results from a study of 160 marketing companies in five countries were explored for their insights into the causes of business performance. Culture, climate, innovativeness, and customer orientation all proved to have an important influence on relative profitability, market share, and sales growth. Equally important, however, the nature of that influence tended to vary significantly from country to country. The "best" type of corporate culture may be specific to a given country in terms of its fit with the national background culture. Likewise, it appears that type of organizational culture, customer orientation, innovativeness, and organizational climate interact in their impacts.

Businesses with organizational cultures with a strong external orientation tend to be the best performers across all five countries studied. Usually, it is the combination of external focus and flexible response that pays the biggest dividends, although the controlled response of the Market type culture appeared to be somewhat more effective in Japanese companies.

Customer orientation has a positive impact on performance, especially when found in combination with an entrepreneurial approach to decision making and a record of innovation on the part of the company. Customer orientation as a set of values, without the follow-through on specific action that serves the customer and responds aggressively to competition, has little direct impact on company performance. Nonetheless, it may be the basic set of values and beliefs, the fundamentals of the corporate culture, without which no positive action is possible.

8 DEVELOPING A CUSTOMER-ORIENTED, MARKET-DRIVEN COMPANY

> Consumption is the sole end and purpose of production; and the interest of the producer ought to be attended to only so far as it may be necessary for promoting that of the consumer.
>
> Adam Smith
> *Wealth of Nations,* 1776

As the marketplace evolves under the converging pressures of changing demographics, politics, economics, technology, and social mores, so do organizations change, along with the nature of cooperation and competition among them. As organizations change, so must the role of marketing within those organizations.

Traditionally, businesses were built for a world of transactions conducted in a competitive marketplace between hierarchical, divisionalized, bureaucratic organizations and their customers. Today, the world is moving rapidly toward a pattern of economic activity based on exchanges in the context of long-term relationships and partnerships among economic actors in the loose coalitional frameworks of network organizations.

To survive in the future, every business will have to be customer focused, market driven, global in scope, and flexible in its ability to deliver superior value to changing customers in the global competitive marketplace. In this chapter, we will summarize the assertions and

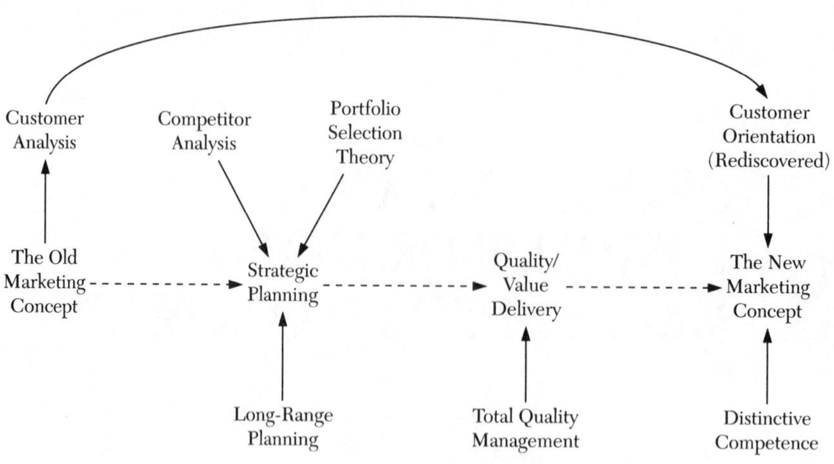

FIGURE 8–1. The evolution of the new marketing concept.

conclusions of the analysis in earlier chapters into an integrated framework for thinking about the new marketing concept.

The new marketing concept has evolved out of the old marketing concept by way of long-range planning, portfolio selection theory, strategic planning, competitor analysis, total quality management, the theory of distinctive or core competence, and a new value-delivery concept of strategy. This evolution is summarized in Figure 8–1.

MARKETING WITH A VIEW TOWARD THE YEAR 2000

The economic environment that spawned the original marketing concept in the 1950s was one of postwar economic growth and pent-up consumer demand. America was rebuilding socially and economically, transforming a wartime economy into a consumer society. The marketing concept focused companies on the need to capture this increasingly affluent and demanding customer, who would be able to choose among a broader variety of competing product offerings. The average age of the population would be trending downward as the postwar baby boom accompanied an increased rate of household formation and laid the basis for the mass consumption and production.

Europe and Japan were rebuilding physically as well as politically, recovering from the effects of the most devastating war in history, which had ended with the advent of the Nuclear Age. The Cold War began almost as soon as World War II ended, as the United States formed alliances with European, Asian, and Latin American countries to counter the aggressive military moves of the Soviet Union under the dictatorship of Joseph Stalin. The phrase "The Cold War," first used by Bernard Baruch in 1947, defined a political, and potentially military, contest between the United States and its allies on one side and the Union of Soviet Socialist Republics and its mostly involuntary satellite countries on the other. The Western bloc, which included Japan, was held together by its focus on a common enemy. The battle between two fundamentally different economic systems, capitalism and communism, was to continue for almost 50 years.

In 1950, the world's population stood at about 2.5 billion, with the United States population at 151 million or about 6.0% of the total. By 1991, world population had more than doubled to 5.4 billion, with the United States at 250 million or 4.6%. World population was galloping toward a predicted 8.2 billion in the year 2020, of which Americans would be perhaps 325 million or 4.0%. Most of the population growth was occurring in the least developed parts of the world, generally in the Southern Hemisphere. The gap between the rich and poor countries continued to widen, although there were some bright spots in Mexico, China, and perhaps India.

As we approach the end of not only a century but a millennium, the world has changed faster, by almost any criterion, in the past half century than at any earlier time in history. We are living in a time that has variously been called the Information Age, the Knowledge Economy, and the Age of Discontinuity.[1] The service economy, with information and information technology at its core, now accounts for more than half of employment and of consumer expenditures in virtually all the developed countries. In the United States, services account for more than three-fourths of both employment and gross national product.[2]

The economic conditions of the 1990s have forced a continued retrenchment and reorganization by businesses around the world. From New York to London to Rome to Tokyo, business firms are downsizing, delayering, and redefining their served markets, attempting to reduce costs and become more efficient while at the same time improving the attractiveness of their product offerings. These fundamental structural changes are having an impact on people at all levels of society, from blue-collar wage earners to high-level executives, with white-collar professionals and middle managers disproportionately affected by the restructurings. These displaced or insecure employees are also cautious, or perhaps pessimistic, consumers.

The Cold War came to a surprisingly fast end in the late 1980s with massive political reforms within the Soviet Union and disintegration of the Soviet bloc. The experiment with centrally planned socialism following the Marxist model had failed. Communism was in ruins. European economic integration, originally dubbed "Europe 1992" and officially planned under the Maastricht Treaty to become a reality in 1994, is struggling to come to fruition. The end of the Cold War resulted in the vicious rebirth of national and ethnic tribalism on a scale not expected by even the most astute political observers. Armed conflict and massive migrations of displaced and unemployed persons were unanticipated facts of European life. While the rest of the world talked about "Europe," the Europeans themselves continued to see the world from a national perspective, especially in terms of employment, economic growth, and trade.

The "German Miracle" that had been expected to be the main engine on the European train had been derailed by the huge burden of welcoming East Germany (formally, The German Democratic Republic, the Soviet orphan) back into the family. The capital investment in plant, equipment, and infrastructure required to rebuild the East German economy had been badly underestimated. (It was part of the Communist dogma that investment in the service sector was wasted; thus none of the former Communist countries had adequate infrastructure to support economic development.[3]) Germany's economy turned in its worst performance in 25 years in the first quarter of 1993, falling almost 4% below the level of the preceding year.[4]

In the United States, the 1980s had seen the longest period of economic growth in history, but this had been followed by serious recession and unemployment of more than 7% in the early 1990s. Slow recovery was underway in 1993, but high levels of unemployment remained. The countries of the European Economic Community and their neighbors were still in recession, in most instances of even more serious magnitude than the United States had experienced, aggravated in many cases by inflationary pressures that resulted in a real decline in the average consumer's standard of living. Unemployment in most of the countries of the European Economic Community exceeded 10%, while in the

United States it continued to decline well below 7% throughout 1993. In 1994, it was clear that the U.S. economy was making a solid, if unexciting, recovery.

Europe and the United States both have large negative trade balances with Japan, the third member of the Northern Hemisphere "Triad" of global trading partners and competitors. Japan's trade surplus exceeded $150 billion, reflecting the global strategies of Japanese manufacturers of consumer electronics, automobiles, photographic equipment and many other products and services, as well as government policies that encouraged exports and foreign investment by Japanese businesses and discouraged imports and investments from abroad. For Europe and the United States, the unfavorable trade balance was an irksome piece of the economic puzzle that included huge budget deficits, unacceptable levels of unemployment, the ever-present threat of inflation, and the cost of government itself. (Despite its negative trade balance, the United States has remained the world's largest exporter. American consumers are important customers for many Asian and European manufacturers.)

Japan, in turn, was suffering from many of the symptoms of the United States' earlier economic malady, including major downward trends in real estate values, severe disruption in the banking system caused by the need to absorb the huge volume of bad loans resulting from the bursting of the bubble of speculation, a major slump in the stock market, and an increase in the rate of inflation. For the first time in five decades, Japanese firms faced decreasing profits and an environment of little or no real economic growth.[5] Japanese firms, like their Western competitors, were being forced to consider employee layoffs and the downsizing of their organizations, severe changes from the traditions of Japanese business. There was little doubt, however, that Japan's economy would recover and that Japanese firms would continue their global quest for increased investment and market share, with a heightened sensitivity to bottom-line profitability and return on investment.[6]

Japan was under intense pressure from the United States and Europe to reduce its huge trade surplus but appeared unwilling to pay the price in national unemployment that would result from reducing its favorable balance of trade with the rest of the world. (Economist Lester Thurow estimated that a $45 billion reduction in the favorable trade balance of Japan would cost one million jobs.[7]) Political turmoil within the

Japanese government further clouded the direction of future economic policy.

Global competition is now a fact of economic life for the industrialized nations as well as for most of the developing economies. The fact of the global marketplace is as real for the small manufacturer and local retailer or bank as it is for the multinational corporation. All customers have purchasing options that span the globe, not just the community or the nation. Economic growth has new political urgency because of the need to create millions of new jobs, in all the western countries. The balance of the 1990s is going to be characterized by freer trade *within* regional trading blocks, such as the European Economic Community and the North American Free Trade Area, and much more competition *among* the trading blocs represented by the old Triad.[8] The "successful" capitalist economies are going to need to change as least as fast as the old Communist countries to meet the challenges that they face. The concept of "global competition" has new reality and urgency for every business and every government policy maker.

MARKETING TO THE GLOBAL CUSTOMER

The *old* marketing concept grew out of the need to serve customers created by the conditions of post-World-War-II affluence and population growth. These consumers would be the beneficiaries of aggressive competition among domestic producers, with new entrants in many industries as firms adjusted from military to peacetime production and entrepreneurs were attracted by the prospect of unprecedented growth in consumer expenditures.

Marketers in the 1950s faced the necessity of becoming truly knowledgeable about and responsive to consumers who had increased discretionary spending power and who were informed, demanding, and confident about the future. Mass production and mass consumption of products with high symbolic value characterized the era of the Consumer Society, dubbed "The Affluent Society" by John Kenneth Galbraith.[9] It was an age of "conspicuous consumption," where products were often purchased based on what they conveyed about the self-concept and lifestyle of the consumer as much as for their specific performance benefits.

The *new* marketing concept is required for today's global customer who can choose among a much larger variety of products and services from producers located throughout the world. The new consumer is much more likely to judge products and services in terms of their fundamental *value,* defined simply as the ratio of benefits to cost/price, including costs-in-use. Customer value is at the heart of the new marketing concept and must be the central element of all business strategy.

The global customer learns quickly about the wide range of choices of products and services available, through modern telecommunications technologies of many kinds giving virtually instant access to cultural events, political news, fashions, and economic developments throughout the world. International travel is increasingly common, giving first-hand exposure to global products and services of all kinds, creating informed, sophisticated, and demanding customers. Travelers likewise inform their host countries' consumers about choices available to them in the global marketplace, helping to spread and homogenize consumer needs and preferences as well as to create the demand for global products and services. Coca-Cola, Levi's, Fritos corn chips, Honda automobiles, McDonald's burgers, Inter-Continental Hotels, Caterpillar tractors, IBM PCs, Avis rental cars, Hermes scarves, Colgate toothpaste, Swissair, Kodak film, Omega watches, the Sony Walkman, Heineken beer, and Madonna are everywhere! For consumers in the developed countries, there are more than enough options to choose from in virtually every category of product and service.

The global customer faces a fundamentally different economic scenario from that offered to the consumer of the 1950s. Instead of scarcity, optimism, and growth, the market environment of the 1990s comprises material abundance and excess productive capacity, pessimism, and stagnation. Economic uncertainty and political instability combine to create low consumer confidence and a high degree of caution. For the near- to intermediate-term future, the outlook is for little or no real economic growth, continued high-level unemployment, increasing taxation, and widespread job insecurity resulting from the attempts of employers in both the private and public sector to control costs and eliminate employees wherever possible.

The global customer is also concerned about the natural environment in fundamentally new ways and increasingly considerate of how the purchase and use of products may deplete natural resources and pollute air, water, and soil. The customer commonly expects the manufacturer or reseller to assist with the recycling or disposal of the spent product and its packaging. The prices of products must reflect the additional costs of responsible product manufacture, use, and disposal, heightening the consumer's sensitivity to both value and price. Companies wishing to do business on a global basis find that they must design products and services for the highest, not the lowest, common denominator in such areas as product recovery and recycling (where Germany appears to be setting the world standard). Whereas the automobile customer of the 1950s was impressed by horsepower and tailfins, the 1990s customer is looking for fuel economy and lowest total costs of ownership. The financial package may be as important as style, with leasing growing in popularity.

While manufacturer brands remain important, and global brands become more dominant, in most product categories there will be fewer manufacturer brands in total and more store or "own" brands promising the customer greater value. In many product categories, we can expect to see only two or three national manufacturer brands survive the 1990s and merchants and their brands will become increasingly powerful in the marketing channel. Although retailing is likely to remain primarily national in scope, global retailers will also appear with increasing frequency, such as Southland Corporation's "7-Eleven" convenience stores that originated in the United States, expanded to Japan, and then were acquired in the United States by their Japanese partner. Other large retailers with a growing international scope include Price Club/Costco, Wal-Mart, Toys "R" Us, and fashion merchandisers such as Louis Vuitton, Jaeger, and Chanel.

THE VALUE-DELIVERY CONCEPT OF STRATEGY

A value-delivery concept of strategy is a necessary response to an increasingly informed, sophisticated, cautious, and value-conscious global customer. Chapter 2 described how a focus on customer value grew out of analysis of the PIMS data showing that *quality*, not market share, was the major driver in the performance of the most profitable companies.

Market share and profitability were both shown to be the result of delivering superior value to customers. By the late 1970s, strategic planning was shifting away from a definition of markets as collections of competitors back toward an emphasis on customers and their definition of quality. The total quality management movement helped to focus the operations of many companies on the concept of customer-defined quality, which is to say *value*. Now, in many companies with successful quality programs, such as Polaroid, where a concern for customer-defined quality has permeated the organization, separate quality departments are disappearing. Quality, like marketing in general, is too important to be left to a specialized department.

Value Delivery and Distinctive Competence

The value-delivery concept of strategy helped to bring customer orientation, as called for by the old marketing concept, back into the forefront. But it also added the fundamental notion that the firm's value-delivery strategy must be based on some *distinctive competence,* a source of unique and sustainable competitive advantage. More often than not, this distinctive competence is based on intellect and knowledge, which is to say *people,* not physical materials, plant, and equipment. In his paradigm of "the intelligent enterprise," James Brian Quinn proposes:

> At their core, most successful enterprises today can be considered "intelligent enterprises," converting intellectual resources into a chain of service outputs and integrating these into a form most useful for certain customers. . . . [M]ost of the processes that add value to materials derive from knowledge-based service activities.[10]

It was proposed in Chapter 3 that all businesses, even manufacturing companies, should define themselves as *service* businesses; customers buy *benefits,* not products. Usually, the physical product itself is only one part of the total value-delivery system for the customer; customer expectations are importantly defined by the service aspects of the product offering. Information has the ability to turn any product into a service and into a customer relationship. For example, a package of Procter & Gamble's Crest toothpaste offers a toll-free telephone number (1-800-543-7270) that a customer can call with questions or comments. The caller's name and address are entered into a database and the consumer can request information about dental care. The product has become a service and a two-way relationship between the marketer and the customer, who is buying improved dental health, not just a physical product.

The ability to command natural resources, technology, and capital for competitive advantage is becoming relatively less important strategically while the ability to control knowledge and information becomes more important. The value-delivery concept of strategy is based on the fundamental assumption that *value is defined in the marketplace,* not in the factory, by customers who are continuously assessing competitive product offerings and their own needs and preferences, which change as the customer learns.

Customer Knowledge as a Source of Competitive Advantage

At the core of the successful business of the future will be a base of knowledge about customers, their characteristics, needs, and preferences, supported by information technology that makes this information instantly available to decision makers throughout the organizational network. *Information about customers* becomes the critical strategic resource because customers define value. Through their definition of value, customers also define the business by the demands they place on it. In a business world increasingly characterized by network organizations—coalitions of firms bringing together their distinctive competences to create customer value—customer knowledge is the link that holds the organization together and defines its shared objective and common purpose.

Customer knowledge is only one of several distinctive competences necessary for survival, and by itself it is inadequate to differentiate the firm from its competitors. The firm must also have other knowledge-based competences, especially those related to technology and other dimensions of the product offering, that allow it to design, develop, and deliver superior customer value. Coming back to the customer-knowledge dimension of competence, there is a prior question to be answered: Knowledge about *which customers?*

SELECTING CUSTOMERS: THE CRITICAL STRATEGIC CHOICE

Customers define the business by placing a set of demands on it for delivering superior value. Customer selection—the market segmentation and targeting decision—thus sets up the criteria by which the firm will be judged in the marketplace. Every firm (and every network organization) is limited in its competences; the firm committed to a strategy of value delivery must therefore *limit* the customers it proposes to do business with. The selection of those customers becomes the critical strategic choice, the polestar for everything that happens in the business and most especially the development of the product offering. The product is a variable; it is the customer that is the given.

Under both the old marketing concept and the new, market segmentation, market targeting, and positioning are the central requirements for effective strategic planning. In the new marketing concept, however, the focus is sharpened by adding the idea of the "value proposition." The value proposition is the verbal statement that matches up the firm's distinctive competences with the needs and preferences of a carefully defined set of potential customers. The value proposition is a communication device that brings together the people in the organization and its customers, concentrating their efforts and expectations on those things that the company can do best in a system for delivering superior value to customers. The value proposition creates a shared understanding that is the necessary basis for a long-term relationship that meets the goals of both the company and its customers.

To maintain its strategic focus, its commitment to its customers and to development of its distinctive competence, the firm must be selective. Opportunism and "the siren song of sales volume" must be avoided; the essence of market targeting and positioning is the willingness to recognize that, in the case of certain customers, both the firm and customers will be better off if those customers are served by competitors. Losing a customer can be the best thing that can happen to a business if it cannot satisfy that customer at a reasonable cost. Not all customers are valuable to a business. However, those customers who value those things the firm does well must be attracted and retained as the critical strategic resource for the business. In the slow-growth markets of the 1990s, the key to survival for most firms will be retaining its present customers rather than attracting hordes of new ones.

MANAGING CUSTOMER LOYALTY

Under the old marketing concept, the objective of marketing was to make a sale. Under the new marketing concept, the objective is *to develop a customer relationship,* in which the sale is only the beginning. The customer is seen as a long-term, strategic business asset. As customer relationships and strategic buyer-seller partnerships replace transactions and simple repeat purchases as the objective of marketing activity, a new definition of customer loyalty emerges.

The old marketing concept encompassed "brand loyalty," usually defined as the portion of a customer's purchases concentrated on the brand. It was a definition based on statistical characteristics of a string of purchases by an anonymous customer. Brand loyalty was specific to a given product, within a given category (e.g., loyalty to Pepsi-Cola within the carbonated soft drinks category). The brand-loyal customers were identified by demographic characteristics (e.g., age, education, occupation, and income). Customers were defined by statistics describing averages and central tendencies within a population, not as individuals.

Customer Loyalty: A Two-Way Street

Customer loyalty replaces brand loyalty in the new marketing concept. It is a two-way street: Customers remain loyal to the company that serves their needs and preferences with a total set of related products and services, while companies demonstrate and maintain their loyalty to customers by becoming knowledgeable about them and responding to them with enhanced product offerings. The commitment to deliver superior value to customers contains an explicit commitment to managing customer loyalty.

Customer loyalty has meaning only within the context of relationship marketing. Relationship marketing is only possible when the company knows the customer as an individual, not as a statistical phenomenon, and can address communications and specific product offerings to that individual. In this way, the customer also develops a relationship with the company, not just a product or brand.

In Chapter 5, we explored why a repeat customer is much more valuable than a new customer:

- Multiple purchases from the same customer.
- The likelihood that the loyal customer will pay a somewhat higher price.
- The opportunity to sell other products and services.
- The benefits of favorable word-of-mouth.
- The avoided costs of finding and attracting new customers.

We saw that price-oriented customer promotions often attract the "wrong" customers, those who are attracted only by price, thus reducing both loyalty and profitability.

The Commitment to Relationship Marketing

With a commitment to relationship marketing, the objective is to retain loyal customers by offering them superior value, defined as the ratio of benefits to cost/price. There is a positive trade-off between spending money to *retain* customers versus spending promotional dollars to *attract new ones.* The assumption being made in any customer retention program, which must be carefully tested, is that the customers in danger of being lost are in fact worth retaining. This is only true if the business has carefully and strategically selected the correct customers in the first place, namely those who value the things the firm tries to do well.

This observation underscores the critical importance of the market segmentation and targeting decision. Customers selected should be those for whom the company can deliver superior value. Pricing should be used as part of the process by which customers and companies select one another, not as an indiscriminate tool for attracting as many customers as possible, good and bad. Then the company should commit the resources necessary to retain those good customers by offering them a broad range of related products and services that will keep them loyal as their needs change and evolve over time.[11]

INNOVATION AND CUSTOMER RETENTION

Retaining customers requires keeping them satisfied, and keeping them satisfied requires innovation. While everyone remembers that customer orientation was the central theme of the old marketing concept, few recall that innovation was given nearly equal importance.

Innovation and Mass Production

Back in the 1950s and 1960s, *innovation* was synonymous with new product development. That was entirely consistent with the growth markets of the time and the opportunity to exploit technology (much of it developed in the military and space exploration programs) for the consumer society. The objective was to invent products that could be produced in large quantities at low cost, allowing the low prices required to create mass markets.

The concept of innovation for mass production created an interesting paradox. Innovation implies dynamic change, whereas mass production calls for an unchanging product and a stable production process. As firms saw the huge growth in consumer markets, it was implicitly assumed that the key to profitability would be efficient production of large quantities of standardized products permitting economies of scale.

Of course, the idea of mass production for mass markets was not new; Henry Ford's dream, beginning with the Model T, was to produce a car cheaply enough that the people who made it could also afford to buy it. In fact, the phrase "Fordism" has been applied to the system of mass production and mass marketing. In the 1950s and 1960s, the concept of market segmentation moved industry well beyond the days of the Model T and "any color you want as long as it's black," but the standard model of efficiency was still the large-scale production of standard products. Once product designs were set, it was marketing's job to generate the necessary volume. Mass marketing was the handmaiden of mass production. Thus, marketing could quickly revert to a sales orientation, and it often did.

The quality movement of the 1970s and 1980s shifted the emphasis in the definition of innovation to the notion of continuous improvement. Innovation in this general sense of continuous improvement and finding new and better solutions to customer problems is another hallmark of the new marketing concept. The dynamic mechanism of customer expectations, as described in Chapter 3, means that the definition of quality keeps changing. The augmented product becomes the expected product. As customers' expectations are met, they are revised upward. Competitors likewise respond with improvements and innovation, adding another stimulus to the firm's own innovation.

Continuous improvement represented a dramatic shift from the ideology of mass production, where the emphasis was on getting an optimum design and process and then maximizing the volume being run through that process. Continuous improvement applied more to processes than products, although product improvement was often a by-product. The new concern for process improvement was closely related to the realization that the supporting service bundle is often at least as important as the physical product in defining customer value and the redefinition of the business as a service business.

Process Improvement and Reengineering

The commitment to continuous improvement has led to the development of the relatively new discipline called "reengineering," defined as a fundamental, radical rethinking of the business from the ground up.[12] To improve customer service and to find and eliminate unnecessary costs, many companies have engaged in in-depth study of the development and delivery of customer value. Reengineering requires looking at the company and its processes of value delivery from the customer's perspective and redesigning those processes and their related organization structure "from scratch." Nothing about the company can be taken as "given" in a true reengineering effort. Today, reengineering is a major part of the practice of many consulting firms. One of the most common results of reengineering is to eliminate layers of bureaucracy, enhancing the ability of the business to respond to customer needs and marketplace developments and bringing top management closer to the customer.

Reengineering concentrates on *process* improvement. While continuous improvement in the pursuit of customer satisfaction and loyalty is an important part of the new marketing concept, the importance of *product* innovation in the more traditional sense of truly new ideas, major technical breakthroughs, and totally new products should not be dismissed. Research with companies in Japan, Europe, and the United States, described in Chapter 7, has shown that a business's ability to innovate in this traditional sense is among the strongest determinants of its growth and profitability. This research finding has been consistent across countries and different corporate cultures.

The lower costs associated with doing business with existing customers is undoubtedly one of the major reasons for the strong, positive relationship between innovativeness and business performance. Innovation results in products in tune with customers' changing needs and preferences, new products with the potential to attract valued new customers with the ability to build customer loyalty. Continuous improvement and new product development are both essential ingredients in relationship marketing.

FROM MASS PRODUCTION TO MASS CUSTOMIZATION

The old marketing concept evolved in a world of standard products, mass production, and mass marketing. Traditional marketing research was built around survey methodologies with the objective of finding the common denominators of customer needs and preferences, the characteristics of the "average" consumer. Once that profile was established, perhaps for multiple market segments in the case of the more sophisticated marketers, a standard product was designed for maximum appeal and mass communications. Other forms of mass marketing were used to attract and persuade the largest possible number of potential buyers.

Mass marketing, using the mass media, especially the new medium of television, provided the sales volume to support the large factories that would deliver the economies of scale in production necessary for low cost and profitability. The legendary mass marketers, such giants as General Motors, Procter & Gamble, General Foods, Gillette, and General Mills, also achieved economies of scale in marketing with their superior ability to purchase hugely expensive television, radio, and magazine advertising time and space on a national basis at lowest possible prices. Mass production and mass marketing depended on highly standardized products and standardized messages that would appeal to the maximum number of potential customers.

The customers of the 1990s demand more precise and more complete response to their needs and preferences. With domestic and foreign producers aggressively competing for business, customers can afford to be demanding. They can ask for a larger variety of products and products tailored specifically to individual needs and wants. And they can get them! We have moved from the age of mass production to mass customization, made possible by the impact of information technology on order entry, product design, production scheduling, manufacturing, inventory management, product delivery and distribution, and customer feedback.

Researchers at IBM have been leading the way in developing a theoretical framework for thinking about the move from mass production to mass customization.[13] The concept of mass customization was originally put forward in 1987 by Stanley Davis.[14] If an increasingly demanding customer is the primary force *pulling* mass customization into being, the primary *driving* force is information technology, essential to the development of the low-cost, flexible production systems that make mass customization feasible. IBM has more than passing interest in the trend toward mass customization because it has great strategic importance for both its products and its customers.

The IBM researchers conceive an evolutionary process that begins with invention. By its very nature, invention is a dynamic process, and the product remains a dynamic concept during the development process. To develop a commercial product, both the product and the manufacturing process must become as stable as possible. In the traditional paradigm, the next step after invention was the development of a stable mass production process that would ensure a low-cost standardized product of consistent quality. This product was aimed at homogeneous markets where mass marketing methods were used to manage and stabilize demand. Stable product, stable process, and stable demand were all required for mass production. A series of product improvements and added features were developed over time to extend the product life cycle and the life expectancy of the plant and equipment that had been committed to the product. Product development cycles were long and expensive as the firm moved cautiously to avoid prematurely making its investment in old products and processes obsolete and to ensure that the new product would have maximum appeal.

Instability in demand levels, caused by economic cycles, changing customer demographics, and competitive moves, resulted in swings in inventory and rates of production and introduced major inefficiencies into a system that had been built on a basic commitment to stability. Further instability could be introduced by product and process technology shocks, as competitors brought innovations to market or achieved a lower cost position with a new production process. Another cause of inefficiency was that most markets were not as homogeneous as assumed and customers often demanded changes in the product to better suit their needs. A standard product was a sitting duck for a niche marketer who could offer a product with features designed for a specific subsegment. Fragmentation of mass markets was a common occurrence as products matured.

The development of cable television and the advent of literally thousands of new special interest magazines aimed at smaller target audiences created a media fragmentation that has decimated the large audiences once delivered by the three leading television networks and the mass, general interest magazines. In the mid-1990s, the mass production and mass consumption view of business is unquestionably obsolete. Mass markets are disintegrating and the costs associated with serving them—both production and marketing costs—are too high. Mass production and mass marketing systems lack the flexibility required by today's global marketplace.

The objective of the old mass-production/mass-marketing paradigm was products in sufficient quality at low cost so that most people could afford them. The new, mass-customization paradigm is based on the goal of developing, producing, and delivering affordable goods and services with enough variety and customization that nearly everyone can find exactly what they want.[15] Low cost remains a necessary condition for profitability. As discussed earlier, the movement toward mass customization as a response to the competitive demands of the global marketplace began with the new focus on continuous improvement and led to the concept of reengineering. This first step introduced new flexibility and responsiveness into the organization and its processes. (See Figure 8–2 for a model of the evolution from mass production to mass customization.) With the commitment to continuous improvement that came out of the total quality movement and rising customer expectations, firms were learning to live with a concept of dynamic process change instead of the old stable processes of a mass production world.

The next and final step is to make the form of the product as dynamic as the process that produces it. In services marketing, process improvement is often synonymous with product improvement. As noted earlier, continuous improvement often concentrated on the service bundle surrounding the product, especially order entry and delivery systems, rather than the product itself. Mass customization as a concept is

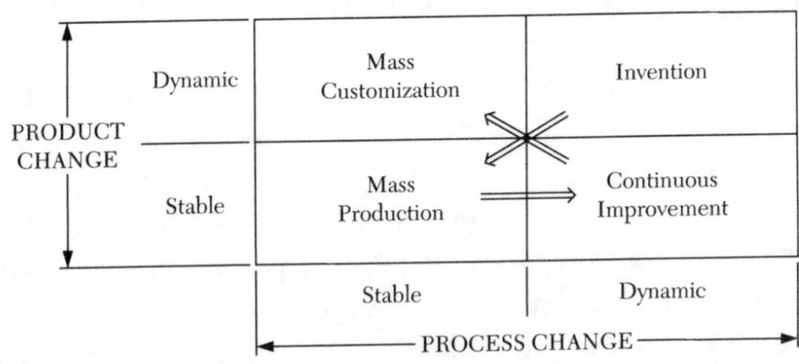

FIGURE 8–2. From mass production to mass customization. *Source:* Adapted from A. C. Boynton, B. Victor, and B. J. Pine II, "New competitive strategies: Challenges to organizations and information technology, *IBM Systems Journal,* Vol. 32, No. 1 (1993), pp. 40–64, at p. 60. Reproduced with permission.

easier to understand in the case of services, where there is no factory that must be tuned for flexibility. (In much services marketing, however, there is a "backroom" operation involving communications and data processing that is very close to a "factory" defined by machines, workstations, and workers.)

In services marketing, the product is often produced at the point of contact with the customer, or even as it is being consumed, as a customized response to that particular customer's needs. Even in the production of services, however, there is usually some technology in the background, such as a computer and a database, which can be accessed in modular form, allowing the service provider to quickly assemble components into a service package that appears to be completely tailored to the customer's needs and wishes.[16]

A traveler who contacts a travel agent or airline sales representative, for example, selects destination, time of day, class of travel, routing, seat location, a special meal, payment terms, and other variables that represent a unique product. The product is "assembled" in the computerized reservations system where it is "held in inventory" until it is delivered at the time of travel. But it is truly a unique product. It literally has the customer's name on it, and he or she is identified in the customer information file by a large amount of data that describe a unique individual to whom communications can be addressed and whose needs and preferences have been duly noted. If the person is a frequent traveler, his or her traveling history (a series of transactions) is noted and the value of the relationship with that customer can be rather precisely determined.

While the concept of mass customization may appear to be more applicable to services, it is increasingly relevant for the production of physical products as well. Even with products as tangible as automobiles, the options available to the consumer in styles, accessories, colors, and so on, make it possible to produce a unique car for each of the millions of people who purchase a car each year. It has been reported that Toyota is working on an information and production system that will make it possible for an individual consumer to specify a car that will be delivered to the person's home within a few days of ordering. A Japanese bicycle company already offers a similar service, tailoring each bike to the physical characteristics of the rider, although delivery takes a few weeks. Personal computers can be assembled with hardware features such as modems and software, chosen from hundreds of options, installed to meet the unique needs of the customer.

With mass customization, the product truly becomes a variable, as called for by the new marketing concept. Mass customization means working with existing product technology, often in modular form, to create specific product bundles for particular customers. From time to time, the whole process is invigorated with the introduction of new technology, created through the ongoing process of invention. In both cases, the process starts with the customers, chosen carefully to match up their needs and preferences with our capabilities; the business then tailors the product offering as precisely as possible to deliver superior value. That is the ultimate fulfillment of the marketing concept!

In the world of mass customization, the task of the marketing function is to understand the needs and preferences of customers *as individuals,* not as part of a mass market. Increasingly, it makes sense for the firm to think of itself not as producing goods or services *for* the customer, but as engaging in codevelopment and coproduction *with* the customer. This concept of coproduction is more easily understood in the context of business-to-business marketing, as when a producer of raw materials plays an integrated role with the customer in the design and management of the customer's manufacturing process. Increasingly, however, the concept also makes sense for marketers of consumer products, from home-office personal computers to banking services to insurance to kitchen appliances and frozen foods. In every instance, the marketer must understand the individual customer and the use-system where the product or service will be applied.

In the new marketing concept, this knowledge, understanding, and commitment is not the special province of the marketing department. Rather it is shared throughout the organization. In the words of B. Joseph Pine, mass customization represents "the death of the marketing function . . . the triumph of the marketing discipline."[17] Marketing becomes part of the organizational culture and the knowledge systems that guide decision making at all levels.

CUSTOMER ORIENTATION AS ORGANIZATIONAL CULTURE

Implementing the new marketing concept requires that organizational culture be actively managed, along with strategy and organization structure. We have defined organizational culture as the basic set of values and beliefs shared throughout the organization, that help members understand its functioning and provide norms for their behavior. We reviewed some research with managers showing that the most effective organizational cultures in terms of growth and profitability are those that maintain an external focus and have flexible processes for responding to a changing environment.

Focusing on the Customer

In a customer-oriented organizational culture, the customer's interests come first, always. The firm stays focused on the customer in everything that it does, and management constantly asks how it can do things better on behalf of the customer. The customer-oriented firm puts the customer's interests ahead of those of the owners, management, and employees. Everyone's job is defined in terms of how it helps to create and deliver value for the customer, and internal processes are designed and managed to ensure responsiveness to customer needs and maximum efficiency in value delivery.

The customer-oriented firm is almost certainly committed to relationship marketing, and employees have a team spirit reflecting that commitment as they work together to solve customer problems. Employee morale is a critical success factor in the customer-oriented company, especially for those employees who deliver some aspect of the service bundle that is part of the product offering. In the customer-oriented company, an explicitly stated value proposition becomes the focal point for the organization. Employees will repeat the value proposition as a rallying cry. It becomes part of the symbols and rituals of the organizational culture.

Hierarchy and authority become relatively unimportant in a customer-oriented company culture. Over time, a value-delivery definition of strategy will likely result in a flattening of the organization and elimination of layers of middle management as the firm attempts to improve its responsiveness by designing a structure that is most appropriate for its strategy.

Conceptually, and as part of the organizational culture, people may talk about the customer being at the top of the organization structure. Next in the hierarchy come the people who have direct contact with the customer and make up the front line of the value-delivery process. Then come those internal job functions that provide support with products, services, and information. The role of "higher-level" managers is to help everyone involved in the value-delivery process by giving them the resources they need, including procedures and policies as well as tangible and financial resources, to do their jobs most effectively and efficiently. The customer comes first and every person and every job is committed to creating a satisfied customer.

Loyal Customers and Loyal Employees

Relationship marketing builds an organizational culture in which the customer comes first. Customers become known by name and may even develop enduring personal relationships with members of the organization. Loyal customers are seen as a key strategic asset and resource that must be preserved and defended.

Loyal employees are essential to maintaining a strong organizational culture, to improving efficiency in the value-delivery process, and to building long-term customer relationships. Customer and employee loyalty are related; each reinforces the other. Experienced employees are very likely to be able to serve the customer best and to understand customers and their needs better. This knowledge is an essential part of continuous improvement. The customer's sense of confidence and trust in the organization is enhanced by knowing the employees as individuals, forming a bond with the organization. Likewise, this ongoing relationship helps to bond the employee to the customer and builds the commitment to customer satisfaction.[18]

Wal-Mart is often used an example of a customer-oriented company with a strong organizational culture. Until his death in 1992, Sam Walton, the founder of the company, was the fountainhead of the Wal-Mart corporate culture, its chief spokesman and cheerleader. Today, top management carries on the tradition vigorously. Among the most important and more tangible aspects of the culture are a commitment to their customers and value based on low prices; a strong dedication to employee welfare and to employees' families; "greeters" who welcome customers at the store door; the famous Saturday morning management staff meeting; and a number of company cheers regularly repeated in employee meetings. Every employee pledges to greet any customer who is within 10 feet, "so help me, Sam!" "Be an agent for the customer" is one of the specific values articulated as part of the Wal-Mart culture.

Top management personnel, buyers, and regional managers, using a fleet of company airplanes, leave company headquarters in Bentonville, Arkansas, every Monday morning to visit stores around the country. These representatives meet with employees, called "associates," in each of the stores visited, averaging two or three stores per day. They can analyze any store's performance using a data terminal to compare it with any other store, for any time period, on any item. The representatives return on Wednesday or Thursday with up-to-the-minute information from the field about conditions in the stores, competition, customer needs and opinions, inventory problems, and personnel. This information is shared in the Saturday morning meetings, which include many other company members and have been described as a combination of business and entertainment. Weekly results are also reviewed based on information provided overnight by a state-of-the-art management information system. Every new store opening that week is reviewed in detail.

When problems are spotted at a particular location, management will often take the blame by identifying things they should have done to prevent or solve the problem. They will examine the underlying processes of personnel selection, order fulfillment, delivery, or whatever that need to be addressed to correct the problem. The discussion usually identifies specific actions that need to be taken immediately with someone volunteering or being appointed to take responsibility to be sure that it happens and that the underlying problem is addressed as well. These meetings, and the culture that they represent, are action oriented. Management spends a lot of time worrying about the details. Especially when it comes to fashion merchandise or out-of-stock conditions, speed is of the essence.

To perpetuate the Wal-Mart culture, each new store is headed up by a manager with at least seven years of Wal-Mart experience. Assistant managers, on the other hand, are moved about every two years to give them additional experience and exposure to the Wal-Mart culture. Most employee/associates own stock in the company. Everyone is focused on serving the customer and beating the competition. It is the essence of a market-driven company, focused on delivering customer value through motivated employees with a sense of ownership. Customer orientation is a core value in the corporate culture.

CUSTOMER ORIENTATION AS MARKET INTELLIGENCE

Customer orientation is more than a set of beliefs, however. It must be supported by up-to-date and accurate information about the customer. That information must focus on the needs, wants, preferences, and buying habits of customers as individuals, obtained through direct contact. The central question that should guide all information gathering is "How does the customer define value and how well are we providing it?"

While there is a still an important role for traditional survey research methods in specific instances, such as routine measurement of customer satisfaction with a large, valid sample of recent customers, other techniques are likely to be more valuable for management problem solving. Small focus groups with actual or potential customers may be particularly helpful in developing new product offerings and service features, for example. For business marketers, carefully planned visits to customer sites can be invaluable in providing information to guide R&D, manufacturing planning, and sales force development. In any company, top management's understanding of market conditions must be obtained first hand by frequent field visits and one-on-one conversations with customers.

The new marketing concept calls for defining the business "from the outside in," being informed and "expert" about the customer and letting the customer define value by matching up the customer's needs and preferences with the firm's capabilities. As Ross Perot would say, "It's just that simple!" Of course, it is a simple idea, but its implementation is not simple at all.

Management of the marketing information function requires top-level professional management. In most companies, it also requires up-to-date knowledge about information technology, commercially available databases, management science methods for building models and analyzing data, and the communication aspects of management information systems.

The principal responsibility of the marketing function in a customer-oriented, market-driven company is to provide decision makers throughout the organization with up-to-date information about customers and competitors, helping everyone to understand the customer's constantly shifting definition of value.

CREATING A LEARNING ORGANIZATION

An important new idea relevant for the implementation of the new marketing concept is that of the learning organization, an organization that is dedicated to continuous improvement and to reinventing itself as market conditions demand. To change productively, any organization must first be able to see the changes occurring in its markets, and it must also be able to capture ideas and learn from experience occurring "on its periphery."[20]

John Seely Brown, Director of the Palo Alto Research Center of Xerox Corporation, believes that many kinds of improvisations and experiments occur within every organization at any time. In the traditional, hierarchical bureaucratic structure of a multi-divisionalized, functional organization, these learning experiences are likely to be ignored if not actively suppressed by normal routines, policies, and procedures. Such improvisations occur as people try in an ad hoc manner to find solutions to problems that arise in the normal course of events but do not respond to old methods for dealing with them. In Brown's view, real learning happens as the result of improvisations and is passed on in the organization by means of informal storytelling, not through formal training programs. He believes that the development of important core competences and improved practices depends on group processes within the organization. In the learning organization, these processes are nurtured and made explicit so that all employees can share the results of experimentation.[21]

We have seen at many points how the concept of organizational learning applies to the implementation of the marketing concept. First, the market intelligence function must be committed to understanding customer needs, defining specific areas that need improvement, and identifying "best practice" wherever it is occurring throughout the organization and in other companies. Organizational learning occurs in the creation and management of strategic alliances with customers and other partners. It is inherent in the definition of an Adhocracy culture as one that is externally focused and capable of quick and flexible response to a changing market.

Market intelligence is a key input to the learning organization. Organizational learning is seen in the progression from mass production to mass customization. The learning organization is part of Jack Welch's concept of GE as a boundaryless organization in which barriers between the company and its customer environment become permeable and the walls that separate functional areas of the business break down. Reengineering is certainly an attempt to make organizational learning occur in a planned way. The concept of the learning organization will become increasingly important in the network organizations of the 1990s, with more opportunities for parts of the organization to learn from one another. In fact, the motivation for many strategic alliances is simply to create a learning organization, introducing change into the existing structure to develop and improve distinctive competence and to learn from the new partner in areas critical for developing and delivering customer value.

STRATEGIC ALLIANCES AND NETWORK ORGANIZATIONS

In the firm committed to a value-delivery concept of strategy, management will have defined those distinctive competences that it must own and develop and those that it needs to acquire through partnership with others in the value chain. These ideas were developed in detail in Chapter 6. The role of marketing in the network organization is to keep all the partners focused on the customer's definition of value. This is a new responsibility for marketing under the new marketing concept, and it requires close cooperation with other management functions including purchasing, R&D, engineering, manufacturing, and distribution.

Responsibilities in Dealing with Marketing Partners

There are many kinds of marketing partners in the network organization. These include procurement, where marketing and purchasing managers must work together to be sure that suppliers of raw materials, components, subassemblies, or complete products with the company's name on them understand the nuances of the company's value proposition and customer needs and preferences. In some companies, managers have been transferred between the marketing and purchasing functions, based on the common value of negotiation skills in both areas and on the recognition that each can benefit from a better understanding of the other.

Technology partnerships, increasingly necessary where distinct and rapidly developing technologies converge on a particular product category, require close cooperation under the guidance of both qualitative and quantitative market research. In really new areas, where customers may not be able to express their preferences for products that do not yet exist, experienced marketing managers must work with their technical colleagues to make the subtle judgments required based on an intimate understanding of customer needs and wants. Their relationship with the customer must be strong enough to lead the customer into the new product future. Managers with experience in both marketing and R&D/engineering may be best able to make the necessary judgments on behalf of the customer.

Partnerships with resellers are perhaps the best known marketing alliances. In fact, the academic study of strategic marketing alliances has been centered in the area of marketing channels and distribution, where there is a useful body of knowledge dealing with power, trust, cooperation and conflict, and other aspects of interorganizational relationships. In network organizations, however, the viewpoint shifts away from the traditional concern for interorganizational conflict between manufacturers and resellers and toward a new emphasis on cooperation in serving the customer. Instead of asking, "Whose customer is it?" and fighting over control of the customer relationship, the participants focus their energies on the shared tasks of understanding and delivering customer value.

Simply defining *the customer* for any company as the party that pays the bill can be very helpful in developing concepts of cooperation in a marketing channel. If I manufacture a branded product and sell it through distributors to retailers who in turn sell it to the household consumer, who is my customer? Under this definition, it is the distributor if the distributor takes legal title to the merchandise, pays me for it based on my invoice, and then resells it to the retailer by means of the distributor's own sales force. If I send the invoice to the retailer, with the distributor physically stocking and delivering the product but not actually taking title, then my customer is the retailer. In this case, my sales force will probably work directly with the retailer as well as with the distributor. (Because I would receive an invoice from the distributor under these circumstances, I become the customer!) The consumer who comes into the store to buy my branded product is the retailer's customer, not mine.

Defining the Customer: How Samuel Cabot, Inc., Succeeds

Different companies will work out this question of customer definition in the network organization in different ways. One company that has recently wrestled with these issues is Samuel Cabot, Inc., a manufacturer of high-quality stains for the exterior surfaces of houses and other buildings. Cabot states its mission as follows:

> Our mission is to provide a full range system of premium quality stains and related products that beautify and protect all exterior wood and wood-related building materials used in the construction industry—combining our products, our expertise, and our service in order for Cabot Stains to be acknowledged as the Wood Care Specialist.
>
> Although the ultimate end-user/purchaser and controller of our brand strategy is the consumer, purchase decisions are greatly influenced by retailers, contractors, builders, and architects. Due to our limited resources, and the competitive environment, the independent dealer is the focus of our selling efforts.

Cabot's strategy is very selective. They focus on the high-quality, high-price end of the market with products that have a higher cost of materials and manufacturing. They make only stains, not paint, although some stain manufacturers such as Olympic have now developed paint lines. They have made a conscious strategic choice not to go to market through mass merchants such as Wal-Mart and Home Depot because this would not be in the best interests of their independent retailer partners and because they do not have the resources to work with the mass merchants as a supplier. They use distributors selectively in some parts of the country, based on their market strength and the availability of strong distributors who meet their strategic needs. However, their main commitment is to the independent retailer as a strategic partner, supported where necessary by a distributor.

Cabot realized that the key to its success, given its limited resources, is the support of the independent retailer in stocking and promoting Cabot Stains. In the Cabot strategy, the focus is on delivering superior value to the retailer in the form of a full product line, a tinting system, a broad spectrum of colors, advertising and sales promotion support, and so on, so that the dealer can obtain superior value from stocking and selling Cabot Stains. Both Cabot and its retailer are committed to a partnership with the objective of delivering superior value to the end-user/customer. Developing and maintaining a strong consumer brand franchise is an important part of the process of delivering superior value to the retailer.

WHAT DOES IT MEAN TO BE "MARKET DRIVEN"?

What it does *not* mean is "market*ing*" driven, in the old sense that a central marketing department must review and approve all activities involving the company's product offering and relationships with customers. A large marketing department may be the antithesis of a market-driven company, especially if it is part of a hierarchical, bureaucratic structure dominated by rules, policies, and procedures. If the marketing department is one link in a chain as ideas get passed along from research to design to engineering to development to manufacturing and so on, it is simply one more step in slowing down the process of responding to customers and competitors. Marketing's job is to provide information to decision makers throughout the organization and to develop total marketing programs including products, prices, distribution, and communications that respond to changing customer needs and preferences.

To be market driven implies more than to be simply "customer-driven," and it requires more than customer orientation. While customer orientation remains as the prime idea within the marketing concept, to be market driven also means being fully aware of competitors' product offerings and capabilities and how those are viewed by customers. It means understanding the intersection of customer needs and company capabilities in the context of competitors' product offerings as these three things come together in the customer's definition of value. To be market driven requires that all decision making is informed by customer information, competitive intelligence, and a clear concept of the company's value proposition.

SUMMARY

The new marketing concept is built around a value-delivery concept of strategy. It recognizes that the individual and business customers of the 1990s have an almost unlimited set of purchase options in the global marketplace. Marketers throughout the world must develop the strategies, skills, and resources required to be competitive as their home countries focus on the fundamental need to create jobs for their citizens.

Companies everywhere are driven by the need for survival to create value propositions built on their distinctive world-class competences and supported by coalitions with multiple strategic partners in network organizations. The old marketing concept was centered on a concept of mass production for mass markets. The new marketing concept calls for 'mass customization" of products and processes to deliver value to customers as individuals, not as part of the mass market. The critical skills are those of sensing and responding to the customer's ever-changing definition of value and competitors' ever-changing product offerings. Every organization must develop processes for continuous innovation and renewal, constantly learning from the experiences and experiments occurring on its periphery. Marketers must assume responsibility not just for responding to customers and their changing needs and definitions of value, but for leading customers into the future with new and better solutions to their problems.

In the final chapter, we will succinctly summarize the new marketing concept as a set of guidelines for creating a customer-focused, market-driven organization as required by the global markets of the 1990s.

9 IMPLEMENTING THE NEW MARKETING CONCEPT

Marketing is too important to be left to the marketing people.

David Packard
Hewlett-Packard Company

FIFTEEN GUIDELINES FOR THE MARKET-DRIVEN MANAGER

We can summarize the key ideas in the new marketing concept with a set of guidelines for its implementation. These 15 interrelated ideas weave the fabric of the new marketing concept. While they are not listed in strict priority, some are precursors to others. All are essential to a full commitment to the new marketing concept. These are 15 things that every business must do to be competitive in the global marketplace:

1. Create customer focus throughout the business.
2. Listen to the customer.
3. Define and nurture your distinctive competences.
4. Define marketing as market intelligence.
5. Target customers precisely.
6. Manage for profitability, not sales volume.
7. Make customer value the guiding star.

8. Let the customer define quality.
9. Measure and manage customer expectations.
10. Build customer relationships and loyalty.
11. Define the business as a service business.
12. Commit to continuous improvement and innovation.
13. Manage culture along with strategy and structure.
14. Grow with partners and alliances.
15. Destroy marketing bureaucracy.

1. CREATE CUSTOMER FOCUS THROUGHOUT THE BUSINESS

As with the original marketing concept, the central idea is customer orientation—putting the customer first, always. From top management on, throughout the entire organization, people must commit to a single overriding purpose: to create a satisfied customer. The customer must be put on a pedestal, standing above all the other stakeholders in the organization including the owners and the managers.

The focus on the customer must pervade the organization, and achieving that focus is a major mission for top management, aided by a strong marketing management team. The CEO must be the chief advocate for the customer, frequently stating the primacy of customer satisfaction as a goal of the business and making the tough decisions when necessary to show the organization that the customer always comes first. A CEO who doesn't put the customer first, inevitably puts some other group's interest first—probably the shareholders. The rest of the organization will sense this and behave accordingly. In the long run, putting the customer first serves all the other constituencies best. Profit is the reward for satisfying a customer.

Customer orientation includes a commitment to quality and a value-driven concept of strategy. To deliver superior value to customers, the customer-oriented company constantly seeks improved efficiency and lower costs. Price is always part of the customer's value calculation, so continuous improvement in pursuit of lower costs is part of being customer oriented.

2. LISTEN TO THE CUSTOMER

Customer orientation has to be more than wishful thinking. To be customer oriented requires, as a first order of business, listening to the customer. Paying lip service to customer orientation doesn't count for anything; it is the customer's voice, not the company's voice, that must be heard. The act of listening is only possible one voice at a time. The customer-oriented company listens to its customers as individuals and understands their perceptions, expectations, needs, and wants. Listening to the customer is not a natural ability; it must be developed, and the instinct to be selective and defensive must be overcome. Opportunities to listen must be sought out and captured whenever they occur, not limited to programmed occasions for soliciting customer feedback.

Customer complaints offer the most valuable opportunity for learning about the customer as well as about the business. When customers complain, they are telling us how they define value and why, in their judgment, we are not delivering it. They may help us to identify a process or a product feature that needs improvement. They may be telling us something we didn't know about our competitors. They also are telling us that they care about our products and our company and want us to do a better job.

Other opportunities for listening to customers occur on every sales call and service call, every time a customer calls in an order, every time there is an inquiry about an order or a delivery or an invoice. Listening to criticism is not something most people do well. Many companies tend to respond to customer complaints and suggestions by "blaming the customer" for not understanding the product and its use well enough, or for expecting too much, or for misusing the product in some way. Instead of reacting defensively, people must learn to listen, not just to respond. When we ask customers what they like and do not like, we must be prepared to hear what they say, to put the information into a form useful to the organization, and to follow up to see that correct action is taken.

To maximize opportunities for listening to customers, steps must be taken so that virtually everyone in the company has some contact with customers on a regular basis:

- Managers must get into the field, make sales calls with the sales representatives, or stand behind the counter in the store.

- Production people can travel with the product to the customer's location to see how it is handled and used.
- Engineering personnel can make site visits to customer facilities. Everyone in the company can benefit from actually watching customers use the product.
- Plant workers can call customers on the telephone, in the evening, to ask them how they like their new purchase, to see if they have any questions, and to learn how the product could be improved.

I have heard literally hundreds of examples of ways to put company people into contact with real customers. In every instance, the report has been positive. Never has someone said it was a waste of time.

3. DEFINE AND NURTURE YOUR DISTINCTIVE COMPETENCES

The old marketing concept lacked strategic impact because it did not consider the difficult task of matching up customer needs with the firm's capabilities. It never really addressed the question of *which* customers, and which customer *needs,* the company should focus on except those that were relatively unsatisfied. The concept of customer value was not part of the definition of customer orientation. What the concept of *value* brings to the equation is the notion that there is a dynamic interaction in the customer's assessment of needs and preferences between the company's product offering and those of its competitors. What can the firm offer that is better than its competitors' offering? What skills, resources, and knowledge are required to deliver superior value to customers?

The notion of distinctive competence requires customer orientation for its definition. A distinctive competence must be something perceived as having value by the customer; otherwise, it has no strategic value. A distinctive competence should also apply across product categories and multiple market segments offering strategic flexibility and opportunities for development and growth. It will almost certainly be knowledge based, which means that it resides in the minds and skills of individuals, a notion that includes but is not limited to technology-based competences. A distinctive competence properly nurtured, developed, and deployed is a source of unique, sustainable competitive advantage.

Customer needs and perceptions are one part of the definition of value; the other part is the set of distinctive competences that the firm brings to the competitive marketplace.

The definition of distinctive competences is the starting point for strategy formulation in the market-driven company. Where in the global market is there an opportunity for us, given our skills and resources, to be the best in the world in delivering customer value? It also leads to the identification of areas where the company does *not* have the competences that it needs for a complete value proposition. This awareness identifies the need for strategic partnering.

4. DEFINE MARKETING AS MARKET INTELLIGENCE

For the market-driven company, *customer knowledge is a distinctive competence* and one of its most important strategic assets. Knowledge about customers is perhaps the critical variable in defining the firm as a distinct entity, not simply as part of a network of partnerships with other organizations. Customers define the business as an economic reality; without its own customers, there is no business.

In the market-driven company, every important judgment made by management is based on current, complete, and correct information about the market including both customers and competitors. Part of the customer-knowledge competence of the organization is the sophisticated understanding of customers and their needs that resides in the minds of management and other decision makers. The other part of the customer-knowledge competence, and another key strategic resource for the business, will be its customer database, probably supported by an investment in computers and telecommunications technology. Customer information files, and the associated hardware and software, are as important a strategic asset today as factories and manufacturing equipment were to the mass producers and mass marketers of the 1950s. Market intelligence cannot consist simply of random insights in the minds of experienced managers scattered throughout the organization. It must be structured, made accessible, analyzed, and constantly available to decision makers as and when they need it.

The essential purpose of a formal marketing function is to be expert on the customer, to advocate on behalf of the customer, and to provide the organization with the information necessary to be customer focused and market driven. Some of the marketing department's tasks will be in response to the specific requests of operating departments—sales, R&D, customer service, quality, manufacturing, and so. In addition, however, marketing management must decide what market information has strategic importance—what the company needs to know that it does not currently know in order to plan for the future and adapt to the customer's ever-changing definition of value. Thus, there is more to market intelligence than simply serving decision maker's defined needs. Even more important is "knowing what we don't know" and identifying the questions that are worth asking strategically. Marketing management must be ahead of the organization when it comes to understanding the customer, leading the way into the markets of the future.

For many critical decisions, the competitive conditions of the global marketplace no longer permit the luxury of a carefully planned test market or customer survey. Increasingly, time is the critical strategic variable. The business must respond quickly to changing customer needs and preferences and competitive moves. Competitors market intelligence systems are such that every move, even an experiment or other attempt to gather market information, is likely to trigger a fast reaction, thus invalidating the research results. Instead of providing one-time, special purpose research, marketing management must create a marketing information system, including a customer information file, that will be a living, growing tool serve the daily information needs of the organization.

5. TARGET CUSTOMERS PRECISELY

The essence of being market driven is to know which customers are the company's and which belong to competitors. This concept of strategic selectivity is often the most difficult for management to accept. It means turning away potential customers and revenue and concentrating on building relationships with customers who have the best probability of being satisfied and loyal.

Market segmentation, targeting, and positioning remain as the critical strategic choices under the new marketing concept, as they were under the old. Positioning now takes on the added meaning of the value proposition, as opposed to the old, narrower definition of positioning as a communication exercise to position the product in the mind of the consumer relative to competition. Market segmentation is an analytical exercise that depends on solid information about customers and about competitors' product offerings. It also requires creativity to define the dimensions on which markets will be segmented. Targeting the customers to be served by the firm involves strategic decision making to match up customer characteristics and company capabilities.

Positioning, developing the value proposition, is the process of putting together the value statement that will be communicated to the customer and throughout the organization. Managers should ask themselves:

- *Who* is our *target customer?*
- *What* are we selling? What is the *frame of reference* we want the customer to use?
- *Why* should the customer do business with us; what are the *benefits* we offer?

The company must select customers carefully because it is going to make a commitment to them and agree to be judged by them. The firm entering into a relationship will try to build customer loyalty. The process of relationship building and loyalty management begins with the market targeting decision.

6. MANAGE FOR PROFITABILITY, NOT SALES VOLUME

As stated several times throughout this book, the strategic importance of market targeting is based on the assumption that the firm should be managed for profitability, not sales volume. Profit is a measure of the *value* that the firm has created for the customer. It indicates the ability of the firm to identify unsatisfied customer needs and to define, develop, and deliver value. Value is the ratio of customer benefits to the costs of the product offering, including both its price and the costs associated with its use.

Profit indicates the efficiency of the firm in delivering value as well as its ability to understand customer value. Profit measures the difference between the value produced in the marketplace and the costs of acquiring the resources, including human and organizational resources, used to create and deliver the product.

Over the long run, creating value for the customer leads to value creation for the shareholder. This article of faith lacked empirical support until recently. Chapter 7, reviewed some new research showing that the best-performing businesses, in terms of return on investment and rate of growth, were those that scored high on measures of customer orientation and innovativeness. Earlier, in Chapter 2, studies were described that discredited the link between market share (sales volume) and profitability. It was seen that quality and market targeting were the driving forces behind both sales volume and above-average pricing, resulting in superior profit margins and better return on investment.

Using low price to build sales volume has proven to be a serious strategic error in many cases for the following reasons:

- It obviously reduces profit margins, which must be made up with even more volume.
- It tends to attract customers who have a low probability of being satisfied and loyal customers who value a relationship with the company.
- Dissatisfied customers in turn generate negative word-of-mouth messages to other potential customers.

Managing for profitability, not sales volume, means that the company is seeking customers who value those things that the firm does well, who need its distinctive competence. Relationships with those customers will help the firm continue to develop its distinctive competence. Those customers will put pressure on the firm to do those things that are in its own best interests, making the necessary investments in resources and skills to maintain its competitive advantage.

7. MAKE CUSTOMER VALUE THE GUIDING STAR

Customer value is defined in the marketplace, not in the factory. The market intelligence function is necessary to make sure that everyone in the company understands how the customer has defined value and how that definition continues to evolve. Customer orientation and market information combine to create a functioning organizational commitment to delivering superior value. The development of business unit strategy and the definition of "how to compete" should be built around a clear concept of customer value. Delivering superior value to customers should be part of the basic culture of the organization, the shared values and beliefs.

The company's mission statement should incorporate the definition of customer value, and specify how the firm proposes to deliver that value, the commitments to excellence that are required to achieve that mission. That vision should be communicated and discussed at every opportunity, helping everyone in the company to maintain that commitment to delivering customer value and thereby maintaining the firm's competitiveness.

8. LET THE CUSTOMER DEFINE QUALITY

In a general sense, quality, value, and customer orientation are all the same thing. However, to be operational, the concept of quality must be translated into specific product performance characteristics that lead to customer satisfaction and can be measured. Under the old definition of quality, product features and specifications were the focus. Product dimensions, failure rates, and so on, as defined by engineering standards, were the benchmarks against which quality was measured. Quality was defined as avoiding mistakes, preventing the things that could go wrong, or at least reducing them to acceptable levels as in "defects per thousand." That is a negative definition of quality. Quality should be defined by customers, not statisticians.

Under the new marketing concept, quality is defined as meeting customer expectations. Chapter 3 included a review of a model of service quality that related this definition to management activities of analyzing customer needs, developing a description of the product offering that will meet those needs, turning that description into a technical specification, creating the product offering, communicating the value proposition back to customers, and measuring the extent to which the company has met customer expectations. The model of service quality has general applicability, especially when every business is defined as a service business.

Total quality management is a process of meeting and exceeding customer expectations. Because customer expectations evolve continuously, quality also must be a dynamic concept coupled with a commitment to continuous improvement.

9. MEASURE AND MANAGE CUSTOMER EXPECTATIONS

Knowing customer expectations is essential to developing a superior product offering and the selling messages that go with it. Measurement of customer expectations is necessary to set the performance standards that are at the core of every quality management program and that drive continuous improvement activity. The measurement task should go beyond routine measures of customer satisfaction and should encompass all dimensions of the customer's purchase and use of the product, not only the product per se but the total service bundle.

Customer expectations are built on several sources of information. By controlling those sources, the company can, to a *degree*, influence and manage customer expectations; this effort should be regarded as part of the value delivery process. Customers' expectations are based on their experiences with the product offering and with those of competitors, word-of-mouth communications from other customers, and marketing communications including advertising, publicity, personal selling, and sales promotion.

Marketing communications must be planned and developed in the context of total quality management, recognizing their crucial role in forming customer expectations. As stated earlier, the business of managing customer expectations begins with market targeting. Different market segments will have different expectations and will respond to marketing communications differently.

There is both a positive and a negative side to be considered. On the negative side, the company must be careful to avoid "overpromising," making product performance claims that are unlikely to be achieved or realized by the consumer. Often, this is the unintentional result of boasting or of creating a message strategy that unwittingly infers the product is better than it really is. This problem is more likely to occur if the company has not segmented and targeted carefully. A firm should not direct communications at potential customers whose expectations it cannot meet successfully.

On the positive side, marketing communications of all kinds can inform and educate customers, creating expectations against which the company wishes to be judged and compared with its competitors. If the company's product offers superior value, that obviously must be communicated through selling messages. The promise is that customers can increase their expectations and have them met by the firm's product.

A recent three-page printed advertisement for Mercedes-Benz automobiles provides an example of this positive approach to managing customer expectations. The first page shows a picture of a car and these words:

> *Some people think*
> *a Mercedes S-Class*
> *is nothing more than*
> *a symbol of how*
> *much you're worth.*

The timely reference to the decline of conspicuous consumption and the increased disdain for displays of wealth suggests the company's research shows this is a major problem that must be overcome, the perception that the large, S-Class automobiles are not worth their very high prices. The balance of the ad attempts to change that perception and enhance the customer's expectations for value delivery. The next two pages, a double-page spread, show the same automobile after it has been in a front-end crash, with these words in the middle of the pages:

> *They couldn't*
> *be more right.*

The surrounding copy explains in detail the many design and engineering features that protect the occupants of the automobile in a crash. The promise is that the owner can expect more from a Mercedes-Benz S-Class than from any other automobile when it comes to preventing or minimizing crash injuries, or better yet avoiding a crash altogether because of superior steering and handling characteristics.

Most customers will never have a chance to test that proposition to the limit, but the expectations themselves become a standard against which other automobiles, and marketing communications about them, will be judged during the buying decision process. The promise of safety becomes part of the product offering.

Managing customer expectations is part of developing and delivering value to customers. It is part of developing the product offering, and of total quality management. It must be accurately focused on customer expectations and aimed toward a vision of what the company wants them to be, its value proposition based on its distinctive competence.

10. BUILD CUSTOMER RELATIONSHIPS AND LOYALTY

As a corollary of customer orientation, market targeting, and managing for profitability, a firm will focus its energy on developing and maintaining customer relationships and building customer loyalty. The objective of marketing effort is to *attract customers,* not to make the next sale. It is another hallmark of the new marketing concept that management sees customers as the single most important business asset. Maintaining the base of loyal customers in an ongoing, two-way relationship with the firm is critical to its survival. Customers, not products, are the lifeblood of the business.

Customer relationships must be developed over time. Not all customers will be interested in a long-term relationship, and this presents the company with a choice. It can either avoid altogether customers who do not want a relationship and the commitments that it involves or it can develop separate, distinct product offerings (including prices and services) for relationship- and transaction-oriented customers. In the latter case, it has the further choice of simply maintaining a base of transactions customers over time, or of trying to convert them to relationships. In most cases, the latter is likely to be a difficult sell.

For most companies, it will be difficult to conduct both types of business at the same time—transactions with some customers and partnerships with others. They require different resource commitments, different skills, different product offerings. Furthermore, customers may not understand what they see. The relationship customers may want the lower prices they know are available to the transactions customers, while the transactions customers may insist on the service bundle provided to the relationship customers.

As stressed throughout this book, existing customers always offer the potential for greater profitability than new customers. Existing customers are likely to perceive greater value and to be willing to pay a bit more for the additional value offered by the total product offering, including the service bundle. They provide a stream of revenue from multiple transactions over time. They may be served at lower total cost because of the operational efficiencies provided by a long-term relationship. They offer an opportunity to sell additional products and services. And they generate favorable word-of-mouth.

It costs more, in terms of communications and related marketing efforts such as developing specific product offerings, to attract new customers. If price has been part of the inducement, as it often is, the new customers, at least initially, provide reduced profit margins. To the extent they were attracted primarily by lower prices, they offer less opportunity for profitable growth in volume, and they have a much higher probability of switching to a competitor. In the worst of all possible worlds, the company spends a lot of money to attract transaction-oriented customers, wastes resources trying to convert them to relationship customers, and then spends even more trying to prevent them from leaving. Such is often the fate of a company that tries to maximize sales volume rather than profitability.

11. DEFINE THE BUSINESS AS A SERVICE BUSINESS

Customers are buying value in the form of benefits provided by the product offering. The product per se may be relatively incidental to the total value provided. Customer expectations are often focused on the service bundle that accompanies the product offering, not the physical product itself. The service aspects of the product offering are usually the dominant *dis*satisfiers. The automobile customer is unhappy with the car because of poor service from the dealer. Insurance customers have problems with agents, not policies.

Defining the product as a service leads to defining the business as a service business. It is usually the service bundle that is dominant in differentiating the product offering from those of competition. It is the *processes* of value delivery that set the firm apart from its competitors and that need continuous monitoring, improvement, and reengineering.

12. COMMIT TO CONTINUOUS IMPROVEMENT AND INNOVATION

Knowing that customers' definition of value keeps changing, and being committed to delivering superior customer value, the company must commit also to continuous improvement and innovation. Global competition offers no other choice. Become complacent and you're dead.

Continuous improvement is part of being customer oriented and of letting the customer define quality. Continuous improvement should lead to lower costs and to a more responsive organization. Sharing the benefits of lower costs with customers in terms of lower prices underscores the value of the long-term relationship for those customers. For the business customer, this support from its vendors is likely to be critical to its survival in the global marketplace. This is seen in the common practice of target pricing, where the vendor agrees to take business at prices that offer little or no profit initially, on the assumption that the customer will work with the vendor to reduce costs so that the relationship becomes mutually profitable over time.

To maximize the value of customer relationships and to build customer loyalty, the company must be able to create new products and services that will enhance the value of the relationship for both itself and its customers. As customers' needs evolve, so must the marketer's product offering. Increasing sales to present customers is a much better path to enhanced profitability than trying to find new customers for existing products. Of course, new products will also attract new customers and expand the base of loyal customers.

13. MANAGE CULTURE ALONG WITH STRATEGY AND STRUCTURE

An awareness of the importance of organizational culture is relatively recent to the field of management and even more recent in the field of marketing. Yet early evidence suggests that it is extremely important and a major determinant of profitability.

Managing culture has two implications. First, customer orientation must be inculcated throughout the organization. This top management responsibility must take the form of both an articulated company mission and vision and a program of action to create customer orientation and drive it throughout the organization. Attention must be devoted to the details of language and other symbols that capture and communicate the vision of customer orientation.

Second, a broader concept of organizational culture must be developed that focuses the firm outward on its customers and competitors and that creates an overwhelming predisposition to entrepreneurial and innovative responsiveness in a changing market. Time and timely action have become the critical strategic variables in the global marketplace. The firm must have a pervasive propensity toward action and flexibility rather than toward preserving, protecting, and defending the organization itself.

It is truly sobering to realize that three of the citadels of management excellence in the 1950s and 1960s—General Motors, Sears, Roebuck & Company, and IBM—are now struggling for survival. The market value of each has declined by tens of billions of dollars, a tragic loss of shareholder wealth with severe consequences for millions of individual investors. In each case, it is fair to say, three things happened that are completely interrelated and interdependent:

1. The company lost touch with its customers.
2. It discounted the threat posed by innovative competitors.
3. It built a bureaucratic structure and culture that was overwhelmingly committed to preserving itself.

None was capable of adapting to its changing markets.[1]

In each instance, the board of directors finally realized that survival required change at the top of the organization as a first step in changing the organizational culture. The culture had to change before anything else—strategy or organization structure—could change in a meaningful way. New leadership has been brought into each organization, either at the level of the chairman of the board or as president/CEO, with the mandate to fundamentally redefine the company. Each firm realizes that the first order of business is to refocus the entire organization on its customers and the delivery of superior value in a devastatingly competitive global marketplace.

14. GROW WITH PARTNERS AND ALLIANCES

In the 1960s and 1970s, guided by the strategic visions of product portfolio models, aggressive companies were committed to growth through acquisitions and mergers. The *only* mandate was to create value for shareholders. Through the minor miracles of leveraged buyouts, junk bonds, and other tricks with tax laws and debt instruments, structures were created that were bigger and more complicated but that did not necessarily have the staying power of a business defined by its distinctive competences and its customer base. Many houses of cards were built out of financial paper.

These conglomerate organizations were often loose confederations of independent businesses, held together in a corporate structure that had legal definition only. This represented a significant shift away from the traditional bureaucratic, hierarchical, divisionalized, functional organizations that had characterized the 1950s and 1960s. Marketing as a competence, if it existed at all in the conglomerates, was found in the strategic business units, not at the corporate level. Markets were defined as collections of competitors, and the battle was for market share.

In the 1990s, we have come back to a definition of markets as customers and a focus on value for customers as the path to value for shareholders. The battles of the 1990s are for customer loyalty and profitability based on efficiency and superior value delivery.

As the firm develops its strategic vision and its definition of the sources of competitive advantage in its distinctive competences, it also identifies the need for partnerships with customers, suppliers, distributors, and competitors, present and potential. The competitors offer the opportunity to exchange distinctive competences, resources, and skills that have value to the other. USAir grows into the European market by forming a strategic alliance with British Airways, which in turn gains access to a feeder system for its routes to Europe. Both gain enhanced access to the skies of the emerging global marketplace.

Even the largest firms, including IBM, General Motors, and Sears, do not have the resources to develop and maintain more than a few distinctive competences. They must focus on those abilities and depend on partners for the other competences needed for their product offering. They partner with key customers, with major vendors, and with their competitors. IBM and Apple are engaged in a number of joint ventures to create new hardware and software designs, often involving converging technologies where each firm needs the other. General Motors has partnered with Toyota, Isuzu, and others to design new cars and to create new, efficient, manufacturing capacity.

These new alliances, called network organizations, are loose coalitions of partnerships among more traditional organization forms. Marketing has a major role to play in keeping the entire network focused on the customer. At the hub of the network, or at the "top" of the flattened organization, marketing managers must be involved in defining the position of the firm in the value chain and in defining its core set of target customers. It must work with top management to develop a customer-focused culture and the symbolic communication that will spread it throughout the organization. In a customer-oriented company, marketing management must participate in the design of the strategy, structure, and culture of the firm. With the focus on customer-defined value and the firm's distinctive competence, marketing management has a critical role to play in defining those areas where the firm will develop its own competences and where it must find strategic partners. In this fundamental sense, marketing management has a major role to play in defining the shape and scope of the firm.

At the strategic business unit level, the key activities requiring professional marketing management are the development of the firm's market intelligence system and its market segmentation, targeting, and positioning. Also at the business unit level, there must be a series of "make versus buy" decisions about both the product offering and marketing services, to define areas where the firm should develop strategic marketing alliances. Marketing management needs to play a key role in these decisions. At the business level, these are strategic activities, as opposed to the "shape of the firm" and "business scope" issues that are addressed primarily at the corporate level. For small business units, however, it may be inappropriate to develop a full-fledged marketing capability, especially in the area of information systems. Then, the responsibility should shift back to the corporate level, but only if so demanded by considerations of efficiency.

At the operating level, professional marketing managers will still be involved in the development of the marketing (as opposed to business-level) strategy and the creation and implementation of the "marketing mix" of products, prices, promotion, and distribution. Even at the operating level, however, marketing takes on new meaning, with the shift in strategic emphasis from creating the next sale to that of building a base of loyal customers. At the operating level, there must also be marketing people who develop and manage strategic relationships with resellers in the channel of distribution, although the day-to-day operating details should be in the hands of the sales organization. At the operating level, marketing people will often work with teams from other parts of the organization to address issues relating to total quality management and continuous improvement on behalf of the customer. Traditional functional boundaries will disappear in the most effective organizations.[2]

15. DESTROY MARKETING BUREAUCRACY

Traditional marketing departments, with managers of advertising, products, brands, sales promotion, market research, distribution, pricing, customer service, and so on, as the places where all marketing gets done, should be a thing of the past. While organizations must still develop professional competence in the many specific areas of marketing management, and while responsibility for achieving results must still be assigned, gone are the days when marketing was the responsibility of the marketing department while the rest of the organization concentrated on other things. Today, the customer must be everyone's shared responsibility.

Especially in traditional product-manager and market-manager organizations, there was a tendency to centralize all decision-making authority and to move with all the slowness and caution associated with bureaucracy. Such organizations cannot survive in the global marketplace of the 1990s. In terms of types of organizational cultures, as defined in Chapter 7, Hierarchies and Clans need to be replaced with Adhocracies, flexible and externally focused. Dinosaurs must develop wings!

The marketing professionals who remain must be experts on the customer, responsible for such areas as product strategy, marketing communications, pricing, and distribution that have traditionally been the responsibility of marketing management; but, even more importantly, they also must be responsible for providing market information to the rest of the organization, working with people in all areas to help them deliver superior value to customers.

SUMMARY

Superior marketing, defined by the preceding 15 guidelines as customer-focused problem solving and the delivery of superior value, is a more sustainable source of unique competitive advantage than superior technology will be in the global markets of the 1990s and beyond.

The new marketing concept is much broader than the old. It is also more pervasive. The old marketing concept encompassed customer orientation, innovation, and profit as the reward for creating a satisfied customer. It looked at the business from the customer's point of view. It was a management philosophy.

The new marketing concept is more than a philosophy; it is a way of doing business. It includes customer orientation, market intelligence, the focus on distinctive competences, value delivery, market targeting and the value proposition, customer-defined total quality management, profitability rather than sales volume, relationship management, continuous improvement, and a customer-focused organizational culture. It requires hands-on involvement by management at all levels and in all functions, throughout the complex networks of strategic partnerships, to develop and deliver superior value to customers. It requires that everyone put the customer first.

To survive in the global marketplace, every business must develop world-class competence in those areas that give it some unique competitive advantage. It is the customer who will decide whether the company has created value. The competitiveness of each business and of the nation it represents depends on its commitment to the new marketing concept.

Notes

Chapter 1
Putting the Customer First—Always!

1. Peter F. Drucker, The Practice of Management (New York: Harper & Row, 1954).

2. Frederick E. Webster, Jr., "The Rediscovery of the Marketing Concept," *Business Horizons,* Vol. 31, No. 3 (May–June, 1988), pp. 29–39.

3. Frederick E. Webster, Jr., "The Changing Role of Marketing in the Corporation," *Journal of Marketing,* Vol. 56 (October, 1992), pp. 1–17.

4. Drucker, *Practice of Management,* pp. 37–41.

5. Ibid., pp. 38–39.

6. *Business Week,* No. 1086 (June 24, 1950), pp. 30–36.

7. General Electric Company, 1952 Annual Report, p. 21.

8. Robert J. Keith, "The Marketing Revolution," *Journal of Marketing,* Vol. 24 (January 1960), pp. 35–38, at p. 38.

9. Carlton P. McNamara, "The Present Status of the Marketing Concept," *Journal of Marketing,* Vol. 36 (January 1972), pp. 50–57.

10. J. B. McKitterick, "What Is the Marketing Management Concept?" in Frank M. Bass (ed.), The Frontiers of Marketing Thought and Science, (Chicago: American Marketing Association, 1957), pp. 71–82.

11. Ibid., p. 77.

12. Theodore Levitt, "Marketing Success through Differentiation—of Anything," *Harvard Business Review,* Vol. 58 (January–February 1980), pp. 83–91.

13. Richard T. Hise, "Have Manufacturing Firms Adopted the Marketing Concept?" *Journal of Marketing,* Vol. 29 (July 1965), pp. 9–12, at p. 9.

14. McNamara, "The Present Status of the Marketing Concept,"

15. Theodore Levitt, "Marketing Myopia," *Harvard Business Review,* Vol. 38 (July–August 1960), pp. 45–56.

16. Andrew G. Kaldor, "Imbricative Marketing," *Journal of Marketing,* Vol. 35 (April 1971), pp. 19–25.

17. Ibid., p. 25.

18. Frederick E. Webster, Jr., *Top Management Views of the Marketing Function,* Report No. 80-108 (Cambridge, MA: Marketing Science Institute, October 1980), p. 5.

19. John G. Myers, Stephen A. Greyser, and William F. Massy, "The Effectiveness of Marketing's "R&D" for Marketing Management: An Assessment," *Journal of Marketing,* Vol. 43 (January 1979), pp. 17–29.

20. Webster, *Top Management Views,* p. 18.

21. Ibid., p. 22.

Chapter 2
Strategic Planning and Marketing

1. Alfred D. Chandler, Jr., *Strategy and Structure* (Cambridge, MA: MIT Press, 1962).

2. H. Igor Ansoff, *Corporate Strategy: An Analytical Approach to Business Policy for Growth and Expansion* (New York: McGraw-Hill, 1965).

3. Ibid., p. 5.

4. Ibid., pp. 8, 40–41.

5. Ibid., p. 93.

6. Ibid., p. 41.

7. G. P. E. Clarkson, *Portfolio Selection: A Simulation of Trust Investment* (Englewood Cliffs, NJ: Prentice-Hall, 1963). Winner of the 1961 Ford Foundation Doctoral Dissertation Award.

8. H. Markowitz, *Portfolio Selection: Efficient Diversification of Investments* (New York: John Wiley & Sons, 1959).

9. Ansoff, *Corporate Strategy,* p. 50.

10. Peter F. Drucker, *The Practice of Management* (New York: Harper & Row, 1954).

11. Theodore Levitt, "Marketing Myopia," *Harvard Business Review,* 38, 4 (July–August, 1960), pp. 45–56.

12. Ansoff, *Corporate Strategy,* pp. 104–109.

13. Walter Kiechel III, "Corporate Strategists under Fire," *Fortune,* December 27, 1982, pp. 34–39.

14. Richard G. Hammermesh, "Strategic Management," in Eliza G. C. Collins and Mary Anne Devanna (eds.), *The Portable MBA* (New York: John Wiley & Sons, 1990), pp. 292–331, at p. 296.

15. George S. Day and David B. Montgomery, "Diagnosing the Experience Curve," *Journal of Marketing,* Vol. 47, 2 (Spring 1983), pp. 44–58, at p. 45.

16. Frederick E. Webster, Jr., *Industrial Marketing Strategy,* 3rd ed. (New York: John Wiley & Sons, 1992), pp. 333–39; see also Hammermesh, "Strategic Management," pp. 297–304.

17. Hammermesh, "Strategic Management," pp. 295–96.

18. Robert D. Buzzell and Bradley T. Gale, *The PIMS Principles: Linking Strategy to Performance* (New York: Free Press, 1987).

19. Sidney Schoeffler, Robert D. Buzzell, and Donald F. Heany, "Impact of Strategic Planning on Profit Performance," *Harvard Business Review,* 52, 2 (March–April 1974), pp. 137–145; and Robert D. Buzzell, Bradley T. Gale, and Ralph G. M. Sultan, "Market Share—Key to Profitability," *Harvard Business Review,* 53, 1 (January–February 1975), pp. 97–106.

20. Paul W. Farris, Mark E. Parry, and Frederick E. Webster, Jr., *Accounting for the Market Share-ROI Relationship,* MSI Technical Working Paper, Report No. 89-118 (Cambridge, MA: Marketing Science Institute), November 1989.

21. Thomas Peters and Nancy Austin, *A Passion for Excellence* (New York: Random House, 1985), p. 82.

22. Cathy Anterasian and Lynn W. Phillips, *Discontinuities, Value Delivery, and the Share-Returns Association: A Re-examination of the "Share-Causes-Profits" Controversy,* Research Program Monograph, Report No. 88-109 (Cambridge, MA: Marketing Science Institute, October 1988), pp. 1–3.

23. Michael E. Porter, *Competitive Strategy* (New York: Free Press, 1980), pp. 42–43.

24. Lynn W. Phillips, Dae R. Chang, and Robert D. Buzzell, "Product Quality, Cost Position, and Business Performance: A Test of Some Key Hypotheses," *Journal of Marketing*, Vol. 47, 2 (Spring 1983), pp. 26–43.

25. Buzzell and Gale, *The PIMS Principles*, pp. 79–82.

26. Ibid., p. 7.

27. Walter Kiechel III, "The Decline of the Experience Curve," *Fortune*, October 5, 1981.

28. Anterasian and Phillips, *Discontinuities*.

29. George S. Day and Robin Wensley, "Assessing Advantage: A Framework for Diagnosing Competitive Superiority," *Journal of Marketing*, Vol. 52, 2 (April 1988), pp. 1–20.

30. *Business Week*, "King Customer," March 12, 1990, pp. 88–92.

Chapter 3
Quality Equals Customer Satisfaction

1. Theodore Levitt, "Marketing Success through Differentiation—of Anything," *Harvard Business Review*, 58, 1 (January–February, 1980, pp. 83–91, or Chap. 4 in *The Marketing Imagination* (New York: Free Press, 1983), pp. 72–93.

2. David A. Garvin, "Competing on the Eight Dimensions of Quality," *Harvard Business Review*, 65, 6 (November–December 1987), pp. 101–109.

3. "The Cracks in Quality," *The Economist*, April 18–24, 1992, pp. 67–68.

4. Garvin, "Competing on the Eight Dimensions."

5. See, for example, A. Parasuraman, Valarie A. Zeithaml, and Leonard L. Berry, "A Conceptual Model of Service Quality and Its Implications for Future Research" *Journal of Marketing*, 49, 3 (Fall 1985), pp. 41–50; Valarie A. Zeithaml, Leonard L. Berry, and A. Parasuraman, *Communication and Control Processes in the Delivery of Service Quality*, Report No. 87-100 (Cambridge, MA: Marketing Science Institute, 1987); and A. Parasuraman, Valarie A. Zeithaml, and Leonard L. Berry, *SERVQUAL: A Multiple-Item Scale for Measuring Customer Perceptions of Service Quality*, Report No. 86-108 (Cambridge, MA: Marketing Science Institute, 1986).

6. Edward F. McQuarrie, "The Customer Visit: Qualitative Research for Business-to-Business Marketers," *Marketing Research* (March, 1991), pp. 15–28.

7. Katherine Tobin, "Hewlett-Packard's Customer Visit Program: Getting Closer to Customers," a presentation to the Marketing Science Institute Conference on Communicating with Industrial Customers, March 8–10, 1989, Melbourne, FL.

8. John R. Hauser and Don Clausing, "The House of Quality," *Harvard Business Review,* 66, 3 (May–June 1988), pp. 63–73.

9. "Special Report: Quality," *Business Week,* November 30, 1992, pp. 66–75, at pp. 74–75.

10. C. K. Prahalad and Gary Hamel, "The Core Competence of the Corporation," *Harvard Business Review,* 68, 3 (May–June 1990), pp. 79–91.

11. Richard C. Whiteley, *The Customer-Driven Company* (Reading, MA: Addison-Wesley, 1991), p. 151.

12. Claes Fornell and Birger Wernerfelt, "Defensive Marketing Strategy by Customer Complaint Management: A Theoretical Analysis," *Journal of Marketing Research,* XXIV, 4 (November 1987), pp. 337–346.

Chapter 4
Market Targeting and "the Value Proposition"

1. Frederick E. Webster, Jr., "Republic Airlines (A) & (B)," case studies developed for classroom use at the Amos Tuck School of Business Administration, Dartmouth College, 1985.

2. Wendell R. Smith, "Product Differentiation and Market Segmentation as Alternative Marketing Strategies," *Journal of Marketing,* Vol. 20 (July 1956), pp. 3–8.

3. Al Ries and Jack Trout, *Positioning: The Battle for Your Mind,* 1st ed.-rev. (New York: Warner Books, 1986), p. 2.

4. "Ford Motor Company (B)," in Kenneth R. Davis, *Marketing Management,* 2nd ed. (New York: Ronald Press, 1966), pp. 659–673.

5. Kevin Lane Keller, "Conceptualizing, Measuring, and Managing Customer-Based Brand Equity," *Journal of Marketing,* Vol. 57 (January 1993), pp. 1–22. See also David A. Aaker, *Managing Brand Equity* (New York: Free Press, 1991).

6. Stuart Elliott, "P&G discovers that a new look to an old product can be seen as betraying customers' brand loyalty," *New York Times,* January 28, 1993, p. D20.

7. "Gould, Inc.—Graphics Division," in E. Raymond Corey, *Industrial Marketing: Cases and Concepts,* 2nd ed. (Englewood Cliffs, NJ: Prentice-Hall, 1976), pp. 119–139, and personal communication with Mr. Daniel Carroll, former President of Gould, Inc.

8. "Amicon Corporation (A)," in E. Raymond Corey, *Industrial Marketing: Cases and Concepts,* 4th ed. (Englewood Cliffs, NJ: Prentice-Hall, 1991), pp. 217–39.

9. Lynn W. Wilson, Allen M. Weiss, and George John, "Unbundling of Industrial Systems," *Journal of Marketing Research,* Vol. XXVII (May 1990), pp. 123–128.

10. Rashi Glazer, "Marketing in an Information-Intensive Environment: Strategic Implications of Knowledge as an Asset," *Journal of Marketing,* Vol. 55 (October 1991), pp. 1–19.

11. Stephen H. Haeckel, *Business Strategies in an Information Economy,* Report No. 90-119 (Cambridge, MA: Marketing Science Institute, December 1990).

12. William Boulding, Eunkyu Lee, and Richard Staelin, *The Long-Term Differentiation Value of Marketing Communication Actions,* Report No. 92-133 (Cambridge, MA: Marketing Science Institute, December 1992).

Chapter 5
Relationship Marketing

1. Frederick E. Webster, Jr., *It's 1990: Do You Know Where Your Marketing Is?* MSI White Paper (Cambridge, MA: Marketing Science Institute, 1989).

2. Attributed to Professor Jagdish Sheth by Richard C. Whiteley, in *The Customer-Driven Company* (Reading, MA: Addison-Wesley, 1991), p. 41.

3. Terry G. Vavra, *Aftermarketing: How to Keep Customers for Life through Relationship Marketing* (Homewood, IL: Business One Irwin, 1992), pp. 203–221.

4. Ibid., p. 203.

5. Robert C. Blattberg, "The Marketing Information Revolution," a presentation to the Marketing Science Institute Board of Trustees, April 25, 1991, at their meeting in Tucson, AZ.

6. Robert C. Blattberg and John Deighton, "Interactive Marketing: Exploiting the Age of Addressability," *Sloan Management Review,* Vol. XX (Fall 1991), pp. 5–14.

7. Russell Johnston and Paul R. Lawrence, "Beyond Vertical Integration—the Rise of the Value-Adding Partnership," *Harvard Business Review,* Vol. 66 (July–August 1988), pp. 94–104.

8. James P. Womack, Daniel T. Jones, and Daniel Roos, *The Machine That Changed the World: The Story of Lean Production* (New York: Harper Perennial, 1991).

9. Ibid., pp. 48–58.

10. Gary L. Frazier, Robert E. Spekman, and Charles R. O'Neal, "Just-in-Time Exchange Relationships in Industrial Markets," *Journal of Marketing,* Vol. 52 (October 1988), pp. 52–67.

11. Robert E. Spekman, "Strategic Supplier Selection: Understanding Long-Term Buyer Relationships," *Business Horizons,* Vol. 31 (July–August 1988), pp. 75–81.

12. Jan B. Heide and George John, "Alliances of Industrial Purchasing: The Determinants of Joint Action in Buyer-Seller Relationships," *Journal of Marketing Research,* Vol. XXVII (February 1990), pp. 24–36, at p. 34.

13. Ibid.

14. Robert E. Spekman and Deborah Salmond, *A Working Consensus to Collaborate: A Field Study of Manufacturer-Supplier Dyads,* MSI Working Paper, Report No. 92-134 (Cambridge, MA: Marketing Science Institute, December 1992).

15. James C. Anderson and James A. Narus, "Partnering as a Focused Market Strategy," *California Management Review,* Vol. 33 (Spring 1991), pp. 95–113.

16. Robert Krapfel, Deborah Salmond, and Robert Spekman, "Strategic Relationship Management: A Conceptual Framework" *European Journal of Marketing,* Vol. 29, No. 9 (1991), pp. 22–37.

17. Rowland T. Moriarty, Gordon S. Swartz, and Charles A. Khuen, *Managing Hybrid Marketing Channels with Automation,* MSI Work Paper, Report No. 88-113 (Cambridge, MA: Marketing Science Institute, December 1988).

Chapter 6
Strategic Alliances and Network Organizations

1. Kenichi Ohmae, "The Global Logic of Strategic Alliances," *Harvard Business Review,* Vol. 67 (March–April 1989), pp. 143–154.

2. Stratford Sherman, "Are Strategic Alliances Working?" *Fortune,* (September 21, 1992), pp. 77–78.

3. See, for example, Jordan D. Lewis, *Partnerships for Profit* (New York: Free Press, 1990); Kathryn R. Harrigan, *Strategies for Joint Ventures,* (Lexington, MA: Lexington Books, 1985); and Joel Bleeke and David Ernst, "The Way to Win in Cross-Border Alliances," *Harvard Business Review,* Vol. 69 (November–December 1991), pp. 127–135.

4. C. K. Prahalad and Gary Hamel, "The Core Competence of the Corporation," *Harvard Business Review,* Vol. 68 (May–June 1990), pp. 79–91.

5. Ibid., at p. 84.

6. Ibid., at p. 89.

7. Louis P. Bucklin and Sanjit Sengupta, *Balancing Co-Marketing Alliances for Effectiveness,* Report No. 92-120 (Cambridge, MA: Marketing Science Institute, 1992).

8. "CLOUT! More and More, Retail Giants Rule the Marketplace," *Business Week,* December 21, 1992, pp. 66–73.

9. Hans Thorelli, "Networks: Between Markets and Hierarchies," *Strategic Management Journal,* Vol. 7 (1986), pp. 37–51.

10. James R. Houghton, "The Age of the Hierarchy Is Over," *New York Times,* September 24, 1989, Sec. 3, p. 3.

11. "The Virtual Corporation," *Business Week,* February 8, 1993, pp. 98–103.

12. General Electric Company, *Annual Report,* 1990.

13. Noel M. Tichy and Stratford Sherman, *Control Your Destiny or Someone Else Will* (New York: Doubleday, 1993). Excerpts from this book were reported in "Jack Welch's Lessons for Success," *Fortune,* January 25, 1993, pp. 86–92.

14. An earlier version of these ideas appeared in Frederick E. Webster, Jr., "The Changing Role of Marketing in the Corporation," *Journal of Marketing,* Vol. 56 (October 1992), pp. 1–17.

15. Regis McKenna, "Marketing Is Everything," *Harvard Business Review,* Vol. 69 (January–February 1991), pp. 65–79.

Chapter 7
Organizational Culture and Customer Orientation

1. Peter F. Drucker, *The Practice of Managment* (New York: Harper & Row, 1954), p. 41.

2. Stanley M. Davis, *Managing Corporate Culture* (Cambridge, MA: Ballinger, 1984).

3. William G. Ouchi, "Markets, Bureaucracies, and Clans," *Administrative Science Quarterly,* Vol. 25 (March 1980), pp. 129–141; Alan Wilkins and William G. Ouchi, "Efficient Cultures: Exploring the Relationship between Culture and Organizational Performance," *Administrative Science Quarterly,* Vol. 28 (September 1983), pp. 468–481.

4. Joanne Martin, *Cultures in Organizations, Three Perspectives,* (New York: Oxford University Press, 1992).

5. Ibid., especially pp. 8–13.

6. This section is based on Rohit Deshpandé and Frederick E. Webster, Jr., "Organizational Culture and Marketing: Defining the Research Agenda," *Journal of Marketing,* Vol. 53 (January 1989), pp. 3–15.

7. Linda Smircich, "Concepts of Culture and Organizational Analysis," *Administrative Science Quarterly,* Vol. 28 (September 1983), pp. 339–358.

8. See, for example, Geert Hofstede, *Culture's Consequences: International Differences in Work-Related Values* (Beverly Hill, CA: Sage, 1980); James R. Lincoln and Arne L. Kalleberg, *Culture, Control and Commitment: A Study of Work Organization and Work Attitudes in the U.S. and Japan* (Cambridge, UK: Cambridge University Press, 1990); Akio Morita, *Made in Japan* (New York: Dutton, 1986); Robert T. Pascale and Anthony Athos, *The Art of Japanese Management* (New York: Simon and Schuster, 1981); John W. Slocum, "A Comparative Study of American and Mexican Operatives," *Academy of Management Journal,* Vol. 14, No. 1 (1971), pp. 89–97; and Michael Y. Yoshino, *Japan's Managerial System: Tradition and Innovation* (Cambridge, MA: MIT Press, 1968).

9. David B. Montgomery, "Understanding the Japanese as Customers, Competitors, and Collaborators," *Japan and the World Economy,* Vol. 3, No. 1 (1991), pp. 61–91.

10. Thomas Peters and Robert Waterman, *In Search of Excellence,* (New York: Harper & Row, 1982).

11. Terence E. Deal and Allen A. Kennedy, *Corporate Culture,* (Reading, MA: Addison-Wesley, 1982).

12. Bro Uttal, "The Corporate Culture Vultures," *Fortune,* October 17, 1983 (unpaged reprint).

13. "I'm Going to Let the Problems Come to Me," *Business Week,* April 12, 1993, pp. 32–33.

14. Joseph A. Litterer and Stanley Young, "The Development of Managerial Reflective Skills," paper presented at Northeast American Institute of Decision Sciences meetings, April 1981.

15. Deborah Dougherty, "The Problem of New Products in Old Organizations: The Myth of the Better Mousetrap in Search of the Beaten Path," unpublished PhD dissertation, Sloan School of Management, Massachusetts Institute of Technology, 1987.

16. Michael W. Miller, "At Many Firms, Employees Speak a Language That's All Their Own," *Wall Street Journal,* December 29, 1987, Sec. 2, p. 1.

17. Claude Lévi-Strauss, *Structural Anthropology* (New York: Basic Books, 1963) and Stephen P. Turner, "Studying Organization through Lévi-Strauss' Structuralism," in *Beyond Method: Social Research Strategies,* Gaeth Morgan, ed. (Beverly Hills, CA: Sage, 1983).

18. Ajay K. Kohli and Bernard J. Jaworski, "Market Orientation: The Construct, Research Propositions, and Managerial Implications," *Journal of Marketing,* Vol. 54 (April 1990), pp. 1–18. The definition quoted appears on p. 6.

19. Bernard Jaworski, "Market Orientation and Business Performance: Where Are We and Where Do We Need to Go?" a presentation at a Marketing Science Institute Conference, *For Good Measure: New Metrics for Improving Business and Marketing Performance,* April 22–23, 1993.

20. John C. Narver and Stanley F. Slater, "The Effect of a Market Orientation on Business Profitability," *Journal of Marketing,* Vol. 54 (October, 1990), pp. 20–35.

21. Michael E. Porter, *Competitive Strategy* (New York: Free Press, 1980), especially pp. 42–43.

22. Noel Capon, John U. Farley, and James Hulbert, *Corporate Strategic Planning* (New York: Columbia University Press, 1988).

23. Kim S. Cameron and Sarah J. Freeman, "Cultural Congruence, Strength and Type: Relationships to Effectiveness," in *Research in Organizational Change and Development,* Vol. 5, R. W. Woodman and W. A. Passmore, eds. (Greenwich, CN: JAI Press, 1991).

24. Robert E. Quinn, *Beyond Rational Management* (San Francisco: Jossey-Bass, 1988).

25. Benjamin Schneider and Joan Rentsch, "Managing Climates and Cultures: A Futures Perspective," in *Futures of Organizations,* Jerald Hage, ed. (Lexington, MA: Lexington Books, 1988).

26. Capon et al., *Corporate Strategic Planning.*

27. Jean L. Johnson, Tomoaki Sakano, Joseph A. Cote, and Naoto Onzo, "The Exercise of Interfirm Power and Its Repercussions in U.S.–Japanese Channel Relationships," *Journal of Marketing,* Vol. 57 (April 1993), pp. 1–10.

28. Rohit Deshpandé, John U. Farley, and Frederick E. Webster, Jr., "Corporate Culture, Customer Orientation, and Innovativeness in Japanese Firms: A Quadrad Analysis," *Journal of Marketing,* Vol. 57 (January 1993), pp. 23–37.

Chapter 8
Developing a Customer-Oriented, Market-Driven Company

1. Peter F. Drucker, *The Age of Discontinuity* (New York: Harper & Row, 1968).

2. James Brian Quinn, *Intelligent Enterprise* (New York: Free Press, 1993).

3. Ibid., p. 6.

4. "Kaput! The End of the German Miracle," *Sunday London Times,* June 6, 1993, pp. 14–15.

5. "Japan Economy, Built on Rapid Expansion, Faces Wrenching Shift," *Wall Street Journal,* December 7, 1992, pp. A1, A9.

6. Emily Thornton, "Japan's Struggle to Restructure," *Fortune,* Vol. 127 (June 28, 1993), pp. 84–88.

7. Lester Thurow, "Marketing in a World of Trading Blocs," address to the 3rd Global Conference on Marketing, Management Centre Europe, London, June 3, 1993.

8. Ibid.

9. John Kenneth Galbraith, *The Affluent Society* (Boston: Houghton Mifflin, 1958).

10. Quinn, *Intelligent Enterprise,* p. 213.

11. Frederick R. Reichheld, "Loyalty-Based Management," *Harvard Business Review,* Vol. 71 (March–April 1993), pp. 64–73.

12. Michael Hammer and James Champey, *Reengineering the Corporation: A Manifesto for Business Revolution* (HarperCollins, 1993).

13. Andrew C. Boynton, Bart Victor, and B. Joseph Pine II, "New Competitive Strategies: Challenges to Organizations and Information Technology," *IBM Systems Journal,* Vol. 32, No. 1 (1993), pp. 40–64; B. Joseph Pine II, *Mass Customization: The New Frontier in Business Competition* (Boston: Harvard Business School Press, 1993).

14. Stanley Davis, *Future Perfect* (Reading, MA: Addison Wesley, 1987).

15. B. Joseph Pine II, "Mass Customisation of Goods and Services: The New Competitive Reality," 3rd Global Conference on Marketing, Management Centre Europe, London, June 3, 1993.

16. Quinn, *Intelligent Enterprise,* pp. 349–350.

17. Pine, "Mass Customisation."

18. Reichheld, "Loyalty-Based Management," at p. 68.

19. Bill Saporito, "A Week Aboard the Wal-Mart Express," *Fortune,* Vol. 126 (August 24, 1992), pp. 77–84; Sam Walton, *Made in America* (New York: Doubleday, 1992).

20. Marjorie Adams, *Seeing Differently: Improving the Ability of Organizations to Anticipate and Respond to Constantly Changing Needs of Customers and Markets,* Conference Summary, Report No. 93-103 (Cambridge, MA: Marketing Science Institute, May, 1993).

21. John Seely Brown, "Keynote Address: Seeing Differently," in ibid., pp. 1–5.

Chapter 9
Implementing the New Marketing Concept

1. Carol J. Loomis, "Dinosaurs?" *Fortune,* May 3, 1993, pp. 36–42.

2. Frederick E. Webster, Jr., "The Changing Role of Marketing in the Corporation," *Journal of Marketing,* Vol. 56 (October 1992), pp. 1–17.

Index